Green Energy and Technology

Climate change, environmental impact and the limited natural resources urge scientific research and novel technical solutions. The monograph series Green Energy and Technology serves as a publishing platform for scientific and technological approaches to "green"—i.e. environmentally friendly and sustainable—technologies. While a focus lies on energy and power supply, it also covers "green" solutions in industrial engineering and engineering design. Green Energy and Technology addresses researchers, advanced students, technical consultants as well as decision makers in industries and politics. Hence, the level of presentation spans from instructional to highly technical.

Indexed in Scopus.

More information about this series at http://www.springer.com/series/8059

Alessandra Battisti · Maurizio Marceca ·
Silvia Iorio
Editors

Urban Health

Participatory Action-research Models Contrasting Socioeconomic Inequalities in the Urban Context

Springer

Editors
Alessandra Battisti
Department of Planning, Design, and Technology of Architecture (PDTA)
Sapienza University of Rome
Rome, Italy

Maurizio Marceca
Department of Public Health and Infectious Diseases (DSPMI)
Sapienza University of Rome
Rome, Italy

Silvia Iorio
Unit of History of Medicine and Bioethics
Sapienza University of Rome
Rome, Italy

ISSN 1865-3529 ISSN 1865-3537 (electronic)
Green Energy and Technology
ISBN 978-3-030-49445-2 ISBN 978-3-030-49446-9 (eBook)
https://doi.org/10.1007/978-3-030-49446-9

This Springer imprint is published by the registered company Springer Nature Switzerland AG
The registered company address is: Gewerbestrasse 11, 6330 Cham, Switzerland

Preface

This book describes and examines, with a qualitative and quantitative approach, the relationships between the constructed environment, health and social vulnerability. It demonstrates that spatial disintegration is quite often intertwined with health and social inequalities; therefore, it is crucial to adopt a methodology of multidisciplinary approach to urban health, in order to investigate the inequalities in healthcare and medical assistance through the analysis of psycho-social–environmental processes and the impact that these aspects can produce on objective and perceived health. The territorial insecurity is a local translation of complex phenomena regarding social 'mobility' (migration, economic crisis and development, restructuring of physical environments, increase in population), a clear reflection of the concept of urban divides where intra-metropolitan duality produces areas that have high levels of quality of life and areas characterized by poverty and spatial segregation. The first are the urban territories that, due to their characteristics, are capable of intercepting the opportunities of the global market; the latter are less attractive areas for investments, trade and tourism that consequently find themselves on the outskirts of society.

Empirical relationships have been observed between urban environment, social vulnerability and health in different contexts; however, we are still scarcely equipped with standardized tools that allow for a clear understanding of the phenomenon of how health inequalities and daily life are generated. In order to face this issue, a national network of active research groups has been created to draft and develop a prototypical analysis infrastructure. This tool will facilitate empirical studies aimed at adequately grasping the complexity of the relationships between health disparities, socio-environmental and economic distress, as well as personal and collective health. Given the interest in achieving meaningful, fair and lasting solutions to the conflict and the reduction of health inequalities, the current lack of an analytical system suggests the need for new multidisciplinary approaches, oriented towards the quality of life within a eco-social model of health. This book mainly addresses researchers and those working in local and government social care, healthcare and administrative institutions. Researchers will particularly benefit from the overall vision and the methodological approach explicated in this work, while those working in these institutions could gain important understanding of good practices as well as the sharing of their experiences in urban contexts.

Rome, Italy

Alessandra Battisti
Maurizio Marceca
Silvia Iorio

Contents

Urban Public Health, a Multidisciplinary Approach

Daniela D'Alessandro

Abstract Urban environment is a highly complex interactive socio-physical system, with competing expectations and priorities. Public health interventions have always had a fundamental role in the control of diseases in cities. WHO considers urbanization as one of the key challenges for public health in the twenty-first century, since cities offer significant opportunities to improve public health if health-enhancing policies and actions are promoted. A multidisciplinary approach is required, but the basic differences existing between technical and health disciplines make the interaction difficult. The multidisciplinary collaboration is still at a very early stage of development, and needs to be further understood and planned. The author concludes stressing the need for a transversal training, but also for sharing knowledge, instruments and methods, involving all the actors in the planning process, to develop a real multidisciplinary approach.

Keywords Urban health · Public health · Planning · Multidisciplinary · Cities

1 Introduction

Public Health interventions have always had a fundamental role in the control of diseases in cities [1–3]. A growing body of research has documented that the action of urban environment in shaping health and disease is itself of interest. Understanding which are the urban factors relevant for health can enrich the positive aspects of urban living and lead to develop appropriate behaviours and to identify preventive measures. This is also the pivotal topic in many documents produced by WHO [4–10].

Actually, we know that the urban environment is a highly complex interactive socio-physical system, with competing expectations and priorities [11]. Several factors, related to the built environment, are directly responsible for health impacts [12]. They include air quality, both indoor and outdoor, climate, water quality and quantity, noise and traffic-related injuries. Much of the evidence concerning direct

D. D'Alessandro (✉)
Full Professor of Environmental Health, Department of Civil Building Environmental Engineering, Sapienza University of Rome, Rome, Italy
e-mail: daniela.dalessandro@uniroma1.it

A. Battisti et al. (eds.), *Urban Health*, Green Energy and Technology,
https://doi.org/10.1007/978-3-030-49446-9_1

impacts is quantifiable and causal effects can precisely be attributed [12, 13]. Other factors, including the ways in which built environment features and their design (housing, neighbourhoods, social environments, connectivity, density, land use mix, accessibility, amenities and decision-making processes), have an indirect impact, because they are able to influence the feeling and behaviour of individuals and population [12]. For most of these impacts in recent years several evidences have been collected, documenting their relationship with health and these results are fundamental in the definition of salutogenic cities [8, 9, 14].

This is nothing of new. In the past, the disciplines of public health and urban planning were tightly intertwined. With the introduction of a deeper knowledge of microorganisms, infectious diseases and vaccinations, however, the focus of public health moved away from community engineering and urban design and going towards a model based only on strict medical principles [15].

These discoveries opened the way to targeted medical interventions aimed at preventing and curing communicable diseases. It was thus possible to control most of them diseases, at least in developed countries [16]. Consequently, from 1850 to 2000 infant mortality rate has been massively reduced. In Italy, for example it dropped from 220 to 5‰. On the contrary, in the same period, life expectancy at birth passed from about 44 to 79.6 years and the natality rate decreased from 33‰ to 9‰ live births, with an acceleration of this decline after the early 1960s. The mortality from all causes decreased from 22‰ to about 10‰ (crude rates), with a cross between natality and mortality curves in 1993 [16]. The fall in mortality for communicable diseases and the exceptional life prolongation explain why chronic diseases became the predominant cause of death during the twentieth century. In fact, the incidence of this kind of diseases grows exponentially with age. At the same time, after smallpox, other epidemiologically important infectious diseases are close to disappearing, but new epidemics are occurring in recent years, mainly related to climate change and to instability, poverty and conflict in many parts of the world. Both chronic diseases and new infections find the cities the place of their most expression.

As argued by WHO [15], following this shift, public health and urban planning became separated across the world. For long time, mainly during the period of economic prosperity and improvements in medical technology, the urban inequalities in health persisted, the divary increased and the dialog among them became more difficult, because objectives and interest felt far one from the other. Those who mostly suffered this dichotomy and the health consequences (both chronic and communicable diseases) were the members of poorer social class and economically disadvantaged urban population [3, 17–22].

In the 1988 the Institute of Medicine published the report "The Future of Public Health", in which leaders in the field agreed that the nation's Public Health activities were in confusion and that the field needed to refocus its efforts to address growing inequalities in health across population groups [10, 17]. By the 1990s, Public Health researchers of some Western Countries began to reconceptualise the risk factors for the uneven distribution of diseases across populations in order to explain health disparities, energizing the field of *social epidemiology* [23]. This discipline, by emphasizing distribution as distinct from causation, pushed Public Health scholars to reconsider how and why poverty, economic inequality, stress, discrimination, and social capital become "*biologically embodied*" and help explain persistent patterns of inequitable distributions of disease and well-being across different population groups and geographic areas [24]. The *Commission on Social Determinants of Health* drew attention to how transport patterns, access to green spaces, pollution effects, housing quality, community participation, and social isolation were all structured by social inequality [3, 10, 17].

As already discussed in some previous papers [3, 17], by the end of the Twentieth century, a split emerged in Public Health between those emphasizing the biomedical model and focusing on fighting individual disease risk factors, and social epidemiologists, who emphasized the idea of improving neighbourhood conditions, eliminating poverty, and enhancing social resources for health.

To find something similar, it is necessary to go back to the second half of the Eighteenth century, when West European Countries understood that better living conditions would have increased city residents' physical and mental health, but also boosted moral and economical status of the population [1, 26]. In the same period, in Germany, Rudolf Virchow, having understood that poverty and hunger lead to epidemics and that, in order to avoid them, political reforms were necessary [26], wrote "*Medicine is a social science, and politics is nothing else but medicine on a larger scale*" [27].

At the end of the second half of the twentieth century the drop of mortality for cardiovascular and cerebrovascular diseases is a reality in most countries in the world, which may be ascribed to important improvement in prevention, diagnosis and therapy, but also to changes in lifestyle and environmental conditions.

Past that era, a lot of things have changed. Today health can mean different things to different people. One of the most pertinent definitions of health is that from the 1948 Constitution of the World Health Organization [28]. This statement is the evidence that 70 years ago, public health moved progressively away from the medical model—focused on the individual and on interventions targeted to treat disease—back towards a social model, considering health as an outcome of the effects of socioeconomic status, culture, environmental conditions, housing, employment and community influences.

Today cities are energetic hubs of creativity and power, learning and culture. They are ecosystems that support growth and change, and are now home to more than half of the world's population—a proportion expected to reach two thirds by 2050 [4].

The WHO has identified urbanization as one of the key challenges for public health in the twenty-first century [5], since cities offer significant opportunities to improve public health if health-enhancing policies and actions are promoted [6, 7].

However, as the World continues to become more complex, the challenge is to fight for a framework in which scholars from multiple disciplines can effectively work together with a common aim: creating healthy, sustainable and equitable cities.

2 Multidisciplinarity as a Response to Complex Problems

While it is true that health and urban planning were successful partners long time ago, this is more difficult to reach today, because rests on building a respectful relationship out of mutual understanding and practical engagement across these disciplines [29].

The theme of multidisciplinarity has been very much discussed along the last decade, since the complexity of problems and processes to be managed at various levels (e.g. research, local governance, policy), need a new approach and methods able to analyse more in depth the problems and to find integrated and effective solutions. In the research field, the importance of multidisciplinarity has been widely recognized. It occurred not only in emerging areas such as the new infectious diseases (e.g. HIV, Ebola, Sars-COV, studies), the nanotechnology applications, etc., but even in more traditional fields, such as physics or applied math.

Multidisciplinarity does not mean a simple cooperation for improvement, at least at academic level. Zuo and Zhao [30], in order to evaluate whether a higher level of multidisciplinarity within an academic institution was associated with true internal collaborations, revised 90,000 publications by 2500 faculty members in over 100 academic institutions belonging to three multidisciplinary areas (information, public policy, and neuroscience). They observed that many multidisciplinary institutions were not necessarily practicing true collaboration, although they did feature collaborations that are more interdisciplinary.

Speaking about urban environment, it is to be underlined that cities around the world face many health challenges, including air, water and soil pollution, traffic congestion and noise, and poor housing conditions, and all these situations are caused and worsened by unsustainable urban development and climate change.

A multidisciplinary assessment of these criticalities offers opportunities for integrated low carbon solutions in the urban environment, that can bring multiple benefits for public health [31]. For example, to achieve high walkability, it is crucial to involve town planners and health workers, but this is not enough; it is mandatory also to incorporate thoughts about health and health promotion into regulation plans, to stimulate cultural and commercial activities, and to ensure good maintenance and safety [8, 32, 33].

The efforts that combine the perspectives of different disciplines, that use quantitative and qualitative approaches when appropriate, are more likely to provide answers about both how and why the characteristics of urban living may affect health. Quantitative and qualitative methods may help each other to minimize the a priori decisions; however, the typical interdisciplinary practice involves people with disparate backgrounds and, frequently, for them, the sense of words assumes different meanings depending on which discipline is involved; and researchers and practitioners, schooled in different academic traditions, have to face considerable challenges when working together [34, 35]. In particular, as argued by Kent et al. [29], health and built environment professionals do not need to become technical experts in each other's field, but they simply must work together to capitalise on each other's particular skill. This requires understanding, and the development of this understanding should be the focus of professional development, rather than the explicit development of a technical skill set.

Actually, there is little shared vocabulary among disciplines and this is a problem, because cities are multi-dimensional systems influenced by trends and processes operating at local, national or supranational levels [e.g. global initiatives that address urban issues, such as the Sustainable Development Goals (SDGs)] [36]. It follows that health and environmental issues, like climate change or the growing populations, need to be addressed using "holistic" approaches that require the development of multidisciplinary research synergies focused on urban health, accompanied by multidisciplinary sustainable interventions. For example, urban energy systems have interactions and influence wherein the socio-technical sphere is expanded to political, environmental and economic spheres as well. In addition to the inter-sectoral linkages, the diverse agents and multilevel governance trends of energy sustainability in the dynamic environment of cities make the urban energy landscape a complex puzzle [37].

A basic difference among technical and health disciplines, that can make interaction difficult, regards the "evidences". For example, the nature of evidence that planners use to develop their policy is different from that used by public health workers (e.g. lack of standardisation in measurement of environmental and health variables). However, as noted by Kent et al. [29], "*it must be recognised that the way people live and move around a place cannot be subject to the methods employed to produce the standard of evidence traditionally used to underpin health policy decisions....*". A more comprehensive way to explore and understand the complex issues needs to be embraced, including the use of case studies, in-depth observations, environmental and social impact assessment, etc.

Lawrence [38] argues that interdisciplinary contributions highlight the difference between disciplines and suggests to apply a *transdisciplinary* approach. This kind of contribution crosses the boundaries of scientific knowledge, to account for other types of knowledge (professional know-how, tacit knowledge, etc.). Transdisciplinary contributions create a knowledge domain broader than interdisciplinary contributions; they are based on the coproduction of knowledge by actors and institutions for socially accepted projects that are meant to impact on real world situations.

In conclusion, the multidisciplinary collaboration is still at a very early stage of development, and needs to be further studied, understood and planned.

3 How to Realize Multidisciplinarity in the Era of Complexity?

As argued by Grant et al. [39], today Public Health needs to add a fourth arm to its traditional remit of "(a) protecting and promoting health, (b) preventing ill-health and (c) prolonging life": it has to actually "create health" by means of investigating and understanding how possible it is to create the conditions for good health and wellbeing and equitable access to them. This concept is central in health promotion activities and it is an integral part of the "salutogenic city" definition [14]. At the same time, urban designers are grappling with a similar concept when they start to define their term *liveability*. To face up to complex issues, whose causes lie beyond the traditional remit of the health sector, it is necessary to share knowledge from many sectors for obtaining that this fourth arm could realize its goals. Nevertheless collaborative activities involving professionals trained in different cultural areas are still marginal.

More transdisciplinary contributions [38] are required in order to address the complexity of health-related problems at urban scale and implement effective responses to real-world situations. These kinds of contributions offer a broad integrated perspective, which should be part of the training in universities and of the professional training in today's era of complexity.

Barton et al. [40] suggest that an ideal health-integrated planning system should have five key elements: (a) acceptance of interdepartmental and intersectorial collaboration to properly explore health implications and to integrate the solutions across institutional remits; (b) strong political support, to ensure a consistent approach and the resources needed; (c) full integration of health with other local policy: placing health at the heart of plan-making; (d) active involvement of stakeholders (e.g. citizens) in the policy process; (e) a planning approach that fully reflects health objectives and makes them explicit (quality-of-life monitoring, health impact assessment, strategic sustainability assessment, urban potential studies).

As argued by Ryden et al. [10], improving health in cities implies to realize numerous small-scale interventions, selecting those effective, encouraging self-organization by citizen, and constantly modifying approaches as the system continually changes and adapts. Obviously, the assessment of these various experiments is fundamental. Such assessment should be based on observation, dialogue, discussion and deliberation, rather than on a technical exercise done by external experts. For example, a regeneration project aimed at increasing social cohesion, must consider the values and the priorities of local dwellers. It could be useful to ask their contribution—involving in vivo actors and stakeholders—to understand whether this project contributes to, or hinders the change. In-depth consultation, mediation, and deliberation are all processes that can be used to engage stakeholders in detailed and problem-orientated argumentation, to deliver potential solutions in the policy-making process.

Transdisciplinary knowledge production has to move beyond conventional research agendas, to address real world concerns, to address societal challenges in many domains that require collective understanding, political commitment, and innovative responses.

As Lawrence argues, speaking about housing and health [38], today there is no shared understanding about an interdisciplinary and a transdisciplinary epistemology in this field. Therefore the formulation and application of shared conceptual and methodological frameworks (for research and action) should be an objective of this field of inquiry in the immediate future.

In conclusion, there is a transversal need of training, but also of sharing of knowledge, instruments and methods, for all the figures involved in the planning process, to develop a real multidisciplinary approach. The road is long, and we have just begun the journey.

References

1. Rosen G (1993) History of public health. Johns Hopkins University Press, Baltimore
2. Vlahov D, Galea S (2003) Urban health: a new discipline. The Lancet 362:1091–1092
3. D'Alessandro D, Appolloni L, Capasso L (2017) Public health and urban planning: a powerful alliance to be enhanced in Italy. Ann Ig 29:453–463
4. World urbanization Prospects: The 2018 Revision (2018) Key facts. United Nations, New York. https://population.un.org/wup/Publications/Files/WUP2018-KeyFacts.pdf. Last visit 10 Aug 2019
5. WHO/UN-Habitat (2016) Global report on urban health: equitable healthier cities for sustainable development. World Health Organization, Geneva. https://www.who.int/topics/urban_health/en. Last visit 10 Aug 2019
6. Frieden TR (2010) A framework for public health action: the health impact pyramid. Am J Public Health 100:590–595. https://doi.org/10.2105/AJPH.2009.185652
7. World Health Organization (2016) Health as the pulse of the new urban agenda: United Nations conference on housing and sustainable urban development, Quito, October 2016. World Health Organization, 2016. https://www.who.int/phe/publications/urban-health/en. Last visit 10th Aug 2019
8. Capolongo S, Rebecchi A, Dettori M, Appolloni L, Azara A et al (2018) Healthy design and urban planning strategies, actions, and policy to achieve salutogenic cities. Int J Environ Res Public Health 15(12), 29 Nov 2018
9. D'Alessandro D, Arletti S, Azara A, Buffoli M, Capasso L et al (2017) Strategies for disease prevention and health promotion in urban areas: the Erice 50 Charter. Ann Ig 29(6):481–493
10. Ryden Y, Bleahu A, Davies M, Dávila JD, Friel S et al (2012) Shaping cities for health: complexity and the planning of urban environments in the 21st century. Lancet 379:2079–2108
11. Barton H, Mitchan C, Tsourou C (2003) Healthy urban planning in practice: experience of European cities. Report of the WHO City Action Group on Healthy Urban Planning. WHO Europe. http://www.euro.who.int/__data/assets/pdf_file/0003/98400/E82657.pdf?ua=1. Last visited 10 Mar 2019
12. GCPH (2013) The built environment and health: an evidence review. https://www.gcph.co.uk/assets/0000/4174/BP_11_-_Built_environment_and_health_-_updated.pdf. Last visited 10 Mar 2019
13. Renalds A, Smith TH, Hale PJ (2010) A systematic review of built environment and health. Fam Commun Health 33(1):68–78
14. Maas R, Lillefjell M, Espnes GA (2017) The application of salutogenesis in cities and towns. In: Mittelmark MB, Sagy S, Eriksson M et al (eds) The handbook of salutogenesis. Springer, Cham
15. Duhl LJ, Sanchez KA (1999) Healthy Cities and the city planning process. A background document on links between health and urban planning. WHO. https://apps.who.int/iris/bitstream/handle/10665/108252/E67843.pdf?sequence=1&isAllowed=y. Last visited 10 Mar 2019
16. De Flora S, Quaglia A, Bennicelli C, Vercelli M (2005) The epidemiological revolution of the 20th century. FASEB J 19:892–897
17. Corburn J (2007) Reconnecting with our roots American urban planning and public health in the twenty-first century. Urb Aff Rev 42:688–712
18. Whitehead M, Dahlgren G (1991) What can be done about inequalities in health? Lancet 338:1059–1063

19. Marmot M, Allen J, Bell R, Bloomer E, Goldblatt P (2012) WHO European review of social determinants of health and the health divide. Lancet 380(9846):1011–1029
20. Braubach M, Fairburn J (2010) Social inequities in environmental risks associated with housing and residential location a review of evidence. Eur J Public Health 20(1):36–42
21. Marmot M, Bell R, Goldblatt P (2013) Action on the social determinants of health. Rev Epidemiol Sante Publique 61(Suppl 3):127–132
22. Adamkiewicz G, Zota AR, Fabian MP, Chahine T, Julien R, Spengler JD, Levy JI (2011) Moving environmental justice indoors: understanding structural influences on residential exposure patterns in low-income communities. Am J Public Health 101(Suppl 1):238–245
23. Berkman L, Kawachi I (2000) Social epidemiology. Oxford University Press, New York
24. Krieger N (2000) Epidemiology and social sciences: Toward a critical reengagement in the 21st century. Epidemiol Rev 22:155–163
25. Hamlin C, Sheard S (1998) Revolutions in public health: 1848, and 1998? BMJ 317(7158):587–591
26. Morbelli G (1997) Città e piani d'Europa. La formazione dell'urbanistica contemporanea. Dedalo Ed. Bari
27. Wittern-Sterzel R (2003) Politics is nothing else than large scale medicine Rudolf Virchow and his role in the development of social medicine. Verh Dtsch Ges Pathol 87:150–157
28. World Health Organization (1994) Constitution of the World Health Organization. In: WHO basic
documents, 40th edn. World Health Organization, Geneva
29. Kent J, Thompson H (2012) health amd the built environment: exploring foundations for a new interdisciplinary profession. J Environ Public Health 1:958175
30. Zuo Z, Zhao K (2018) The more multidisciplinary the better?—The prevalence and interdisciplinary of research collaborations in multidisciplinary institutions. J Inform 12:736–756
31. Vardoulakis S, Dear K, Wilkinson P (2016) Challenges and opportunities for urban environmental health and sustainability: the HEALTHY-POLIS initiative. Environ Health 15:30–33
32. D'Alessandro D, Appolloni L, Capasso L (2016) How walkable is the city? Application of the Walking Suitability Index of the Territory (T-WSI) to the city of Rieti (Lazio Region, Central Italy). Epidemiol Prev 40:237–242
33. Appolloni L, Corazza MV, D'Alessandro D (2019) The pleasure of walking: an innovative methodology to assess appropriate walkable performance in urban areas to support transport planning. Sustainability 11:3467. https://doi.org/10.3390/su11123467
34. NSF (2005) Facilitating interdisciplinary research. Technical Report National Academy of Sciences, Washington, DC. http://dx.doi.org/10.17226/11153. Last visited 10 Mar 2019
35. Galea S, Vlahov D (2005) Urban health: evidence, challenges ad direction. Annu Rev Public Health 26:341–365
36. Andrianou XD, Markis KC (2018) The framework of urban exposome: application of the exposome concept in urban health studies. Sci Total Environ 636:963–967
37. Basu S, Bale CSE, Wehnert T, Topp K (2019) A complex approach to defining urban energy systems. Cities 95:102358
38. Lawrence RJ (2017) Constancy and change: key issues in housing and health research, 1987-2017. Int J Environ Res Public Health 14:763–769
39. Grant M, Brown C, Caiaffa WT, Capon A, Colburn J et al (2017) Cities and health: an evolving global conversation. Cities & Health 1:1–9
40. Barton H, Grant M, Claire M, Tsourou C (2009) Healthy urban planning in European cities. Health Promot Int 24(S1). https://doi.org/10.1093/heapro/dap059

Participatory Governance and Healthcare. Opportunities and Perils

Edoardo Esposto and Giulio Moini

Abstract Since the 1990s, public policy has made incremental transformations towards greater involvement of common citizens in policymaking. The vast body of literature on healthcare service co-production and patient empowerment testifies to the persistent relevance of participatory ideas and practices in the healthcare debate. This chapter analyzes participation through the lens of an interpretative approach to public policy. It discusses the macro, meso and micro connections between participation and the evolution of contemporary democracies. Secondly, it explores the dilemmas and unintended consequences that result from using participation as the ultimate justification for policy interventions. Finally, it highlights the potential depoliticizing effect of participatory procedures on decisions about collective problems and social goals.

Keywords Community engagement · Depoliticization · Health policy · Participatory governance · Public policy theory

1 Introduction: Framing Participation in Public Policy

Since the 1990s, public policy has made incremental transformations towards greater involvement of common citizens in policymaking. Scholars and practitioners adopted the term 'deliberative turn' [1] to characterise this newly acquired centrality of reflexivity and civic engagement.

The participation of the public in debating and deciding about collective issues was conceived of as a tool for consolidating representative democracies, while expanding the democratic premises of liberal regimes: a form of 'democratization of democracy' [2]. This overarching goal translated into a multiplicity of practices that retained certain procedural commonalities yet had different objectives, origins, degrees of

E. Esposto (✉) · G. Moini
Department of Social Sciences and Economics, Sapienza University of Rome, Rome, Italy
e-mail: edoardo.esposto@uniroma1.it

G. Moini
e-mail: giulio.moini@uniorma1.it

A. Battisti et al. (eds.), *Urban Health*, Green Energy and Technology,
https://doi.org/10.1007/978-3-030-49446-9_2

organizational complexity, and preferred modes of interaction between participants. Deliberative polling, citizen juries, town meetings, open space technology, consensus building, public hearings, participatory budgeting, and action planning are some examples of such practices.

Welfare services planning and provision is a policy area where participatory processes have been widely applied in the last decades, and the vast body of literature on participation in healthcare testifies to the extent of this adoption. A brief survey of the literature identified three broad research interests actively pursued by scholars: (1) the nexus between community participation and improving the provision and customisation of healthcare services; (2) the participation of patients and their families in therapeutic practices; and (3) the comparative review of case studies centered around the participatory governance of policymaking in healthcare.

In their recent and comprehensive review of the literature concerning the first topic, Bath and Wakerman [3] highlighted the solid, but limited, body of evidence linking community-based design and implementation of healthcare interventions to service improvements. A fundamental limitation of the reviewed studies was the lack of clarity over the nature of the participants targeted by the participatory processes (e.g. the general public, community members, service users) [4]. This conceptual ambiguity risks overlooking the underrepresentation of marginalised groups in healthcare governance [5]. Moreover, a clear link between various participatory designs—and their degree of structuration into institutional decision making—and the type of improvement that could be expected by their implementation has yet to be established by empirical research [6].

The notion of 'patient empowerment' is central to the second strand of the debate. The concept—a sectorial application of the vast and ambiguous idea of empowerment—refers to the recognition of the capability of patients to voice their needs and devise contributions to their treatment [7]. Patients are here recognized to have an expert knowledge on their bodies, feelings, and symptoms. They thus should be granted spaces for meaningfully influencing decisions regarding their health [8] through involvement in the organizational and practical operations of hospitals and nursing homes [9].

The idea of healthcare service co-production [10], a research interest influenced by the burgeoning debate on co-production of human services, is bridging these first two dimensions [11] and shaping the 'zeitgeist' of the debate [12].

While these two research topics are mostly concerned with micro and meso analyses of individual or community participation, the third is more closely related to a macro approach, focusing on cases of sub-national or national participatory healthcare reforms. Authors explored the connections between meaningful participatory designs (i.e. endowing participants with a substantive decision-making power) and the production of broad and lasting health reforms [13]. The commitment of institutional actors and healthcare professionals to ensure meaningful engagement is deemed essential to the effectiveness of the reforms [14]. However, a tension exists between institutionally embedded participatory policymaking (usually initiated by public officials in a top-down fashion) and those initiated by citizens mobilization (often stemming from the contestation of existing healthcare policies and service provision) [15].

Empirical examinations confirmed the usefulness of participatory processes to tackle decisions over health policies involving difficult trade-offs, e.g. the expansion of healthcare coverage vis-à-vis the increase of insurance premiums [16]. A prominent empirical experimentation of participation in health policymaking is the sectoral application of participatory budgeting, i.e. the involvement of citizens in crafting public budgets, setting priorities, and devising alternatives for the allocation of public health expenditures [17].

The diffusion and resilience of participation can be interpreted as a reflex of its status as a frame of reference, or *référentiel,* for public policy [18]. *Référentiel* is an analytical concept describing a normative and cognitive representation which defines a policy field and situates it in the broader structure of collective and political action [19].

We can distinguish between a global dimension of a *référentiel,* which encompasses the ideas and beliefs that form the ideational background of a society in a particular moment, and a sectorial dimension, which adapts those ideas and beliefs to specific policy fields [20].

The theory of *référentiel* is a useful interpretative tool for questioning participatory practices, offering an analytical frame for establishing connections between participation and the evolution of public policy in contemporary democracies. This chapter explores the dilemmas and unintended consequences that result from using participation as the ultimate justification for policy interventions.

2 Explanatory Variables of the Success of Participation

It is useful to give a general, if provisional, definition of the new forms of political participation that we will refer to in this chapter. They are new modes of organizing the relationships between institutions and civil society, an incentive to the direct involvement of the latter in the former [21]. Participatory practices are a supplement and/or substitute to institutional mediation and representativeness, aiming at a greater engagement of citizens and their spontaneous associative bodies in the management of collective issues.

Individual or collective actors involved in public decision making through participatory forums do not represent the interests, goals or opinions of larger social groups or classes. Although they do not represent others, they present their own positions and ideas and confront those of other participants.

Beyond nomenclature, the new forms of participation share little in common with the claims to direct democracy which characterized social movements in the 1960s and 1970s. Pateman [22] distinguishes between (older) participatory and (newer) deliberative forms of direct democracy, although her criteria for discerning between the two do not coincide with those discussed here.

In a brief summary, participatory practices in the 1960s and 1970s were (I) initiated by bottom-up pressure to enter in the decision-making process; (II) sustained by the agency of collective actors (e.g. workers' movement, student movement, feminist movement), through a repertoire of conflictual actions; (III) characterized by high ideological stakes, and embedded into an alternative view of the social system; and (IV) loosely structured and with little or no technical support by experts.

By contrast, the forms of participation which became prevalent in the 1990s were (i) initiated by top-down invitations of institutional actors; (ii) joined by individual citizens or formal associations, rather than by informal collective entities; (iii) devoid of ideological content and oriented towards problem-solving; (iv) highly structured and supported by expert knowledge in their design and implementation.

The new forms of participation have a preferred scale of action too. They pose a greater emphasis on proximity and tend to be implemented by local communities. In more rigorous terms, new participatory practices are framed by an idea of social relationships as networks of interactions within a territorial and spatially limited context.

One defining characteristic of the 'second generation' participation is thus the formation of local public arenas, i.e. spaces where all who have a stake in the management of a community can express their interests and opinions and contribute to the formation of collective decisions by employing their resources and expertise.

There are several variables that may explain the success of new participatory practices. We will base our explanation on a hypothesis of interconnection between these variables, namely the interrelation between the macro, meso and micro dimensions of participation.

The macro level variables correspond to the historical process of change undertaken by contemporary politics and society. Considering the transformations in the political sphere, we can identify two broad phenomena linked to the success of participatory practices.

On the supply-side of political transformations, the late twentieth and the early twenty-first century have been characterised by the weakening of representative democracy. The higher rate of abstentionism and the drop in party membership are signs of the well-known crisis of mass parties, the organizational backbone of representation. The importance of elected assemblies—where political conflicts are translated into pluralistic public debates—declined in favour of the executive branches of the state, first and foremost the government. This shift in the institutional balance of power was coupled with the personalization of politics, where individual politicians increasingly competed for popular appeal to gain party and government leadership. As a result, political discourse has simplified and shows little concern for systematic argumentation, while decision-making power is increasingly attributed to experts, pre-politically legitimized by their technical knowledge and by the ideal of meritocracy. Finally, and at a more fundamental level, the belief in the superior allocative capacity of markets vis-à-vis politics has been cemented, in the last decades, in the political élite and in the broader public alike.

On the demand-side, political institutions have suffered from a deficit of legitimacy, expressed by the decreasing confidence they inspire in citizens.

New participatory practices, which bypass institutional mediation and directly engage social actors in collective decisions and responsibilities, were touted as an antidote to the crisis of representative democracy—a statement that would deserve a closer examination, that is not fitting into the limited scope of this chapter.

Moving to the macro variables connected to social transformations, the first element to be considered is the complexification of collective problems. Institutional and political actors often lack the material and, crucially, cognitive resources for confronting these new problems. They thus seek the support of civil society, which can contribute solutions through voluntarism and reflexivity. This supplementary role of social actors is compounded by the growth of new social mobilizations centered around the promotion of active citizenship (e.g. community-supported urban farming). One of the consequences of the reinvigoration of civic activism and civic engagement is the renewed trust in the reservoirs of knowledge dispersed across the social body, which can be accessed through partecipatory tecniques.

The meso variables are related to the normative and cognitive blueprints—produced by global or sectoral mediators, as for the theory of *référentiel* discussed previously—which circulate in the policy space and act as models for legislation enhancing participation. The European Commission's *European Governance—A White Paper* [23], the OECD's *Citizens as Partners* [24], or the World Bank's *Participatory Budgeting* [25] are examples of publications with long-lasting influence on the planning of participatory practices worldwide. Participation is nowadays a recognizable area of operation for organizations dealing with global governance [26], and it has been embedded in most international policy frameworks (e.g. the SDG 16.7 of UN Sustainable Development Goals).

Participatory practices follow these meso-level circuits and move from local or national experimental responses to contingent issues to templates for solving similar impasses in other jurisdictions and, eventually, to standards of global policy.

Finally, the micro-level variables are connected to concrete aspects of decision-making processes. At this level, participation is an instrument for reaching decisions about contentious issues, such as the distribution of social resources that benefits some social groups at the expense of others. Participatory processes incentivize collaboration to reach shared decisions and help gather a wider knowledge and resource pool for selecting and implementing a course of action. Micro-level participation is thus a tool for overcoming decisional stalls and for avoiding impractical choices, which would imply high costs and conflicts. An example of this is the adoption of participatory techniques in the sensitive context of large infrastructure projects, particularly when they are met by the opposition of local communities.

3 Impacts and Perils of Participation

When the outcomes of participatory processes are considered, a paradox becomes evident: participation was widely adopted, but concrete experiences show it only had a limited impact on policy choices. This weak and uncertain impact is greatly relevant for understanding participation, even though it is not a new problem. It was already scrutinized by S. Arnstein in her seminal work from the late 1960s, *A Ladder of Citizen Participation* [27]. Much research has since concluded that available evidence about the effective impact of participatory mechanisms are sparse [28]. Studies in the United Kingdom [29] and Spain [30], for example, found that participatory processes have had limited efficacy, despite a growing political interest in implementing them.

Scholars argued that these results were consistent with a critical understanding of new participation as primarily symbolic and consultative in nature [31]. The issue has been related to other alleged limitations of participation, such as the tendency to be confined to the micro level [32]—both in terms of its narrow spatial scope and its focus on policy niches—and to overlook the asymmetrical power relations inside and outside participatory forums [33].

The seemingly contradictory relationship between impact and diffusion of participation can be better explained by addressing the reasons that motivate the adoption of participatory techniques. We can roughly distinguish three main types of expected impacts justifying the implementation of participatory processes.

First, we can identify a functional impact. Here, participation should enhance the efficiency and efficacy of administrative actions, particularly in the case of local governments. When, for example, citizens are engaged in the requalification of a local public space (e.g. a park, a square), one central assumption is that participation will cement their support for the project, increasing the responsibility they perceive to have over its usage and maintenance. This, in turn, will help reduce the future scarce public resources allocated to its upkeep.

Second, participatory practices are initiated to achieve social impact. Participation is expected to help create community ties, strengthen social cohesion, or experiment with new forms of social relationship. It is not uncommon to find that a participatory process led participants to form associations, or merge existing ones, to undertake a new project or tackling a common problem.

Finally, participation may be utilized to achieve political impact. In this case, it should redistribute decision-making power from the political to the social sphere. Through the means of participatory mechanisms, social actors can acquire a meaningful influence over a wide range of public choices, and participatory forums are thus institutionalized into public governance. However, when the stakes are high (e.g. for decisions over the distribution of collective resources), participation risks to be 'colonized' by actors possessing the material and ideational resources to bend participatory decision making towards their interests and goals.

The more participation is skewed towards political impact, the higher the risk of participation being co-opted by few resourceful actors (i.e. the pledge to equally include everyone who is affected becomes more rhetorical). Conversely, the more the functional impact is preeminent, the narrower the participatory practice is in scope and content (i.e. the promise to democratize the political sphere becomes less meaningful) [34].

This heuristic principle may help us reconsider the opportunities and risks of participation. If planned and managed carefully, participatory techniques may improve the quality of public decisions. By including the stakeholders affected by a policy choice in the decision-making process, these techniques enable policymakers to collect relevant information that they may have lacked about a collective problem. Participation may also activate networks of social relationships, reconstituting the social capital of local communities. The deliberative (i.e. reflexive and argumentative) character of new participation should enhance the legitimacy of decisions, even when they concern difficult or contentious issues. Finally, by bringing together different perspectives and opinions, participatory practices may incentivize creative and genuinely new solutions to collective problems.

On the other hand, the new forms of political participation are confronted with the pitfall of window dressing, or the risk of becoming purely rhetorical devices for justifying predetermined choices on the basis of the alleged engagement of the public in decision making.

Even when participatory practices are effectively seeking to form decisions through an open-ended deliberation, they are exposed to the pitfall of liturgical proceduralism, i.e. following a rigorous and demanding procedure that is ultimately devoid of any type of impact. Empty proceduralism is often the unintended consequence of poor planning and unforeseen contingencies, hence it is detectable only in an a posteriori reconsideration, after the participatory process has ended.

Both these shortcomings expose participation, and the institutional actors who promote it, to potential backlashes. Quite obviously, activating participatory processes that do not affect decisions, do not strengthen social cohesion, and do not share decision-making power with citizens is likely to be perceived as a waste of public resources. Moreover, purely rhetorical or grossly inefficacious practices can be—and, in most of the cases, are—recognized as such by participants and commentators, subjecting the promoters to the risk of public denunciation and delegitimization. The perception of being caught in an instrumental or meaningless process has consequences on the disposition of citizens towards future participation, reducing their commitment and depleting the 'participatory capital' of local communities.

A second set of problems arises from the tendency towards the 'technicization' of participation. Examples of this tendency are the prominent role that experts and facilitators play in the design and implementation of participatory practices, as well as the vast array of techniques and sectoral knowledge developed in the last decades. Facilitators frame the issues, the interactions, and the stakes of participatory practices through expert knowledge and procedural tools. Moreover, this epistemic community [35] helps to move the legitimacy of the outcomes of participation to a technical ground. The last part of this chapter is devoted to discussing the potential depoliticizing effect of this technical posture on the process and the results of participation.

The 'technicization' of participatory procedures implies the formalization of citizen engagement. The pace of decision and the modes of interaction among participants are increasingly predetermined by facilitators, following the criteria of efficiency and responsiveness of decision making. By abiding by those rules, participants internalize a sense of their own responsibility towards the development of the process and of active involvement in its results. While formalization is instrumental to increasing the legitimacy of participation, it may foster an uncritical acceptance of the scope and targets of deliberation set by facilitators (on the behalf of institutional promoters). Hence, the 'technicization' of procedures is a crucial component of the top-down structuring of participatory forums which characterizes new participation.

By narrowing down the alternative scenarios which are considered and deliberated upon by participants, these 'invited' spaces [36] of participation have a depoliticizing effect. Empirical studies [37] confirm that the rules of the game shape participant perceptions of what can be achieved by the participatory process. This, in turn, leads participants to adjust their expectations to allegedly realistic, rather than desirable, outcomes.

On the other hand, depoliticized procedures favor the depoliticization of the results of participation by downplaying or removing the conflictual aspects of decision making. Techniques and procedural tools tend to normalize the emergence of conflicts by confining it to specific moments and forms of expression. At a more fundamental level, for turning political and economic conflicts into argumentative disagreements, expert knowledge reframes contentious issues and conflictual stakes into technical problems and differing viewpoints. This discursive depoliticization does not remove the reality of conflicting interests and goals over the distribution of collective resources: it is merely set aside, on the premise that rational argumentation leads to consensus decisions, which are considered both 'competent' and 'impartial' [38].

The more participation is institutionalized into the public governance of collective resources—thereby increasing the stakes—the more actors possessing social and economic power (according to the present unbalanced social structuration) are incentivized to achieve a leading position in participatory processes.

In the past decades, stakeholder networks were increasingly presented as a solution to both the rigidity of traditional governmental bureaucracy and the fragmentation and exclusionary potential of market governance, and adopted as a model of horizontal distribution of decision-making power [39]. In light of this historical development towards network governance, participatory practices are increasingly at risk of becoming a 'flanking mechanism' for the hegemony of the interests and goals of resourceful private actors in decisions about collective problems and social goals [40].

Following an interpretative approach centered around the nexus between depoliticization and politicization [41], this last incarnation of participation risks to depoliticize collective issues, by removing them from the responsibility of elected officials, and to politicize the demands of the private actors that possess enough resources to align decision making to their own interests and goals.

This scenario is especially concerning for a field devoted to the preservation of the collective right to wellbeing and to the provision of essential public goods, such as healthcare.

References

1. Dryzek JS (2000) Deliberative democracy and beyond: liberals, critics, contestations. Oxford University Press, Oxford
2. de Sousa Santos B, Avritzer L (2005) Introduction: opening up the canon of democracy. In: de Sousa Santos B (ed) Democratizing democracy: beyond the liberal democratic canon. Verso, London, pp xxxiv–lxxiv
3. Bath J, Wakerman J (2015) Impact of community participation in primary health care: what is the evidence? Aust J Primary Health 21(1):2–8
4. Degeling C, Carter SM, Rychetnik L (2015) Which public and why deliberate?—a scoping review of public deliberation in public health and health policy research. Soc Sci Med 131:114–121
5. De Freitas C, Martin G (2015) Inclusive public participation in health: policy, practice and theoretical contributions to promote the involvement of marginalised groups in healthcare. Soc Sci Med 135:31–39
6. Conklin A, Morris Z, Nolte E (2015) What is the evidence base for public involvement in health-care policy?: results of a systematic scoping review. Health Expect 18(2):153–165
7. Castro EM, Van Regenmortel T, Vanhaecht K, Sermeus W, Van Hecke A (2016) Patient empowerment, patient participation and patient-centeredness in hospital care: a concept analysis based on a literature review. Patient Educ Couns 99(12):1923–1939
8. Renedo A, Marston CA, Spyridonidis D, Barlow J (2015) Patient and public involvement in healthcare quality improvement: how organizations can help patients and professionals to collaborate. Public Manage Rev 17(1):17–34
9. Tobiano G, Bucknall T, Marshall A, Guinane J, Chaboyer W (2016) Patients' perceptions of participation in nursing care on medical wards. Scand J Caring Sci 30(2):260–270
10. Batalden M, Batalden P, Margolis P, Seid M, Armstrong G, Opipari-Arrigan L, Hartung H (2016) Coproduction of healthcare service. BMJ Qual Saf 25(7):509–517
11. Ocloo J, Matthews R (2016) From tokenism to empowerment: progressing patient and public involvement in healthcare improvement. BMJ Qual Saf 25(8):626–632
12. Palmer VJ, Weavell W, Callander R, Piper D, Richard L, Maher L, Boyd H, Herrman H, Furler J, Gunn J, Iedema R, Robert G (2019) The Participatory Zeitgeist: an explanatory theoretical model of change in an era of coproduction and codesign in healthcare improvement. Med Humanit 45(3):247–257
13. Mayka L (2019) The origins of strong institutional design: Policy reform and participatory institutions in Brazil's health sector. Comp Polit 51(2):275–294
14. Pagatpatan CP, Ward PR (2018) Understanding the factors that make public participation effective in health policy and planning: a realist synthesis. Aust J Prim Health 23(6):516–530
15. Slutsky J, Tumilty E, Max C, Lu L, Tantivess S, Hauegen RC, Whitty JA, Weale A, Pearson SD, Tugendhaft A, Wang H, Staniszewska S, Weerasuriya K, Ahn J, Cubillos L (2016) Patterns of public participation: opportunity structures and mobilization from a cross-national perspective. J Health, Org Manage 30(5):751–768
16. Oh J, Ko Y, Baer Alley A, Kwon S (2015) Participation of the lay public in decision-making for benefit coverage of national health insurance in South Korea. Health Syst Reform 1(1):62–71
17. Campbell M, Escobar O, Fenton C, Craig P (2018) The impact of participatory budgeting on health and wellbeing: a scoping review of evaluations. BMC Public Health 18(822):1–11
18. Jobert B, Muller P (1987) L'État en action: politiques publiques et corporatismes. Presses Universitaire de France, Paris
19. Muller P (2003) Les politiques publiques. 5e édition. Presses Universitaire de France, Paris
20. Zittoun P, Demongeot B (2010) Debates in French policy studies: from cognitive to discursive approaches. Crit Policy Stud 3(3–4):391–406
21. Saurugger S (2010) The social construction of the participatory turn: the emergence of a norm in the European Union. Eur J Polit Res 49(4):471–495
22. Pateman C (2012) Participatory democracy revisited. Perspectives on politics 10(1):7–19

23. European Commission (2001) European Governance—A White Paper. Available at: https://ec.europa.eu/commission/presscorner/detail/en/DOC_01_10
24. OECD (2001) Citizens as partners: OECD handbook on information, consultation and public participation in policy-making. Available at: https://www.oecd-ilibrary.org/governance/citizens-as-partners_9789264195578-en
25. Shah A (ed) (2007) Participatory budgeting. Available at: https://elibrary.worldbank.org/doi/abs/10.1596/978–0-8213-6923-4
26. For an example, see the OECD's Innovative Citizen Participation initiative (https://www.oecd.org/gov/innovative-citizen-participation.htm) or the World Bank's Strategic Framework for citizen engagement (http://documents.worldbank.org/curated/en/266371468124780089/Strategic-framework-for-mainstreaming-citizen-engagement-in-World-Bank-Group-operations-engaging-with-citizens-for-improved-results)
27. Arnstein SR (1969) A ladder of citizen participation. J Am Plan Assoc 35(4):216–224
28. Papadopoulos Y, Warin P (2007) Major findings and paths for research: a concluding note. Eur J Polit Res 46(4):591–605
29. Newman J, Barnes M, Sullivan H, Knops A (2004) Public participation and collaborative governance. J Soc Policy 33(2):203–223
30. Font J, Blanco I (2007) Procedural legitimacy and political trust: the case of citizen juries in Spain. Eur J Polit Res 46(4):557–589
31. Papadopoulos Y, Warin P (2007) Are innovative, participatory and deliberative procedures in policy making democratic and effective? Eur J Polit Res 46(4):445–472
32. Sintomer Y, De Maillard J (2007) The limits to local participation and deliberation in the French 'politique de la ville'. Eur J Polit Res 46(4):503–529
33. Fischer F (2012) Participatory governance: from theory to practice. In: Levi-Faur D (ed) The Oxford handbook of governance. Oxford University Press, Oxford, pp 457–471
34. Moini G (2012) Teoria critica della partecipazione. Un approccio sociologico, FrancoAngeli, Milano
35. Haas PM (1992) Introduction: epistemic communities and international policy coordination. Int Org 46(1):1–35
36. Boswell J, Settle C, Dugdale A (2015) Who speaks, and in what voice? The challenge of engaging 'the public' in health policy decision-making. Public Manage Rev 17(9):1358–1374
37. Barnes M, Newman J, Sullivan HC (2007) Power, participation and political renewal: Case studies in public participation. The Policy Press, Bristol
38. Urbinati N (2014) Democracy disfigured. Harvard University Press, Cambridge
39. Klijn E, Skelcher C (2007) Democracy and governance networks: compatible or not? Public Adm 85(3):587–608
40. Davies JS (2012) Network governance theory: a Gramscian critique. Environ Plan A 44(11):2687–2704
41. d'Albergo E, Moini G (2017) Depoliticizing public action by politicizing issues, practices and actors. The role of Resilience Thinking in a program of the Cariplo Foundation. Partecipazione e Conflitto 10(2): 381–420

Urban Health Multidisciplinary Actions Promoting Health in an Urban Environment

Alessandra Battisti and Maurizio Marceca

1 Urban Health: The Link Between Well-Being and the Urban Environment

The crisis faced by the Western lifestyle model when dealing with problems associated with climate change and the new roles that cities and buildings must play in a world of globalisation fosters the rise of a new approach that marks a necessary turning point for our civilisation. For decades now, the fight against climate change has seen many of the world's most important countries committing themselves to agreements—from the Kyoto Protocol of 1992 to the Paris COP21 in 2015—that are gradually getting better at establishing goals, strategies and actions for improving quality of life and protecting the entire planet, even if some venture doubts on the concrete possibility of achieving them [1].

Today, over half the world's population lives in an urban environment (a proportion that is estimated to reach 70% by 2050) [2]. Moreover, as part of this evolving scenario, modern-day cities are experiencing an era of considerable contradictions not only in terms of demographic growth but also as regards the unequal distribution of wealth, social inequality, unequal exposure to risk, unbridled consumption of land and energy, high levels of pollution and the exponential increase in associated diseases.

Urban sustainability is one of the significant themes of the 2030 Agenda for Sustainable Development [3], which considers urban space one of the crucial factors for development. In this document, the analysis of this issue does not limit itself to urban sustainability in the 'strict' sense, but rather applies it across the board and

A. Battisti (✉)
Department of Planning, Design, and Technology of Architecture, Sapienza University of Rome, Rome, Italy
e-mail: alessandra.battisti@uniroma1.it

M. Marceca
Department of Public Health and Infectious Diseases, Sapienza University of Rome, Rome, Italy

A. Battisti et al. (eds.), *Urban Health*, Green Energy and Technology,
https://doi.org/10.1007/978-3-030-49446-9_3

takes into consideration, wherever possible, the level of urbanisation as regards other indicators linked to sustainable development as well. Thus there are many facets that should be considered in a systemic, inclusive and integrated way in order to analyse urban sustainability, such as poverty and exclusion, which for some time now have no longer been merely urban or metropolitan phenomena typical of less developed cities or in so-called 'underdeveloped countries'; instead they are also clearly visible in more developed countries and cities, significantly diminishing the proportion of traditional urban middle classes and average conditions of wealth and well-being. According to studies and research carried out by the world's foremost international organisations (the OECD and the UN) who have been following the transformation of large urban and metropolitan areas as well as the main trends found there for over a decade, the acceleration of urbanisation has strengthened the importance of big cities and metropolitan areas. Thanks to their role as centres managing and responding to demographic and epidemiological change, they are in the front line when tackling the issue of public health, one of the most pressing problems in global development. Increasing cases of chronic-degenerative diseases, the constant threat of epidemics (take the recent case of the coronavirus epidemic, which forced the Chinese authorities to 'seal off' entire cities with millions of inhabitants) [4] and the constant risk of violence (particularly against women) and injury (take the number of road accidents) are the main concerns as regards public health in urban areas, where progress in health not only depends on the strength of health care systems but, above all, on the creation of healthier urban environments.

This awareness of the positive and negative effects of urban demographic growth (particularly as regards the adult population) and social change, as well as those of innovation and technological development, should not merely result in the abandonment of policies fostering growth and the competitive appeal of cities and territories. Instead, it means not simply considering the links between economic-urban development, public health and social integration as natural and therefore given, but rather as a political objective that must be continually reconstructed and which must complement policies, living spaces and services that adapt to changing circumstances.

It means no longer considering urban health a side issue of public housing policies, and going beyond actions that are strictly focused on social welfare, making the issue of public health one of the lynchpins of policies to do with local development, town planning redevelopment, housing policies, policies addressing safety, education services and employment opportunities, as well as those designed to increase social capital. In the end, it means considering such actions a response to the rights of citizens and residents, particularly as regards the weakest and most vulnerable groups and, furthermore, as a response to the increased need for social cohesion and an acceptable quality of life in cities and on the planet. To this end, the WHO's longstanding, gradual redefinition of the concept of health has shifted its focus from a bio-medical model, centred on individuals and limited to the health sector, to a bio-psycho-anthropo-social model where health is the result of a number of different political, socio-economic, cultural and environmental factors (known as 'determinants').

Now, more than ever before, health is no longer an issue that is strictly associated with medical services; instead, it is a priority goal that is strongly influenced by the environment in which people live and therefore a product of fundamental development strategies implemented by local authorities using intersectoral policies that converge.

We need healthy cities that are 'continually creating and improving those physical and social environments and expanding those community resources which enable people to mutually support each other in performing all the functions of life', as stated by the WHO in 2012 [5], while a year later another WHO publication stated: 'the current arrangement of cities and urbanisation in general create as many risks as opportunities for public and individual health. If cities were properly planned, well organised and conscientiously managed, it would be possible to foster synergy between institutions, citizens and experts that could improve the living standards and health of the population' [6].

All this therefore requires a democratic and intersectoral approach that allows us to implement improvements that considerably boost individual and community empowerment and create environmental conditions that foster a change in unhealthy lifestyles and objective improvements in health that can be detected in the spirit of the Ottawa charter [7]. Interrelated strategies for regions, cities, citizens, communities, businesses and civil society are required, such as: a shift from a linear economy to a circular economy that can reuse resources, reduce the need to resort to the planet's natural capital and at the same time reduce greenhouse gas emissions; a guarantee of sustainability as regards energy and mobility from producers to consumers; and the technological, structural and demographic evolution of a more interconnected world in order to ensure sustainable equality. In recent years, an awareness of the need to look more closely at the link between health and the built environment has increased, and not just in the academic world, as part of a framework created by a new 'urban question' [8]. As regards this matter, we cannot overlook the strong moral boost provided by Pope Francis with the publication of his encyclical Laudato Si', which aims to awaken a deep consciousness amongst all people and at all levels and trigger nothing short of a revival of the neo-humanistic ethic of responsibility [9].

Reflections regarding health and the urban environment have adopted many of the assumptions, approaches and instruments of analysis typical of what is known as Global Health: the paradigm that stresses the many different dimensions of health, which depends to a large extent on context and on 'Social—later termed "structural"—determinants of Health' [10]. This model not only includes working and living environments as determinants of health, but also the built environment with its particular characteristics [11] and, above all, intangible characteristics affecting communities, particularly urban communities, such as 'social cohesion' and 'social capital' [12]. The unequal distribution of social determinants, as highlighted by the model proposed by Global Health, generates 'social inequalities in health'. The impact of inequalities in urban environments is a growing problem and a source—as in the mid-nineteenth century—of extreme social injustice [13]. The social epidemiologist Michael Marmot is currently a particularly important researcher on the world stage who, above and beyond his scientific commitment to demonstrating the existence, nature and scale of health inequalities, is flagging up the real possibility of combining responsibilities and improvements at a local level with all institutional and non-institutional players involved, as shown by his ground-breaking 'Marmot cities' experiment [14].

This is why a systemic and integrated approach is necessary if we want to guarantee sustainable urban development that takes into account climate change, factors of economic growth and of social and environmental development, as well as issues regarding urban health.

This is the orientation of global policies inspired by the clear and tangible objectives found in the UN's Sustainable Development Goals [15, 16], particularly the possible achievement of Goal 3 ('Ensure healthy lives and promote well-being for all at all ages') and Goal 11 ('Make cities and human settlements inclusive, safe, resilient and sustainable').

Goal 3 aims to guarantee health and promote the well-being of 'all at all ages'. This aim focuses on various objectives: reducing maternal and infant mortality, eradicating epidemics, fighting both infectious and chronic diseases, promoting well-being and mental health. Much progress has been made, as demonstrated by the continual increase in life expectancy and the positive results obtained in the fields of reproductive health and mother and infant health. The widespread improvement of hygiene and, generally speaking, the care taken over environmental factors have proved to be the backbone of these improvements, particularly as regards reducing infectious diseases. Some of this Goal's targets refer to the health conditions and risks faced by populations experiencing the early stages of a health transition, where mortality is still high. In contrast, there is less margin for improvement in Italy when it comes to maternal mortality and infectious diseases, while the more pressing issues concern the new epidemiological and environmental situation, not to mention the aging population. The spread of chronic-degenerative diseases (including, for example, chronic obstructive pulmonary disease-COPD and bronchial pneumonia, which are perhaps the most variable sensors of urban health) are of more concern, as are access to prevention and the correction of unhealthy lifestyles (alcohol consumption, smoking and drug addiction).

In contrast, Goal 11 addresses the issue of urban sustainability. Cities are responsible for the largest proportion of carbon emissions and energy consumption, for the increasing pressure put on the environment and problems associated with public health. The administration of the urban environment is therefore a crucial development factor that poses challenges and offers opportunities. There are many aspects that should be considered in a systemic, inclusive and integrated way so as to ensure that cities prosper in a sustainable way. The safety of people who live, work or pass through cities should be guaranteed both as regards the structural conditions of buildings and private and public infrastructure and as regards protection from crime, violence and/or public or domestic maltreatment. As regards public health, the reduction of pollution and the improvement of air quality are central aspects, combined with the proper management of waste, the water supply and sewage. The most underprivileged groups (which also include people with disabilities, the elderly, children, immigrants, the homeless, etc.) should be guaranteed the same access to services, universal access to public gardens and parks that are safe and accessible, support involving positive economic, social and environmental links between urban, periurban and rural areas, strengthening regional and national development planning, access to mobility and adequate, safe and low-cost housing, adopting and implementing integrated policies and plans that foster inclusion, the efficient use of resources, climate change adaptation and mitigation and resilience when faced with natural disasters.

Today's continually evolving cities are having to deal with much greater social diversity than before. 'We are the 99%' was one of the slogans of the Occupy Wall Street protest movement, which became its motto after the publication of Noam Chomsky's book, who chose it as the title when writing about the movement that first emerged in New York in 2011 and then spread to other American cities such as Los Angeles, Boston and Chicago. The slogan refers to the inequality with which the economic crisis of recent years has hit most Americans. A small minority is flourishing, sharing amongst its members over a third of the country's wealth. The slogan means: we are the 99% and we are suffering because of you, the 1% [17]. Furthermore, the borderline between 'centre' and 'periphery' or between 'rich' and 'poor' areas is often invisible, and yet city residents are often grouped into those who use services and benefit from urbanisation and those who find it hard (or fail) to meet their needs for reasons to do with—for example—the availability of resources, cultural characteristics, ethnic origins, gender or age. In other words, this separation of groups of city residents—known as the 'urban divide'—is basically linked to socio-economic status [18].

2 Interdisciplinarity and Multiprofessionality When Practices Meet

A series of different perspectives and interests regarding this issue are incorporated in this vision, perspectives that have encouraged the experimental and practical work presented in this book. Such work is geared towards developing a model of planned improvements that, in doing away with any type of 'greenwashing',[1] efficiently links up the various approaches emerging from field literature: from bottom-up approaches linked to the needs of the individual and the resident community (and therefore greatly affected by the problems of a society that is rapidly evolving, with a particular focus on social inclusion), to top-down approaches that address policies that develop integrated actions of a physical or economic nature.

The shift in attention that takes place in this book is inspired by an awareness that the link between health and the urban context creates complex problems that require appropriate answers, answers that must take into account the peculiarities

[1] A term that describes projects that appear environmentally sustainable but whose sustainability is only superficial.

and features of the urbs as object—i.e. the physical city—and at the same time those of the civitas as subject—understood to mean urban society, the community. Throughout the book, one consideration remains constant: an awareness that the issues for which we are trying to find and propose possible solutions for future scenarios and development are complex problems. The situation is therefore one of enormous diversity and has to tackle interdependent problems caused by a range of different factors that often don't suggest an obvious solution or easily foreseeable results and instead imply, first of all, the borrowing of know how and tools from a number of different disciplines, including social sciences such as technosciences [19], applying them within a theoretical framework and, secondly, changing the point of view and behaviour of town planners and residents themselves.

Above and beyond the required planning instruments and guidelines, the book also envisages: the use of coordinating measures that can apply improvements within a common approach; commonly adopted guidelines in favour of an intersectoral project, where strong commitment and support from political and administrative decision-makers is necessary in order to achieve authoritative institutional governance; a systemic approach that guarantees the inclusion of policies from different fields and fosters the involvement of a number of different players with clearly defined goals, roles and responsibilities; the health service's will/ability to carry out a role of advocacy and guide people towards a process of change and growth, helping the various different stakeholders to make choices that will have beneficial consequences on residents' health; and the recognition of health as a right that must be protected, considering the centrality of individuals, their rights, choices and living circumstances.

To this end, the wide range of multidisciplinary contributions found in the research presented in this book has proven extremely useful. Such research makes it possible to assess and analyse using tools that have been tried and tested in different professional fields: from the medical field of public health to architecture and town planning as well as the socio-anthropological field.

In short, the challenge is to 'interpret' this combination of social, economic, engineering and planning mechanisms within a unified approach. This has been made possible thanks to exchanges between authors and researchers concerning theoretical concepts, practices and methods, taking advantage of the specific expertise of each contributor when examining a particular aspect of urban life and working on a specific facet of the communities involved. Opportunities for discussion and sharing have created greater know how, and that is why it was decided to gather all this in a book. This has led to the description of individual improvement projects in a spirit of sharing not only approaches but above all practices that have been tried and tested in the field and through constant cooperation with the communities involved. The text focuses on individual examples and attempts to highlight their potential, their limitations and the problems that emerged during the various phases in which such projects were implemented. This has been done with a view to improving the efficacy of those projects as well as contribute the experience gained from practical applications to a field that has promising prospects for future development. This operation required a cross-contamination between different cultures and experiences (getting to know one another so as to understand each other, sharing and building alliances without one attempting to dominate the other, developing a common terminology and intentions that are in tune with each other); cooperative relationships, alliances and enduring and systematic collaboration in order to achieve the goals of sectors that, though different, also improve health and well-being. Given the need to interpret the combination of different mechanisms that affect urban environments and the need to inform, enhance and improve existing field work as part of a unified approach, the book also aims to compile templates—for each example of research-action—arranged in a mutually agreed form. This has been done so as to discuss and compare the implementation methods and content of the five multidisciplinary urban health projects presented here, addressing: (1) the methodological/experimental aspects, i.e. the study methodologies and examination of context, with a view to integrating tools (qualitative and quantitative methodologies), particularly as regards the possibility of analysing the state of health and needs of populations suffering from housing problems and high levels of unauthorised housing turn-over; (2) the relationship with residents, i.e. the ways in which a community can be involved, not merely using passive information channels, but also in ways that inform people and encourage them to get actively involved in projects (ensuring that the population can understand the technical language used and can autonomously tackle the problems of its environment, identifying the priorities and interacting in an organic and independent way with institutions such as local authorities, health services and universities); (3) the relationship with and between institutions (what is known as horizontal and vertical 'subsidiarity'), i.e. the measures that various working groups have at their disposal (institutional protocols, regular meetings, etc.), so as to share positive experiences of cooperation with a view to promoting health, advocacy processes, etc.

3 Conclusions … Combining Technical Expertise and Humanity

Alongside the methodological approach the book has chosen and the contribution made by various different disciplines to the comprehension of the complex issue tackled, the book also includes a review of the results of research that recommends turning to the weight of a systemic paradigm and sees cooperation between disciplines as a necessary process of development if we want to manage not only the future of town planning, but also that of our way of inhabiting the Earth. As Howard Zinn once said: 'To be hopeful in bad times is not just foolishly romantic. It is based on the fact that human history is a history not only of cruelty, but also of compassion, sacrifice, courage, kindness. What we choose to emphasize in this complex history will determine our lives. If we see only the worst, it destroys our capacity to do something. If we remember those times and places—and there are so many—where people have behaved magnificently, this gives us the energy to act, and at least the possibility of sending this spinning top of a world in a different direction. And if we do act, in however small a way, we don't have to wait for some grand utopian future. The future is an infinite succession of presents, and to live now as we think human beings should live, in defiance of all that is bad around us, is itself a marvelous victory' [20].

References

1. Morin E (2015) Penser global. L'homme et son univers. Editions Robert Laffont, Paris. [trad. it. '7 lezioni sul pensiero globale'. Raffaello Cortina Editore, Milan]
2. UN (2014) World urbanization prospects. United Nations, Department of Economic and Social Affairs, Population Division, New York
3. UN (2017) New urban agenda. United Nations. Available at: http://habitat3.org/documents-and-archive/new-urban-agenda/. Last accessed: Sept 2019
4. World Health Organisation (2020) China leaders discuss next steps in battle against coronavirus outbreak. Available at: https://www.who.int/news-room/detail/28-01-2020-who-china-leaders-discuss-next-steps-in-battle-against-coronavirus-outbreak
5. World Health Organisation (2012) Health 2020: a European policy framework supporting action across government and society for health and well-being. WHO Regional Committee for Europe, sixty-second session. WHO Regional Office for Europe, Copenhagen
6. World Health Organisation (2013) European Healthy Cities Network. Phase VI (2014–2018): goals and requirements. WHO Regional Office for Europe, Copenhagen
7. World Health Organisation (1986) WHO: Ottawa Charter for Health Promotion. First International Conference on Health Promotion, Ottawa, 21 Nov 1986. Available at: https://www.who.int/healthpromotion/conferences/previous/ottawa/en/. Last accessed: Nov 2019
8. Harvey D (2015) Città Ribelli. Il Saggiatore, Milan
9. Pope Francis (2015) Encyclical Letter 'Laudato si" on care for our common home. Libreria Editrice vaticana
10. World Health Organisation (2008) Closing the gap in a generation: health equity through action on the social determinants of health. Final report. WHO, Geneva
11. Barton H, Grant M (2006) A health map for the local human habitat. J R Soc Promot Public Health 126(6):252–261
12. Cattell V (2001) Poor people, poor places, and poor health: the mediating role of social networks and social capital. Soc Sci Med 52(10):1501–1516
13. Gelormino E, Melis G, Marietta C, Costa G (2015) From built environment to health inequalities: an explanatory framework based on evidence. Prev Med Reports 2:737–745
14. Marmot M (2015) The health gap: the challenge of an unequal world. Bloomsbury Ed., London
15. UN (2015) 17 goals for sustainable development. Available at: http://www.un.org/sustainabledevelopment/sustainable-development-goals/
16. UN (2018) Global indicator framework for the sustainable development goals and targets of the 2030 agenda for sustainable development. Available at: https://unstats.un.org/sdgs/indicators/Global%20Indicator%20Framework%20after%202019%20refinement_Eng.pdf. Last accessed: Sept 2019
17. Chomsky N (2012) Siamo il 99%. Edizioni Nottetempo, Milan
18. UN-HABITAT (2010) State of the World's Cities 2010/11. Cities for all: bridging the urban divide, 1st edn. United Nations Human Settlements Programme, Earthscan, Sterling
19. Corburn J (2004) Confronting the challenges in reconnecting urban planning and public health. Am J Public Health 94:541–546
20. Zinn H (2002) You can't be neutral on a moving train and a power governments cannot suppress. Beacon Press, Boston

Equity in Health. Community-Based Action Research in a Compound of the Metropolitan Area of Rome an Experience of Urban Health

Silvia Iorio, Alessandra Battisti, Livia Maria Salvatori, Marco Tofani, Aurora Angelozzi, Susanna Caminada, Lorenzo Paglione, Alessandro Rinaldi, Asia Barnocchi, Alberto Calenzo, Giuseppe Ricotta, Alessandra Brandimarte, and Maurizio Marceca

Abstract In some urban areas, there are veritable islands of spatial segregation, whose effects on health are current the subject of in-depth analysis. However, these studies involve disciplines and expertise that too often lack proper interaction. This action research project was developed through the community-based approach. Moreover, a research model and structured intervention were created in order to adequately grasp the complexity of the relationships among health disparities, socio-environmental and economic distress in an "ecological" perspective of health. The proper study of social determinants of health and their unequal spatial distribution can allow researchers to reach significant, fair and lasting solutions in order to challenge and reduce disparities in health.

S. Iorio (✉)
Unit of History of Medicine and Bioethics, Sapienza University of Rome, Rome, Italy
e-mail: silvia.iorio@uniroma1.it

A. Battisti · A. Barnocchi · A. Calenzo
Department of Planning, Design, and Technology of Architecture, Sapienza University of Rome, Rome, Italy

L. M. Salvatori · M. Tofani · A. Angelozzi · S. Caminada · M. Marceca
Department of Public Health and Infectious Diseases, Sapienza University of Rome, Rome, Italy
e-mail: liviamaria.salvatori@uniroma1.it

L. Paglione
Department of Civil, Building and Environmental Engineering DICEA, Sapienza University of Rome, Rome, Italy

A. Rinaldi
ASL Roma 2, Rome, Italy

G. Ricotta
Department of Social Sciences and Economics, Sapienza University of Rome, Rome, Italy

A. Brandimarte
Department of Prevention, ASL Roma 1, Rome, Italy

A. Battisti et al. (eds.), *Urban Health*, Green Energy and Technology,
https://doi.org/10.1007/978-3-030-49446-9_4

Keywords Inter-disciplinary and inter-institutional project design · Community based · Ecological approach to health

1 Spatial Segregation and Socio-environmental Marginality in a Neighbourhood on the Outskirts of Rome

Investigating how and the extent to which the spatial structuring of neighbourhoods and their interaction within the urban environment affects health in a specific social context requires a strong commitment to designing innovative tools and methods in the field of urban health. If it is true that socio-economic status is today one of the most important predictors of morbidity and premature mortality at a global level, it is also true that literature has highlighted the need to consider in the genesis of health inequalities a wide range of aspects [1]. These studies must not be limited simply to economics, demonstrating the influence of social, but also purely cultural and environmental aspects [2]. Thanks to the increasingly strong connection among urbanism, architecture, anthropology, sociology and medicine, we are now reaching an "ecological" health perspective [3, 4], through which the study of social health determinants and their unequal distribution in the population [5], resulting in the study of the generation of structurally determined health differences. In the international scientific field, the impact that the social gradient can have on the well-being of a specific population group has been established. The study of the greater frequency of mortality and morbidity in the most vulnerable groups, discriminated on the basis of population groups, has assumed a central role in their social and economic position [6]. In Italy, as in all of Europe, in the last twenty years there has been a notable reversal of the social gradient that, as can be observed specifically in Rome, is associated with the vast presence of areas subject to socio-environmental segregation [7]. The area known as the ex-Bastogi residence (or simply Bastogi in this article), which is the subject of our study, is certainly emblematic in this regard. The Bastogi residential complex is an enclave in Northwest Rome, characterized by multi-storey buildings settled in a connective tissue of little value and quality (Fig. 1).

Bastogi is a sort of island in the city, where social degradation is quite evident in people with serious conditions of socio-economic and occupational distress. In addition, building degradation caused by a physical decay of the housing facilities and public outdoor spaces give the whole area a sense of evident marginality.

1.1 Description of the Setting

Built by the Bastogi Construction Company in the 1980s, these apartment buildings never used for their original purpose of accommodating flight personnel of the national airline company. Subsequently, after patients were gradually phased out from the Santa Maria della Pietà psychiatric hospital, the area was squatted in the early

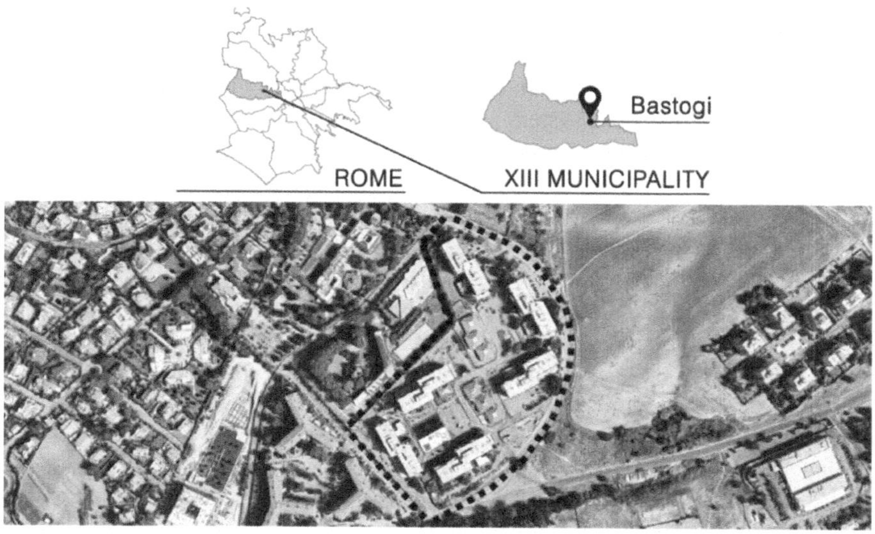

Fig. 1 Location and top view of the Bastogi compound in 2019 *Source* Sustainability [35]. Modified by the authors

1990s by organized groups of citizens with housing problems [8]. The area was taken over by the Municipality of Rome in 1992, which formalized its use for temporary housing assistance. Bastogi is a residential area of 5 ha of land surrounded by large perimeter containment walls, in turn surrounded by a ring road without sidewalks [9].

Current estimates show that around 2000 people live in the area, of which 1033 are formally 'registered' by the ISTAT National Statistics Institute in 2011 [10]. The 'resident' population shows a strong prevalence of subjects in young adulthood. In addition to Italians, there is a notable percentage of the Italian Roma population from Campania, as well as an equally significant presence of non-Italian citizens. Data shows that 18% of the total [10] come mainly from Eastern Europe, North Africa and Latin America. Many of the families are long-term occupants, others are quite recent, while some, even today after 28 years, have unregistered status since there are no official lists of assignees [9]. Only a part of the residents is included in the official register. The building complex, including the illegally squatted buildings, is no longer part of the original classification of Temporary Housing Assistance Centres. Moreover, they are not part of the ERP Public Buildings, due to the fact that the apartments are not up to permanent housing standards. No administrative legal provisions are feasible, given the hybrid and undetermined nature of the Bastogi residence. Although it is owned by the Municipality of Roma Capitale, the complex does not fall under any official classification. All residents are distributed in six buildings of five floors each. Based on the territorial social plan, there are about 450 one-room and two-room apartments, whose size varies mainly between 26 m^2 (although the minimum required by the Health Ministry [11] decree 5/07/1975 is

28 m^2) and 60 m^2, hosting nuclei that often exceed 4 people. Furthermore, since these buildings are made of prefabricated lightweight concrete panels, they do not provide suitable insulation. The fixtures are also obsolete with uninsulated single glass. The lack of a heating system aggravates the sensation of indoor discomfort. There are infiltrations from air and water everywhere, with condensation and mould that are harmful to the people's health. Pipe and drain failures are commonplace, and water supply is sometimes non-existent. Problems are also caused by a lack of regular maintenance.

Compounding the situation, the organization and state of building systems and technology are dismal. This has the greatest impact on the level of degradation and, favouring spatial marginalization. All the residents use gas cylinders for cooking food. The drains of the bathrooms in some cases flow into the garages at the base of buildings. Many apartments—around 50%—lack hot water and heating. Other factors that aggravate the social unease of the residents are the inadequacy of the housing and the overpopulation of the buildings, while the lack of formal transfer to permanent housing creates a sense of transience [9].

In addition, the structural conditions as well as the social image of the neighbourhood clearly underline how serious the implications of perceived well-being may be. The subjective well-being perceived, defined as the overall assessment of one's physical, psychic and socio-emotional conditions, influences individual health, quality of social relations, work productivity and adherence to socially acceptable behaviour and attitudes [12]. Subjective well-being can become a problem not only for the individual, but for the entire community. The feeling of anxiety is exacerbated by these factors, triggering a downward spiral in which the widespread perceived malaise feeds systematic and equally pervasive attitudes of self-destructive and anti-social behaviour in life and at work. Consequently, many governments and international organizations have recently begun to compare the subjective well-being perceived in various nations in order to identify the social and economic policies that allow for the sustainable social development of a nation [13]. Consistent with the biopsychosocial model, research indicates that this perceived well-being can be influenced by numerous factors, which include innate genetic variables as well as various situational and circumstantial determinants that originate in the interaction with a person's socio-cultural context [14]. It is therefore reasonable to assume that the physical, mental and social well-being of people can also be connected to the perception of living in an area that they value positively and that are equally positively valued at a social level. In fact, in the ex Bastogi context, as demonstrated by the qualitative research carried out in 2015 [15], the sense of belonging to the local community is determined by self-recognition as a group made up of subjects who live in conditions of great social and economic hardship with a high dependence on institutions and scarce integration into the legal labour market. It is a sense of belonging that does not exclude in any way the frustration and suffering experienced in recognizing oneself as belonging to a specific social marginality [16].

Two perspectives in fact prevail. The first is defined by a closed perspective around a suffering corporeity that is progressively reduced to isolation, from which the subject finds no other exit than that of painful emotions. The second is a resistance, embodied in an oppositional behavioral style that often results in violence and abuse. That said, it is possible to identify different types of vulnerable groups, though not mutually exclusive: children and elderly people in a state of neglect, irregular migrants, ex-inmates, drug addicts, alcoholics and people with HIV [15]. This is often paired with widespread problems that include household violence, child abuse, prostitution and crime.

With the aim of facing an increase of social unease, over the years public institutions have made several attempts at interventions and actions [17]. However, these actions have been limited due to bias and extemporaneousness. The lack of a definitive answer to the housing problem in particular, has ended up producing an attitude of indiscriminate mistrust, if not outright hostility (especially in those who have lived there longer) towards institutions. More generally, this negative attitude is also towards those who propose initiatives to support the present community. Therefore, the precariousness of the housing situation, due to the scant possibility of finding proper housing from the Municipality, have strongly influenced the daily life of Bastogi's inhabitants, negatively affecting efforts to reintegrate with the rest of the city, and nullifying the hopes for an actual recovery. The lack of a home is often the cause of social problems while instability and inferior housing contribute to a feeling of exclusion from society.

In this regard, the words Pierre Bourdieu offer some clarity:

> To consider the home as a mere capital characterized by a rate of depreciation and the purchase of a house as an economic strategy in the strict sense, would be like stripping the product and the economic act of all historical properties. What is tacitly affirmed through the creation of a house is the will to create a permanent group, united by stable social relations, a lineage capable of perpetuating itself over time, as lasting, unchanging and stable; it is a project or a collective challenge on the future of domestic unity, that is on its cohesion, its integration, or if you prefer, on its ability to resist disintegration and dispersion [...] it is a product of affective cohesion which is strengthened and confirmed over time. Bourdieu [18]

This description helps us understand the condition of degradation and marginality experienced by the inhabitants of the residential complex, combined with obstacles to access and use of public services and assistance. These obstacles are generated in part by bureaucratic and organizational barriers. Above all, however, they are structural barriers, creating significant risks to individual and collective well-being.

1.2 Description of the Planning Process. the Community-Based Approach

The study on the Bastogi residential area began in 2015 [15]. The group applied the action-research methodology, developing the project around the community-based method [19] with an approach strongly aimed at having an impact in terms of policies towards health equality. Moreover, current cultural, scientific and epistemological paradigms do not adequately grasp the complexity of the relationships existing between personal and collective health, socio-environmental and economic discomfort and the generation of mechanisms for health and assistance inequalities [5].

Consequently, the research was designed by integrating different learning paradigms that come from sociology, architecture, medicine, history and bioethics. This approach was carried out through an institutional collaboration that involved the respective departments present in the Sapienza University of Rome, also integrating, through an inter-institutional collaboration, the local, regional and national institutions respectively the ASL Roma1 of the Public Health System, the Municipality XIII, the DEP (Department of Epidemiology of the Health Service of Lazio), the INMP (National Institute of Health, Migration and Poverty).

The general intention of the project is to put together an infrastructure of analysis and prototypical intervention that facilitates empirical studies aimed at adequately grasping the complexity of the relationships among health disparities, socio-environmental and economic discomfort, personal and collective health, involving the population and institutions in this process of analysis and implementation proposals [20]. Given the interest in achieving significant, fair and lasting solutions in the conflict, while also reducing health disparities in a context like Bastogi, the current lack of analytical systems and action-research projects involving institutions and the population suggests the need for new multidisciplinary approaches, oriented to quality of life within an ecological model of health. Consequently, the implementation of this project created a system in which the different institutions, each referring to their respective mandate, participate in the different activities and maintain a certain degree of sharing thanks to the technical round tables that meet periodically. Moreover, in the event of new activities or specific needs, meetings are organized into specific discussions and smaller round-talbers [21].

Currently, an institutional process agreement has been structured through which the local authorities and the other institutions listed above have committed themselves for the next three years to carry out studies, projects and actions that, through the direct involvement of the resident population, can carry forward an initiative to combat inequalities [22]. The epistemological view behind this research is that reality is a process of change that takes place when the people involved in a given field of action actively participate in the project. This approach differs significantly from the belief that there is an objective reality outside the observing subject, independent of its presence and its intervention. According to action-research, scientific theories and transformative practices can and must intertwine with each other in a fertile, reciprocal process, in which hypotheses guide actions and these actions generate and modify knowledge in order to formulate new hypotheses and ideas.

The emancipatory character of research lies in a methodological process. It is also a strategy that actively includes people who encounter or experience a problem, making them co-researchers through their own actions and practices. This implies that we work to establish relationships of reciprocity, fairness and trust with the population. A plan of action is developed in a collaborative manner, focusing on significant and relevant issues for those who participate, in order to recognize, respect, value and prioritize local knowledge, facilitate learning and capacity building [22]. These actions offer a constant contribution to the practice by questioning one's role, position and use of power. Therefore, the credibility of emerging knowledge is ensured among the participants.

Specifically, the project involved the participation of the population through the "Community Consultations" process or group meetings organized in order to identify, starting from the statements of the premises, the different research activities and the various initiatives to be carried out. The monthly meetings held during the first year of research took place in the common areas of the residence and in some cases in private homes. All meetings were recorded and then transcribed.

The analysis of the pertinent themes that emerged during the course of the "Community Consultations" was conducted together with the participants. The research team acted firstly to identify the different community leaders by way of a spokesperson for each of the six buildings in the area. By creating a solid group, the consultations allowed for the collection of information that could not be produced by individual interviews. The average number of participants was 10 during each meeting, and the total number of meetings to date is 20. The age groups represented by the participants start from 20 years old and reached the age of 70, encompassing all intermediate age classes. The most represented gender is women, around 80% of the participants.

During the group sessions, all participants were given the opportunity to express their point of view on the perception of the health of the community as well as their own personal experiences regarding relationships with the area and local public institutions [23]. The main criticism concerned the difficulty in involving the local community. Importantly, action-research means focusing on participation processes in which the community itself identifies the needs and solutions to their various problems. In contexts characterized by high vulnerability and marginality, this is not an easy process. In a general sense, the number of people involved in this stage of the project has certainly not been completely satisfactory. However, considering the institutional mistrust that has defined the Bastogi population for years, it is still a good start. Certainly, in places like Bastogi—where agency and empowerment are nearly entirely absent and an attitude of passive welfare is growing—the convincing solution appeared to be the participation and the activation of direct dialogue between institutions that are territorial, professional and the population [24]. Another criticism is the ability to keep the interest of local institutions constantly active. In this case, the lack of funds and the problems related to the investment of personnel outside the conventional activities by the health and social services can make ensuring effective continuity on the territory particularly difficult [25].

2 Qualitative Research

Qualitative research and participation, articulated through three different methodologies, is the foundation of all the different project actions. Specifically, qualitative research was implemented through participation in community consultations, as well as through participant observation and through semi-structured interviews and lastly through the focus groups. The first phase of the project involved an ethnographic research carried out between 2014 and 2015, which responded to two main requirements. The first looked at the representation, perception and management of the social suffering [26] of the local population. The second, through the stories of the inhabitants, investigated the different forms of inequality, social injustice and environmental discomfort. Starting from these results and from the obvious need to act through proximity operating models, work began with the engagement of the inter-institutional group. This initially set up a first phase of work through the focus group methodology carried out in 2016, which was aimed at recording the perception of the population with regard to the conditions of well-being or biological, psychological, social and environmental malaise within the area.

Specifically, the critical issues that emerged concerned the ability of the population to make proper use of services in the area and the difficulties of living in a context defined by social insecurity and a complete state of environmental degradation. The challenges of moving within the area due to the perception of a well-founded insecurity clearly emerged, as well as the pronounced feeling of unease in the relationship with the world outside of Bastogi. Many of the public services were completely abandoned as were many of the free services offered by these groups. The main contacts, according to the results of the focus groups, are limited to access to emergency healthcare services, quite often in the absence of a GP or family doctor who could instruct people in the proper use of healthcare services. From this first and initial qualitative analysis, the team decided to proceed along three paths: continuing contacts through more freely-structured focus groups, launching a quantitative research line involving social health services, while also structuring this approach through participation of the inhabitants in a questionnaire given to the residents. The questionnaire would investigate the living conditions of the local population through the analysis of housing, areas outside the home and inside Bastogi, while also analysing the theme of mobility. In addition, the various institutions worked for almost a year in order to discuss the actions with the inhabitants. With regard to the problems that could emerge during the project, possible solutions would be applied through four fundamental steps:

(1) Knowledge: through small talk and conversations, a concept developed in the field of game theory;
(2) Mapping: the mapping phase saw participatory work with the inhabitants in analysis and identification of the common assets and their activators on the territory;
(3) Experimentation: planning phase and implementation of civic collaboration and actions, including soccer fields and small parks for children (age group: 6–12 years old).

With this goal in mind, the meetings were structured through sessions of open discussion and active participation for all interested parties in order to express their personal ideas and allow moderators to methodically collect inputs. Graphic and visual tools helped facilitate more direct comprehension and understanding of the discussion topics in a participatory design process.

3 Quantitative Research

Public institutions and services decided to carry out a project that began with their relationship with the local community, often pushed by qualitative research and community consultations, in order to define and design quantitative elements that can measure and tackle inequalities in health.

Quantitative research—largely based on the results of the community consultations or focus groups—consisted primarily in the characterisation of the territory through an initial assessment of the distribution of social determinants of health within the Urban Zones adjacent to Bastogi, starting from the data of the general ISTAT Census of population and housing in 2011. The organization of the census results, available in a disaggregated manner of these "Census Sections", highlighted significant differences in the distribution of social determinants of health between Bastogi and neighbouring "Urban Zones" [27]. These differences, analysed in a recent publication [9] were nearly always statistically significant, in particular with regard to education and the physical conditions and upkeep of buildings. This allowed researchers to develop a true centre-periphery gradient in the distribution of determinants, including employment, education, income and building conditions. In conjunction with this characterisation, architectural urban planning also took place. Through an initial documentary analysis, territorial surveys were carried out on excerpts from the general regulatory plans of Rome [28] (1965 and 2008). This operation made it possible to assess the adequacy of the buildings compared to the current legislation for the purpose of safeguarding and enhancing public spaces and the individual buildings [29]. A map of past and present uses was implemented: ownership distribution; analysis of the provision of services; accessibility status detection; on-site analysis carried out through inspections with spatial and energy dimensional measurements (photographs, surveys, thermographic studies, etc.); meetings and questionnaires with the inhabitants. The questionnaires concerning the living conditions at Bastogi were administered to 100 people and 100% of the questionnaires highlighted the inadequacy of the accommodations as well as the perception of living in an insecure and hostile place with reference to the community and the physical environment. Another characteristic that emerged concerned the widespread perception of isolation and the objective difficulty in order to reach public services (100%). Again, starting from the results emerged from the focus groups, in particular those concerning the difficulties with the territorial services, the questionnaires were administered to the social services and medical staff of the ASL [local health unit] in order to understand what could be the problems in the relationship between the population and the services.

Moreover, based on the perspective of professionals working in the area, the following points were studied: knowledge of the Bastogi area; perception of the relationship between Bastogi residents and services, as well as between Bastogi operators and users; and lastly, the training needs of operators and professionals. A descriptive and univariate analysis of the data was carried out with the Chi2 and T-Student tests using the STATA software 13. Of the 148 employees involved, 73 responded (22 doctors, 25 nurses, 16 administrators, 6 other roles). From the results that emerged, although the territorial services appear adequate to the interviewees, the local professionals believe there are inequalities in access to services between the inhabitants of Bastogi—in part held responsible for these problems—and those in the neighbouring areas. Lastly, results also showed a specific difficulty for operators in establishing a profitable relationship with end-users from Bastogi [30].

Another result of the consultations and focus groups was the administration of the National Monitoring questionnaire called Progress of Healthcare Companies for Health in Italy (or *Progressi delle Aziende Sanitarie per la Salute in Italia*, with the acronym "PASSI", meaning "STEPS"). At national level, the National Centre for Disease Prevention and Control (CCM) has entrusted the National Centre for Epidemiology, Surveillance and Health Promotion (CNNEPS) with the task of designing and experimenting with a system for the monitoring of progress towards national health plan objectives. These questionnaires have a national, regional and also local importance—and are therefore also fundamental for healthcare companies. These questionnaires are also used to plan the activities of the healthcare companies and the region, offering a way to assess public health policies also at local level.

Consequently, the action research project on Bastogi has proposed to integrate the community health profile by using this method consolidated on a national scale. However, the project also broadens its analytical possibilities by applying this method to contexts of marginality and spatial segregation that today completely escape the possibilities of study and interventions by public institutions and social and health services [31]. Therefore, the applicative utility of national health monitoring systems has been recognized, including the questionnaire on Healthcare Progress for Healthcare in Italy (PASSI). Furthermore, these studies and actions also broaden this scope by producing a study that highlights not only to the complexity of the relationships among health disparities, education and economic hardship, but also on the relationship between these determinants and the socio-environmental discomfort typical of marginalised urban areas.

Together with the standard PASSI questionnaire [32], three other questionnaires were developed as a direct result of the focus groups and community consultations: one concerning health literacy, one concerning living conditions, and lastly a questionnaire that investigates the perception of the difficulties encountered by the local population in dealing with local social and health services. Administration and analysis carried out by ASL Rome 1 reached 210 subjects residing at Bastogi. At present, they study has used this information to compare the results of the PASSI Questionnaire obtained from the administration in Bastogi with the PASSI administered annually to the neighbouring Urban Zones in order to obtain an assessment of the distribution of the social determinants of health [33]. Moreover, in order to strengthen this analytical approach involving the comparative study of areas and also ensure more solid results regarding the unequal distribution of determinants, the research team decided to extend the quantitative analysis by using information extracted from three information flows identified to carry out the assessment: Hospital Information System (SIO), the Health Emergency Information System (SIES) the Register of the Causes of Death (ReNCaM). The three databases were structured starting from the ISTAT Census Sections and aggregated in urban areas in such a way as to allow for the identification and comparison of the Bastogi area and the surrounding areas [34]. The comparative study on Bastogi and the surrounding areas shows clear results, in line with what arose from the focus groups. The population in Bastogi has clearcut difficulties in accessing social and health services, prefering direct contact with the emergency room for any health problems, without any kind of intermediation. Overall, based the results of the study on these Information Systems, it was possible to conclude that Bastogi, despite being embedded in a territory characterized by strong criticalities and health inequalities, presents some singular aspects. In short, Bastogi is a sort of pocket of deprivation with strong problems regarding the use and accessibility of services.

4 Project Actions

The proposals developed by the population and public institutions during community consultations—as well as the problems encountered during the focus groups or emerging from the different questionnaires regarding living discomforts in Bastogi and relations with surrounding areas and local services—helped define the actions to be taken [20]. As a result of the analysis and elaboration of design guidelines, paired with the resulting proposals and a greater understanding gained during the work meetings, the initial regeneration actions were set in motion. The group decided to start with a pilot project of a football field and a small playground, due to the fact that the data from questionnaires revealed that 100% of the inhabitants suffer from the total lack of meeting places and public areas. On October 23rd, 2017, the park was inaugurated. The playground and football pitch cover an area of 1350 m^2 and were built using recycled pneumatics. This was the first step in reaching the regeneration of the outdoor areas [35].

The guidelines for the design and regeneration of places were based on the three groups of indicators that were analysed, processed and agreed upon during the development of the project: territorial management and urban planning; the management of natural resources and the ecological footprint; and lastly, economic and social cohesion. Consequently, the group's actions were the direct consequence of the community consultations and results from the questionnaire, specifically the information provided in the open-ended section on how to increase well-being in Bastogi. Their answers highlighted the importance of the redevelopment of outdoor areas through the creation of places where a better sense of community and social cohesion could be developed for the all those living in Bastogi. Furthermore, the choice of facilities, location, and all aspects of their realization were reached by bringing high-level professionals together with the local population, while also focusing on the cost sustainability. The amount allocated for this initial redevelopment was set by the Prosolidar Foundation, which donated the funds for their construction [35].

Therefore, the team decided to work along two lines of action, selected together with the population as the most urgent, while also being identified with public institutions as the most feasible in the short term. This meant starting to act on urban regeneration through the restructuring of the common areas [36] as well as the development of local medical actions in order to respond to the difficulties encountered in the population's relationship with local services. In order to properly unify these two actions, the team organized a day of health promotion within the redeveloped areas [37]. Moreover, in order to increase the involvement of the population—in addition to those who had participated in community consultations, focus groups and the day of health promotion—tools such as social networks were used. The aim was that of publicising all actions to the largest number of people, as well as the project's goals, in order to reach even those who were not physically present at the initiatives carried out at Bastogi. The hope was that the people could be informed and therefore interested in participating. Medical and health-related actions, together with an open dialogue with the community and activities promoted at Bastogi, are aimed at trying to approach the concept of what Michael Marmot defined as "proportional universalism" [38]. This concept allows researchers and professionals to modulate the social and health actions based on specific needs. These needs help define the services provided, resources used and intensity of interventions and actions, according to an inclusive and open approach to the entire population. Specifically, we decided to create, in a community meeting place in Bastogi, a Single Access Point set up by the Local Health Authority, for two days a month, for a period of at least three months, with the presence of health and social workers trained to increase awareness of and access to local social and health services and reduce the feeling of exclusion or inequality in the community. This action was aimed at creating the prerequisites for the future use, by the Bastogi population, of the Single Access Point at conventional service locations. In conjunction with the activation of this access point to services, a community nursing role was defined. This action has the task of implementing primary care models according to the comprehensive primary health care and initiative healthcare, with particular reference to the prevention and control of chronic diseases (also by following specific diagnostic-therapeutic-assistance approaches). Moreover, community nursing is also aimed at favouring the empowerment of individuals, groups and the community towards their own health, while also promoting experimental community participation interventions aimed at better health, support for self-care and family learning. Awareness and understanding shared by and with public institutions, the fundamental structure of the project, explicitly rejects a reductionist approach aimed at evaluating the impact that a given intervention or action has on the community. Therefore, this work moves closer towards an ecological or systemic approach that can shed light on the relationship that it is created between the intervention itself and the community. This means recognizing the community as part of institutional services and therefore considering how it is able to reduce the barriers to services and connect people, seeing the community and access to services as factors that affect determinants of health in general. For these reasons, local healthcare has been joined by the community care through activities focusing on community therapy and motor rehabilitation for a period of one year. Community care, reversing the concept of dependence by giving value to that of healthy precariousness, tries to create bonds of solidarity, through the sharing of the resources that each individual possesses. This work is aimed at creating a social space in which people's daily physical, mental and social suffering can be accepted, shared and addressed, starting with people sharing their life experiences. This social space is a tool through which information and emotions can be exchanged and social support networks can be created. Lastly, the building networks of solidarity and social inclusion, mobilizing local resources as well as individual skills, families and communities, is also an attempt to strengthen ties among people while also respecting their specific needs and beliefs.

5 Conclusions

In every action research process, the community and Institutions should both be responsible for defining the objectives, as well as the choice of the tools needed to achieve these goals. This method of carrying out interventions and actions falls quite close to the fields of cultural psycho-pedagogy and community psychology. Due to the fact that the participation process is in the hands of the participants themselves, the intervention or action, unlike classic approaches, is not based on *ex-ante* construction of objectives to be achieved by the institution. The latter finds itself in the condition of not knowing exactly where the action taken will lead the community, and tries to find—together with the participants—the very meaning behind the action [39]. In Bastogi, a place in which tragic economic and political dynamics are strongly reflected in the social and environmental landscape, action research must come to terms with numerous inter-dependent domains of analysis. These areas of analysis include: the physical domain, the social domain, the domain of physical and functional health, the psychological domain, as well as that of economics and institutions.

The spatial distribution of inequalities is directly linked to the variable configurations that these domains take on in different parts of life. Bastogi's territorial insecurity is consequently a local translation of complex phenomena regarding social 'mobility' (migration, economic crisis and development, restructuring of physical environments, increase in population), a clear reflection of the concept of urban divides where intra-metropolitan duality produces areas that have high levels of quality of life and areas characterized by poverty and spatial segregation [40]. The first are the urban territories that, due to their characteristics, are capable of intercepting the opportunities of the global market; the latter are less attractive areas for investments, trade and tourism that consequently find themselves on the outskirts of society.

On the one hand, this project an attempt to create an innovative model of multidisciplinary analysis, applicable to those contexts of marginalization and spatial segregation that today entirely escape the possibility of study and intervention by the Institutions and the Services [41]. On the other hand, the project is also trying to create innovation through a participatory process that is not always feasible [22]. As in the case of Bastogi, interventions and actions involving the community often face complex problems. Moreover, there are situations in which there is neither clear evidence of cause-effect relationship within the problem nor solutions of proven efficacy for their resolution. Due to the fact that the various elements that constitute the whole are inseparable and interdependent, it is difficult to isolate each individual cause from the entire group to which they belong. As we navigate this sea of complexity [42], we need to replace rational logic with the ecology [37] of each action.

References

1. Braveman P, Gottlieb L (2014) The social determinants of health: it's time to consider the causes of the causes. Public Health Rep 129:19–31
2. Braveman P, Gruskin S (2003) Defining equity in health. J Epidemiol Commun Health 57:254–258
3. Corburn J (2004) Confronting the challenges in reconnecting urban planning and public health. Am J Public Health 94:541–546
4. Kruize H, Droomers M, van Kamp I, Ruijsbroek A (2014) What causes environmental inequalities and related health effects? An analysis of evolving concepts. Int J Environ Res Public Health 11:5807–5827
5. Marmot M (2005) Social determinants of health inequalities. Lancet 365:1099–1104. https://doi.org/10.1016/S0140-6736-(05)71146-6
6. Cardano M (2014) Etnography and reflexivity. Eur Q Political Attitudes Ment 3:1–11
7. Trabalzi F (1989) Primavalle: urban reservation in Rome. J Archit Educ 42(3):38–46
8. Caporilli Razza S (2012) L'inadeguatezza urbanistica e la precarietà abitativa come condizioni di esclusione sociale. Il caso dell'Ex Bastogi a Roma. In: Pompeo F (2012) Paesaggi dell'esclusione sociale. Politiche degli spazi, Re-indigenizzazione ed altre malattie del territorio romano. Utet, Torino
9. Iorio S, Salvatori LM, Barnocchi A, Battisti A, Rinaldi A, Marceca M, Ricotta G, Brandimarte AM, Baglio G, Gazzaniga V et al (2019) Social inequalities in the metropolitan area of Rome. a multidisciplinary analysis of the urban segregation of the "formerly—Bastogi" compound. Ann Ig 31:211–229
10. ISTAT. Portale GIS. Available on: http://gispor-tal.istat.it/bt.viewer/. Last accessed: 9 Oct 2018
11. Decreto Ministeriale (DM) (1975) Published on Gazzetta Ufficiale, Serie Generale No. 190 del 18/07/1975. Available at: http://urbanistica.comune.trieste.it/ediliziaprivata/wp-content/uploads/2014/06/DM_5_7_75_req-uisiti-abitazioni.pdf
12. Diener E, Heintzelman SJ, Kushlev K, Tay L, Wirtz D, Lutes LD (2017) Findings all psychologists should know from the new science on subjective well-being. Can Psychol 58(2):87–104
13. Diener E, Oishi S, Lucas RE (2015) National accounts of subjective well-being. Am Psychol 70:234–242
14. Diener E, Tray L (2015) Subjective well-being and human welfare around the world as reflected in the Gallup World Poll. Int J Psychol 50:135–149
15. Iorio S (2016) Health equity? Social exclusion and mental health within a housing assistance program in Rome, Italy. Edizioni Nuova Cultura, Roma
16. Bourgois P (2010) Recognizing invisible violence: a thirty-year ethnographic retrospective. In: Rylko-Bauer B, Whiteford L, Farmer P (eds) Global health in times of violence. School for Advanced Research Press, NM, Santa Fe, pp 17–40
17. Farmer P (2003) Pathologies of power health, human rights and the new war on the poor. University of California Press, Berkeley
18. Bourdieu P (1993) Per una teoria della pratica. Con tre studi di etnologia cabila. Raffaello Cortina, Milano

19. Guta A, Flicker S, Roche B (2013) Governing through community allegiance: a qualitative examination of peer research in community-based participatory research. Critical Public Health 23(4):432–451
20. Loewenson R, Laurell AC, Hogstedt C, D'Ambruoso L, Shroff Z (2014) Participatory action research in health systems: a methods reader. TARSC, AHPSR, WHO, IDRC Canada, EQUINET, Harare, Zimbabwe
21. Alison O'Mara-Eves A, Brunton G, Oliver S, Kavanagh J, Farah JF, Thomas J (2015) The effectiveness of community engagement in public health interventions for disadvantaged groups: a meta-analysis. BMC Public Health 15:129
22. Dooris M, Heritage Z (2011) Healthy cities: facilitating the active participation and empowerment of local people. J Urb Health: Bull N Y Acad Med 90(1):74–91
23. World Health Organisation (2002) Community participation in local health and sustainable development: approaches and techniques. WHO, Genevra
24. Cyril S, Smith BJ, Possamai-Inesedy A, Renzaho AMN (2015) Exploring the role of community engagement in improving the health of disadvantaged populations: a systematic review. Glob Health Action 8
25. Guldan GS (1996) Obstacles to community health promotion. Soc Sci Med 43(5):689–695
26. Kleinman A, Das V, Lock M (1997) Social suffering. University of California Press, Berkeley-Los Angeles-London
27. Roma Capitale. Denominazione Municipi e Zone Urbanistiche. Available online: https://www.comune.roma.it/web-resources/cms/documents/ElencoZ_Urbanistiche_rg_A.pdf. Accessed on 9 May 2019
28. Nuovo Piano Regolatore Generale di Roma (2008) Available online: http://www.urbanistica.comune.roma.it/prg-2008-vigente.html. Accessed on 30 July 2019
29. Battisti A, Tucci F (2015) Urban regeneration featuring environmental quality, the management of resources and social cohesion. TECHNE J Technol Archit Environ 10:141–152
30. Borrell C, Pons-Vigués M, Morrison J, Díez È (2013) Factors and processes influencing health inequalities in urban areas. J Epidemiol Commun Health 67(5):389–391
31. Cattell V (2001) Poor people, poor places, and poor health: the mediating role of social networks and social capital. Soc Sci Med 52(10):1501–1516
32. Istituto Superiore di Sanità—Roma (IT) (2007) Coordinating Technical Group of the Behavioral Risk Factor System. PASSI (Progressi delle Aziende Sanitarie per la Salute in Italia): an Italian behavioral risk factor system. Rapporti ISTISAN: 07/30. Accessed 19 Dec 2007
33. Diez Roux AV, Mair C (2010) Neighborhoods and health. Ann N Y Acad Sci 1186:125–145
34. Pickett KE, Pearl M (2001) Multilevel analyses of neighbourhood socioeconomic context and health outcomes: a critical review. J Epidemiol Commun Health 55(2):111–122
35. Battisti A, Barnocchi A, Iorio S (2019) Urban regeneration process: The case of a residential complex in a suburb of Rome, Italy. Sustainability 11(21):6122
36. RomaToday (2017) Bastogi un campo di calcetto e due aree gioco con pneumatici fuori uso. AurelioToday, Rome. Available online: https://aurelio.romatoday.it/monte-spaccato/bastogi-campo-calcetto-pneumatici.html. Accessed on 19 July 2019
37. D'Alessandro D, Arletti S, Azara A, Buffoli M, Capasso L, Cappuccitti A, Casuccio A et al (2017) Strategies for disease prevention and health promotion in urban areas: the Erice 50 Charter. Ann Ig 29:481–493
38. Marmot M (2010) Fair society, healthy lives: the marmot review. Strategic Review of Health Inequalitites in England post-2010, London
39. Jackson S, Birn AE, Fawcett SB, Poland B, Schultz JA (2013) Synergy for health equity: integrating health promotion and social determinants of health approaches in and beyond the Americas. Rev Panam Salud Publica 34(6):473–480
40. Lelo K, Monni S, Tomassi F (2018) Urban inequalities in Italy: a comparison between Rome, Milan and Naples. Tvaronavičienė M (ed) Entrep Sustain Issues 6(2):939–957
41. Davidson LF, Doyle M, Silver EJ (2015) Multidisciplinary support for healthcare transitioning across an urban healthcare network. J Pediatr Nurs 30:677–683

42. Capolongo S, Rebecchi A, Dettori M et al (2018) Healthy design and urban planning strategies, actions, and policy to achieve salutogenic cities. Int J Environ Res Public Health 15:2698

Urban Regeneration for Urban Health

Alessandra Battisti, Asia Barnocchi, and Silvia Iorio

Abstract For some years now when attempting to regenerate the urban fabric of big cities, the field of environmental design has been tackling the challenges posed by ongoing climate change, extreme poverty, social marginalisation and health problems, where these are neither occasional nor residual situations that arise as part of development processes but emerge as social diseases with deep-rooted characteristics in places that are already under significant man-made pressure, a type of pressure that causes serious environmental problems (air and water pollution, urban heat islands, increasing temperatures) and social problems (criminality, drug addiction, mental illness and nutritional disorders). With the lack of radical policies designed to foster inclusion, the growth of areas characterised by marginalisation and extreme poverty in cities is affecting these districts, creating what are to all intents and purposes mono-social and mono-cultural enclaves that lack services and where we constantly witness the gradual exclusion of residents from public spaces. The urban metropolis of Rome is afflicted by significant spatial segregation, and the residential area examined in this study, known as the former Bastogi housing estate, is undoubtedly particularly suited to the application of experimental design approaches, given the complexity of the relationships that form there between the consolidated built environment, health problems, social problems and urban poverty.

Keywords Urban health · Urban enclave · Social disease · Regeneration strategies · Well-being · Participation

---

Alessandra Battisti is the author of the Abstract, 1. Introduction, 3. Regeneration Strategies, 5. Conclusions and References sections; Asia Barnocchi is the author of the 2.1 The Urban Focus; Alessandra Battisti, Asia Barnocchi and Silvia Iorio are the authors of 2. The Results of our Analysis, 2.2. The Architectural Focus, 2.3 The Focus on Social Living and 4. Experimentation sections.

A. Battisti (✉) · A. Barnocchi
Department of Planning, Design and Technology of Architecture, Sapienza University of Rome, Rome, Italy
e-mail: alessandra.battisti@uniroma1.it

S. Iorio
Unit of History of Medicine and Bioethics, Sapienza University of Rome, Rome, Italy

A. Battisti et al. (eds.), *Urban Health*, Green Energy and Technology,
https://doi.org/10.1007/978-3-030-49446-9_5

1 Introduction

This study applies research methodology [1] to the case study of a housing estate in Rome, located in the north-west quadrant of the city, known as the former Bastogi estate, which features a single-function fabric where extremely underprivileged families reside. It is a peripheral housing estate that is not properly served by functional or institutional public services, and features many dangerous empty lots that are subject to environmental degradation, criminal occupation and recurring illegal activities [2]. The characteristics of the natural, built and social environment on this estate are risk factors for health, as well as for resilience; fear for one's own safety, social isolation and poor hygienic/sanitary conditions within the apartments are tangible threats to residents' health.

A great deal of research carried out in different fields highlights how the built environment (run-down buildings, homes that are too small to meet the needs of households, the decay of technological elements) [3], the physical environment (noise, air pollution, lack of access to green spaces) [4], the lack of access to services and public transportation [5] and the socio-economic characteristics of peripheral areas (fear of crime and violence, socio-economic deprivation and segregation) [6] all heighten the risk of health problems for the communities who live there, as well as increase the cost of national health care.

Moreover, what emerges from a perusal of field literature is how environmental design can make 'pathways' the focus of social policies, so as to improve the built environment and have a beneficial effect on the health of residents with improvements designed to achieve the following:

- To design public spaces that are perceived as safe, good social capital, comfortable and appealing; living spaces that can serve a number of purposes and uses [7] with benefits particularly for mental health [6];
- To construct spaces that foster relationships, creating social connections so as to encourage residents to do physical activities and create relationships in outdoor, common spaces, diminishing medical risks (sedentary lifestyle, obesity, diabetes and high blood pressure) [7, 8], particularly in more underprivileged communities from a socio-economic point of view, and amongst the vulnerable (the elderly and children), who are mainly discouraged from adopting a healthy, active lifestyle by their perception of social and architectural barriers [9];
- To use nature-based technologies to reduce summer overheating, thus combating the phenomenon of urban heat islands, which have been shown to contribute to chronic cardiovascular disease [10], respiratory illnesses, tumours [11] and neuropsychiatric disorders [12].

A key indicator of the growing importance of health and urban issues is the inclusion of two objectives—SDG 3 'Ensure healthy lives and promote well-being for all at all ages' and SDG 11 'Make cities and human settlements inclusive, safe, resilient and sustainable'—in the set of 17 Goals that the UN's General Assembly adopted in 2015 [13], alongside the 2030 Agenda for Sustainable Development [14], where the global directives for the next few years are established (UN Resolution A7RES/70/1, New York, September 2015), supported by the guidelines of the global agreement signed at the Paris COP21 conference and the objectives established by the European Union concerning the target of zero land consumption to be reached by 2050, adopted in Europe in the Urban and Urbact plans, and in Italy in the *Contratti di Quartiere* ('neighbourhood contracts'), the 2012 *Piano Città* town plans, the *Piano Nazionale per la Riqualificazione e Rigenerazione delle Aree Urbane* national plan to redevelop and regenerate urban areas and, finally, in the *Programma straordinario di intervento per la riqualificazione urbana e la sicurezza delle periferie delle città metropolitane e dei comuni capoluogo di provincia* (the 'Emergency programme for urban regeneration and safety in the suburbs of metropolitan cities and provincial capitals') included in the 2016 Finance Bill which created the *Bando Periferie* suburban call for tenders, Prime Minister's Decree 25/05/2016, which involved 20 Italian cities and four metropolitan areas in 2017. Last but not least, a number of national laws (legislative degree D.lgs. 3 April 2006, no. 152; part V of legislative degree D.lgs. 18 April 2016, no. 50) implement town planning improvements that focus on the reduction of land consumption and the regeneration of brownfield sites.

In methodological terms, our research was divided into a number of different phases: an analysis of the territory in question based on size, statistical indicators and sustainability indicators; the creation of a planning framework, verifying the degree to which it is consistent with current planning and actions; the identification of strategies and the organisation of action to be carried out on the built environment; and the development and completion of the first part of a pilot project.

2 The Results of Our Analysis

2.1 The Urban Focus

A reading of the New PRG General Regulatory Plan of Rome [15] reveals an urban divide between the central areas of the XIII Municipality and marginal areas, where the Bastogi estate is located. As we move out from the centre, the parts of the city that are in good condition gradually make way for derelict areas. In this particular case study, this situation is further aggravated by the estate's spatial segregation and environmental degradation.

Under the 'settlement system' heading of the *Sistemi e Regole 1:10,000* table in the New PRG, what emerges are territorial inequalities with the division of the metropolitan area into four types of 'cities': the 'historical city', the 'consolidated city', the 'city requiring renovation' and the 'city requiring redevelopment'. The first two are the saturated, completed parts of the metropolis, with the 'historical city' given greater attention than the 'consolidated city', due to a recognition of its historical and qualitative value. The other two categories (the latter in particular) are parts of the city that require renovation and renewal, due to the presence of what were previously illegal settlements (built in defiance of the rules specified in the 1965 City Plan of Rome) or were previously spontaneous (built beyond the administrative limits of the 1965 City Plan of Rome, and therefore unplanned) [16, 17]. What emerges is a gradual transition from the 'historical' and 'consolidated' cities of the XIII Municipality's central areas to the 'city requiring renovation' and the 'city requiring redevelopment' of peripheral areas. Despite having become a housing estate through illegal occupation, Bastogi arose in accordance with the 1965 Plan of Rome, categorised under the intended use of a 'private service' (zone M2), which is why it is currently part of the 'consolidated city'. However, it is surrounded by fragmentary, uncontrolled housing (previously illegal or spontaneous low houses), which created districts almost entirely lacking primary services (sewers, adequate roads, lighting, water, electricity and gas networks, equipped green spaces) and secondary services.

The mapping of green spaces and services using a GIS tool provided a closer view of the context. The green fields in the surrounding areas are publicly owned, only 3% of which are properly equipped, whereas the remaining 97% are made up of abandoned and degraded areas. The mapping of services in the Municipality of Rome [15] revealed that local public services are few and hard to access. Within a 2-km radius, there are three churches, two schools, a playing field, a post office and a supermarket. The lack of services of common interest is exacerbated by the absence of facilities that could carry out tertiary functions. Moreover, the distance between Bastogi and the first road offering services is one km, with the exception of a single supermarket, 800 m from the estate. In addition, there are few city squares, meeting places and pedestrian paths or pavements (Fig. 1).

For this reason, the lack of mobility significantly contributes to the estate's isolation from its urban context. Although the Bastogi area is served by local and urban roads, several bus routes and is just two km from the underground (an underground station), these stretches of road are narrow and inadequate and lack footpaths or pavements, a factor that discourages daily travel. As a result, the area is surrounded by a ring road with no pavements or proper paving, spatially marginalised from the

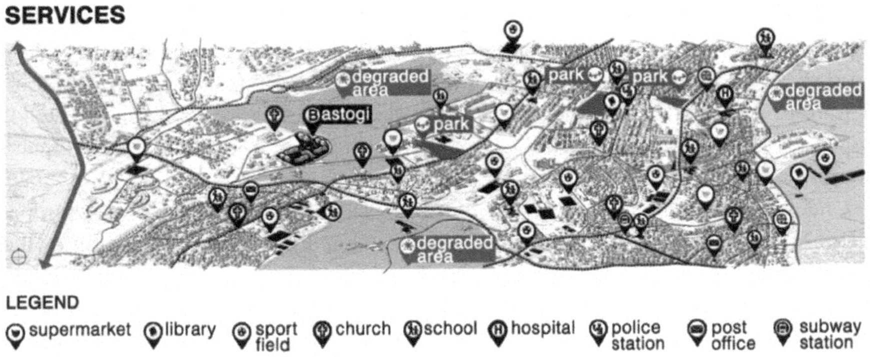

Fig. 1 Aerial photograph of the area surrounding Bastogi. Mapping of parks, green areas. *Source* Sustainability [2] Modified by the authors

outside by a high retaining wall: a kind of 'island within the city' whose morphological layout mirrors the ghettoisation of its residents, and their marginalisation from the rest of the city.

2.2 The Architectural Focus

Having been constructed under the intended use of 'private services' as far as its town planning permissions were concerned, the estate does not possess the requisites that would make it suitable for properly housing families. It is a five-hectare commuter suburb consisting of six linear five-storey buildings whose layout and distribution create interstitial spaces that are not clearly identifiable.

The grounds feature degraded green spaces along the borders and two main squares, more than half of which are asphalted driveway while the rest consist of small paved areas and two football pitches, in a poor state at the time of our analysis. The whole is submerged under piles of waste: a vast 'non-place' that discourages residents from spending time outside and forming social relationships (Fig. 2). The environmental analysis of external spaces revealed the presence of cold winds during the winter from the north side of the site and of cooling winds from the south-west during the summer. What also emerged is that both of the squares offer no shade in the summer.

There are six five-storey buildings in a row along the edge of the estate. The ground floors of each of these buildings—with a surface area of 1400 m^2, a third of which was originally earmarked as common space and the remaining two-thirds as housing—currently lack any practical purpose and have fallen into total disrepair. The only exceptions are two 500-m^2 rooms in two different buildings: one where two

Fig. 2 A picture of the main outdoor area of the Bastogi compound before the realization of the soccer field and playground. *Source* Google Maps 2016

nuns live, carrying out voluntary work, and another where there is an unauthorised boxing gym.

Each of the six buildings features four 1240-m^2 upper floors of housing. The apartments consist of what were once single rooms with a bathroom (totalling 26 m^2 each), now used as 'studio-apartments' (despite the 28-m^2 minimum requirement in Rome, according to Ministerial Decree 15/7/1975) [18], some of which have been merged into 54-m^2 'apartments'. Istat census data [18] reveals that these small homes are inhabited by households consisting of one to six or more people, although the minimum living space required in Italy is 14 m^2 per person, for the first four inhabitants, and 10 m^2 for each additional member of a household [19]. In addition, there are six small 130-m^2 buildings in the middle of the site, occupied by unauthorised activities except for a nursery school and a centre for disabled people, run by a local institution.

Lastly, our environmental analysis highlighted the inadequacy of the technological-construction conditions. The outer walls provide no thermal insulation due to the fact that they are made of single, prefabricated concrete panels and obsolete, unsealed single-glazed windows. There is no central heating and there are no air-conditioning or cooling units anywhere to be found. There is no gas line, so gas cylinders are used, and the apartments often lack hot running water. Drafts and leaks are common, as are condensation and mould. Moreover, the lack of regular maintenance causes numerous problems for pipes and drains, which often flood the underground floors originally intended as garages, where unauthorised activities are carried out.

2.3 *The Focus on 'Social Living'*

One hundred Bastogi residents filled out our Social Living Survey, which asked questions about their homes, work, mobility and leisure. The findings are reported here. As regards the first category, 20% of the interviewees are living in the original single-room layout of 26 m^2, while the remaining 80% live in merged dwellings of 54 m^2. In particular, only 20% of the applicants reside in those apartments alone or as a couple, while 60% reside as a family made up of three to six members, and the remaining 20% are families of over six people. One respondent in particular stated that their 54-m^2 home houses seven people and three pets. In addition, 80% of the respondents claimed the existence of serious problems such as bad thermal insulation, drafts and leaks, condensation and mould. One reported that 'there are cockroaches in my house'.

Data emerging from the work section showed that only 20% of the residents are employed, while the rest are students, unemployed or retired. All those with jobs stated that they are blue-collar workers, while the unemployed and the retired stated that they spend their time at home (45%), with the nuns (30%) or around the neighbourhood (25%). Residents travel on a daily basis by car, public transport and on foot, in equal measure. Lastly, 100% of the participants complained that there is a total absence of meeting places on the estate, though 50% expressed a strong affection for Bastogi.

The survey featured a section for comments, entitled 'The Bastogi I wish for', which revealed residents' wishlist: meeting places, playgrounds, central heating, green spaces, common rooms, as well as education, job opportunities, security and civility. The people that participated in this study felt that a welcoming common place could encourage residents to leave their apartments, thus reducing that sense of painful isolation and marginalisation that many of them feel. Moreover, the authors noticed a common desire for redemption and self-expression.

3 Regeneration Strategies

The analysis carried out on the study area allowed us to establish guidelines for developing experimental projects, strategies and actions that should be launched on the estate.

Using HIA procedures conducted by the Sapienza University research group, we particularly identified best practices and projects designed to support decision-making in the following categories:

- Environmental regeneration projects featuring the implementation of nature-based solutions; green spaces of all types can absorb toxic substances, filtering polluted air and releasing oxygen into the atmosphere, and can reduce sound pollution, particularly in city districts plagued by high levels of traffic. Moreover, an increase in green spaces is linked to better health outcomes (lower mortality rates linked to all causes, including cardiovascular disease). Such benefits are even more noticeable when green spaces are created in areas that are socio-economically underprivileged [20];
- Urban regeneration processes that envisage a focus on tending plants and land, managing water resources, combating urban heat islands and redeveloping brownfield sites, so as to improve the liveability and sustainability of the territorial system;
- Urban regeneration processes that involve improvements to the town planning fabric and buildings, as well as the social and economic fabric of an area, by turning public spaces into safe places for exercise, into allotments and places that foster relationships and 'neighbourliness' as part of an urban regeneration that fosters physical activity and social participation;
- Building renovation processes that involve the improvement of the estate using carefully targeted repairs and the improvement of the existing construction/planning structures, inspired by principles that look to greater energy and bioclimate efficiency, to upgrading the technical quality and layout of the apartments and the air quality inside so as to improve environmental health, sanitation and psychological conditions;

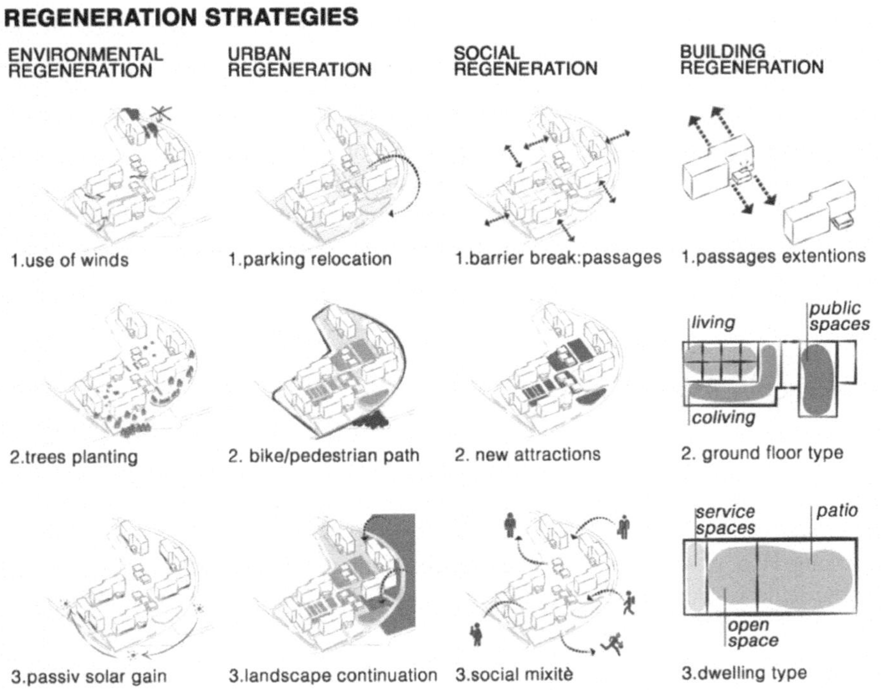

Fig. 3 Regeneration strategies. *Source* Sustainability [2] Modified by the authors

- Projects that focus on safety and social inclusion, which envisage detailed micro-improvements, or 'urban acupuncture', including the support of innovative micro-enterprises, craft workshops, cultural start-ups, social projects designed for the urban community and the creation of a zero-food-mile market, all set up on the ground floors of the six row buildings. Such actions will undoubtedly improve residents' sense of self-worth (Fig. 3).

In order to pursue such a strategy of environmental regeneration, the urban regeneration project includes the most commonly implemented nature-based solutions for carrying out sustainable and resilient improvements in metropolitan areas: tree planting, including hedges and bushes; green roofs and green walls.

We can perceive the benefits of these actions from the following:

- The management and enhancement of flora in its role as a filter between environmental factors and the physical use of outdoor areas;
- The improvement of outdoor areas in a way that will foster relationships and meetings between people, as part of an overall reorganisation of paths and mobility;
- The enhancement of the relationship between mobility, vegetation, bioclimate and street funiture when designing the outdoor areas 'between' buildings;

- The improvement of the psycho-perceptive comfort provided by the morphological layouts typical of intermediate outdoor areas;
- The improvement of residents' mood and an increase in social interaction.

As regards urban regeneration processes applied to the territory using improvements that focus on caring for the land, managing water resources and combating urban heat islands, natural systems for rainwater channelling and storage were adopted (bioswales, rain gardens and ponds), as well as non-nature-based solutions (semi-natural elements), such as highly reflective, permeable draining pavements and artificial water recycling systems (irrigation systems in green spaces and vegetable gardens, etc.).

We can perceive the benefits of these actions from the following:

- A reduction in the amount of rain water that flows into the sewage system, diminishing the probability of waste water flooding during spells of heavy rain;
- A reduction in the total demand for drinking water on the estate, thus reducing water consumption, thanks to the use of rain water collected for irrigation purposes;
- Vegetation's ability to purify the air of pollutants, reducing air and ground temperatures thanks to the shade it provides, not to mention its ability to break the fall of raindrops with its leaves;
- The reduction of urban heat islands, lowering extreme temperatures during the hottest times of the year and lowering the health risks associated with them (heart problems, chronic cardiovascular diseases, respiratory illnesses and neuropsychiatric disorders).

Urban regeneration processes that can improve the estate's town planning fabric and construction, as well as the social and economic fabric of the area, involved a project for public spaces catering to: sport (a five-a-side football pitch), socialisation (the repair of street furniture) and games (a small playground for children aged between six and 10), and allotments with a zero-food-mile market.

We can perceive the benefits of these actions from the following:

- Psychomotor functions for the difficult adolescent age group;
- Psychomotor functions for small children;
- The holding of well-organised sports courses on the five-a-side football pitch;
- The fostering of social relations and physical activity amongst all ages;
- The cultivation, consumption and sale of vegetables from specifically designed allotments and greenhouses;
- The attraction of people from neighbouring districts, interested in the sporting activities and market;
- A reduction in feelings of solitude and associated risks (depression, alcoholism, drug addiction);
- The combating of sedentary lifestyles and associated risks (obesity, sedentary habits, diabetes, high blood pressure, etc.).

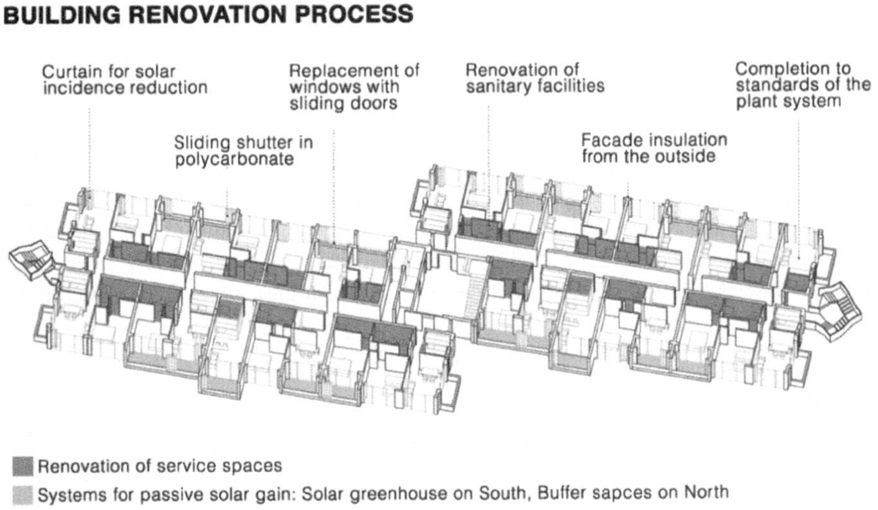

Fig. 4 Building renovation processes. *Source* Sustainability [2] Modified by the authors

As regards building renovation processes, apartments whose architecture is typical and recurring on the estate were chosen in order to simulate a planned renovation, based on an assessment of their current state and the identification of improvement strategies (Fig. 4).

We decided to analyse types of apartments on a typical floor of one of the row buildings. The case studies we analysed provided an overview of recurring problems linked to particular technical, distributional and size characteristics. Each case study was made the object of a design simulation of possible improvements that not only took into account their upgrading to minimum town planning standards of occupancy, energy efficiency and indoor comfort, but also considered the economic feasibility of such improvements. We then assessed the situation pre-renovation and post-renovation using Docet calculation software, so that it proved possible to compare the two situations and verify the benefits gained from the renovation work.

The benefits gained from this process were the following:

- Techno-morphological innovation completed at low cost on existing buildings, involving the fitting of: passive heat gain systems, greenhouses facing south and thermal buffer zones placed facing north; EIFS used to clad the building envelope; insulating double-glazed windows;
- The replacement of the current wiring in common spaces with highly efficient LED systems;
- The installation of a heat pump (run on electricity and, therefore, a kind that does not produce CO_2) for heating and cooling apartments;
- The improvement of living standards inside the apramtents with an increase in space;

- The improvement of air quality and psycho-perceptive well-being thanks to the increased use of natural ventilation and lighting;
- Energy savings created by the improvement of insulation and passive solar gain;
- Energy savings created by the use of more efficient heat production systems.

Projects that focus on safety and social inclusion were developed with the redesign of the neglected common spaces on the ground floors of the estate and plans for the creation of craft workshops, educational and training areas and cultural venues located in four small one-storey pavilions that are currently unused in the green spaces and ground floors of four of the six row buildings (500 m^2 each).

We can perceive the benefits of these actions from the following:

- The creation of a cultural activity that would act as the heart of a district and a community that previously boasted very few services;
- Employment opportunities for many of the young unemployed people living in the neighbourhood;
- Opportunities for participation and learning provided by specially organised seminars, courses and workshops;
- Opportunities for social mixing and interaction with residents of other neighbourhoods attracted by the courses and workshops;
- The organisation of events that can improve the vitality of the estate.

4 Experimentation

Having established which regeneration strategies were preferable, a first phase of renovation was developed and proposed as a pilot urban regeneration project. The authors decided to start the regeneration process with the creation of a football pitch and a playground for two main reasons. Firstly, the questionnaire highlighted the fact that 100% of residents suffer the total lack of meeting places on the estate; in addition, the authors felt it was fair to start the regeneration process with a project that the whole community could enjoy. On 23rd October 2017, the park was inaugurated: an area of 1350 m^2, created using recycled tyres [2]. This proposal formed the guidelines for the design and regeneration of sites, according to four thematic groups of indicators that were analysed, processed and agreed upon during the project's development: territorial management and urban planning; renovation through zero land consumption; the management of natural resources and the ecological footprint; economic and social cohesion. This action was the direct consequence of community discussion groups, thanks to an open-ended section where residents were invited to express their feelings on how to increase well-being in Bastogi. According to them, people's well-being starts with the redevelopment of outdoor spaces through the creation of places where a better sense of community and social cohesion can be developed. Furthermore, as regards the choice of facilities to be added and their location, these were completed thanks to the joint efforts of technical professionals and the local population, where everything done had to be financially sustainable,

Fig. 5 Pilot urban regeneration project. *Source* Sustainability [2] Modified by the authors

given that the figure for this initial redevelopment was established by the Prosolidar Foundation, which donated the funds for its completion (Fig. 5).

5 Conclusions

The urban regeneration process involving the former Bastogi housing estate is an innovative way of working, due to, firstly, a research methodology that brings together academic groups from different fields and local authorities and, secondly, due to the attempt to implement a policy that sets up a true partnership between a community and the public and private sectors that can foster the creation of new production activities within a marginal strip of Rome, in keeping with the preferences that the residents themselves voiced. Following the completion of the first phase where an initial nucleus of functional activities was set up and launched (the five-a-side football pitch and the playground), and ongoing work on the second phase, which will see the creation of the urban allotments and the zero-food-mile market, as well as identity-forming workshops, we should move on to a third phase that will combine those first two phases in a sophisticated administrative approach where the community itself will manage these new facilities.

It is a rather ambitious challenge, whose benefits—both those that have already emerged and those expected in future—can indicate new ways of economically and productively converting the consolidated city using a process that is driven by the community itself. From an organisational and managerial point of view, the project could potentially face a number of obstacles:

- The spaces and activities set up by this project require a strong managerial lead, able to coordinate all the contributions made from the grassroots up and direct them towards the common objectives made available to all. Such a task will be entrusted to the Sapienza working group during the first two years, but will then need to be managed by the local population. This could prove to be a problem, particularly as regards the expertise required;
- Participation is a process that needs to be constantly encouraged with the continual involvement of those affected, and this requires massive resources (in terms of time, effort and money). This project is based on a process where local authorities should make a series of investments, but the economic conditions for a long-term project currently seem to be lacking.

References

1. Loewenson R, Laurell AC, Hogstedt C, D'Ambruoso L, Shroff Z (2014) Participatory action research in health systems: a methods reader. TARSC, AHPSR, WHO, IDRC Canada, EQUINET, Harare, Zimbabwe
2. Battisti A, Barnocchi A, Iorio S (2019) Urban regeneration process: the case of a residential complex in a suburb of Rome, Italy. Sustainability 11(21):6122
3. Barton H, Tsourou C (2000) Healthy urban planning. WHO Copenhagen and Spon, London
4. Abhijith KV et al (2017) Air pollution abatement performances of green infrastructure in open road and built-up street canyon environ-ments—a review. Department of Civil and Environmental Engineering, Faculty of Engineering and Physical Sciences, University of Surrey, Guildford GU2 7XH, United Kingdom
5. The AIE (Italian Association of Epidemiology) Group on Crisis and Health (2012) Health indicators in the time of crisis in Italy. Epidemiol Prev 36(6):337–366
6. Araya R, Dunstan F, Playle R, Thomas H, Palmer S, Lewis G (2006) Perceptions of social capital and the built environment and mental health. Soc Sci Med 62(12):3072–3083
7. Quachioni E, Ferrante G et al (2014) Forte associazione fra depressione e svantaggio socioeconomico negli italiani. Epidemiol Prev 38(1):62
8. Melis G, Gelormino E, Marra G, Ferracin E, Costa G (2015) The effects of the urban built environment on mental health: a cohort study in a large Northern Italian City. Int J Environ Res Public Health 12(11):14898–14915
9. Borgogni A, Farinella R (2017) Le Città Attive: Percorsi pubblici nel corpo urbano. Franco Angeli, Milan
10. Liu L, Núñez AE (2014) Multilevel and urban health modeling of risk factors for diabetes mellitus: a new insight into public health and preventive medicine. Adv Prev Med 2014:246049
11. Buys DR, Howard VJ, McClure LA, Buys KC, Sawyer P, Allman RM et al (2015) 'Association between neighborhood disadvantage and hypertension prevalence, awareness, treatment, and control in older adults': results from the University of Alabama at Birmingham Study of Aging. Am J Public Health 105(6):1181–1188. Public Health 11, 7094–7115
12. Rugel E (2015) Green space and mental health: pathways, impacts, and gaps. National Collaborating Centre for Environmental Health at the British Columbia Centre for Disease Control
13. UN (2015) 17 goals for sustainable development. Available at: http://www.un.org/sustainabledevelopment/sustainable-development-goals/

14. UN (2015) Resolution adopted by the General Assembly on 25 September 2015. Transforming our world: the 2030 Agenda for Sustainable Development. New York City, New York. Available at: https://www.un.org/en/development/desa/population/migration/generalassembly/docs/globalcompact/A_RES_70_1_E.pdf
15. Nuovo Piano Regolatore Generale di Roma (2008) Available at: http://www.urbanistica.comune.roma.it/prg.html. Last accessed: 30 July 2019
16. Piano Regolatore Generale di Roma (1965) Available at: http://www.cittasostenibili.it/urbana/Scheda-13/Fig%203%20Prg_62.jpg
17. Battisti A (2014) Rinnovare le Periferie. Riqualificazione bioclimatica e ambientale delle aree urbane periferiche, Alinea, Florence
18. Zindato D (2011) 15° Censimento generale della popolazione e delle abitazioni. Manuale della Rilevazione. ISTAT 2011: 248. Available at: http://www3.istat.it/censimenti/popolazione2011/allegati_rete_rilevazione/18_ManualedellaRilevazione.pdf. Last accessed: 12 June 2019
19. Dooris M, Heritage Z (2011) Healthy cities: facilitating the active participation and empowerment of local people. J Urb Health: Bull N Y Acad Med 90(1):74–91
20. UNEP United Nations Environment Programme (2016) Health environment, Healthy people. Thematic report Ministerial policy review session, Second session of the United Nations Environment Assembly of the United Nations Environment Programme Nairobi, 23–27 May 2016. Available at: http://www.unep.org/about/sgb/Portals/50153/UNEA/K1602727%20INF%205.pdf

Characterising a Setting with a High Level of Informality, Integrating National and Specialised Surveys, Administrative and Census Data

Lorenzo Paglione, Laura Cacciani, Giovanni Baglio, Maria Alessandra Brandimarte, Elisabetta Confaloni, Adelaide Landi, Livia Maria Salvatori, Aurora Angelozzi, Susanna Caminada, Massimo Napoli, Miriam Errigo, Silvia Iorio, Anna Maria Bargagli, Maurizio Marceca, Enrico Di Rosa, Nera Agabiti, and Marina Davoli

Abstract The history of the urbanization process can determine the social identity of specific places and neighbourhoods. Understanding historical processes behind the physical environment of a city is the first step in an action-research in an urban setting. The characterisation of a neighbourhood, especially in a deprived and segregated urban context, requires a multidisciplinary approach that cannot be separated from a dedicated quantitative analysis, integrating various tools and approaches. In this study's setting, defined by a high level of informality due to a history of exclusion from the surrounding area and a structural segregation from the city's fabric, the integration of tools and point of views had to be used to detect and assess the presence of any inequalities in health. We used administrative health data, census information, and a customised version of a national health survey, integrating different baseline populations in order to develop a global vision of the state of health. This research also includes an evaluation of social determinants of health, hospitalisation rates

L. Paglione (✉) · L. Cacciani · A. M. Bargagli · N. Agabiti · M. Davoli
Department of Epidemiology, Lazio Regional Health Service, ASL RM1, Rome, Italy
e-mail: lorenzo.paglione@uniroma1.it

L. Paglione
Department of Civil, Building and Environmental Engineering DICEA, Sapienza University of Rome, Rome, Italy

G. Baglio
National Institute for Health, Migration and Poverty (NIHMP), Rome, Italy

L. Paglione · M. A. Brandimarte · A. Landi · M. Napoli · E. Di Rosa
Department of Prevention, ASL RM1, Rome, Italy

E. Confaloni
Health District II, ASL RM1, Rome, Italy

L. M. Salvatori · A. Angelozzi · S. Caminada · M. Errigo · M. Marceca
Department of Public Health and Infectious Diseases, Sapienza University of Rome, Rome, Italy

S. Iorio
Unit of History of Medicine and Bioethics, Sapienza University of Rome, Rome, Italy

A. Battisti et al. (eds.), *Urban Health*, Green Energy and Technology,
https://doi.org/10.1007/978-3-030-49446-9_6

and access to the emergency room, as well as the general self-perception of the population's health compared to the surrounding neighbourhoods.

Keywords Urban health · Urban segregation · Social determinant of health · Social inequalities in health

1 Background, Defining the "Informal" Rome

Cities go through overlapping stages of development, leaving legible traces in the social and urban fabric. The understanding of these dynamics and the elements that fuel them is crucial for the analysis of urban exclusion. Moreover, this understanding is essential in order to tackle social inequalities, which have direct consequences on the health of populations and communities.

Within most cities, there are veritable islands of segregation. While in some contexts, such as U.S. cities with marked ethnic segregation [1], in European cities, with some exceptions especially due to the colonial heritage, they are particularly characterized by economic deprivation and social exclusion, as in the case of the city of Rome [2] and of the "ex-Bastogi" residential complex [3].

1.1 A Historic Overview

Italy shows some peculiarities in terms of urban development [4]. In addition to historical urbanization, mainly concerning the Roman era and the Renaissance (XVI and XVII century), the proper development of Italian urban areas in modern and contemporary terms took place in the immediate post-unification period. This led to the industrialization of the "Padania" Plain and the renovation and expansion of the main cities of the Kingdom, following by growth in the second half of the nineteenth century as well as the reconstruction phase following WWII [4, 5].

Urban expansion, with a mass move of the population from agricultural areas at the expense of a large internal migration, took place during the so-called "economic boom" or what was also called the "Italian miracle" [6]. This period was followed by a long wave of unbridled and disorganized urbanization, despite the fact that planning had been carried out. This growth lasted about two decades between the '60s and the '80s, with serious environmental, urban and social consequences [7].

Along with this "formal" urbanization, driven by speculation, throughout the entire history of modern Italy, the phenomenon of the informal settlements has been a constant factor. Since the turn of the twentieth century, around these rapidly growing cities, various "informal" areas developed, often with housing facilities defined by extremely poor quality, when not directly in the form of shacks and slums. Entire population groups resided in these areas, drawn by the employment opportunities and wellbeing that cities were beginning to offer. However, these areas were unable to fully become part of the "civitas", part of the urban social community. This phenomenon affected in particular the city of Rome [8, 9], that became the new Capital of the Kingdom of Italy in 1871.

At the time of the Savoy troops entry, on September 20th, 1870, the city of Rome had a population of little more than 200,000 inhabitants, enclosed within the Aurelian Walls, the late-imperial historical walls of the city. [8] Rome's entrance into modernity coincides with rapid, vast urban development, as well as changes to the city's infrastructure. This period also saw the construction of public and administration buildings, and entire neighbourhoods intended both for the ministerial ruling class as well as the administrative middle-class [8]. Nevertheless, the mass influx of people, especially from central and southern Italy, employed for the construction of the Capital, was not accompanied by adequate housing allocation and programming. Consequently, a large part of such population was simply obliged to make the best of their situation [8]. On the one hand, the "*borgate*" (hamlets) arose, from scheduled subdivisions of the Roman countryside, run and developed by cooperatives and workers' associations. On the other hand, the "*baraccamenti*" (barracks) were built, makeshift buildings that were not proper homes, close to the Roman construction sites and along the main consular roads [8]. While the *borgate* immediately took their own neighbourhood identity, the *baraccamenti* became slums. The next urbanization stage, during the Fascist period, was simply a confirmation of this division between the "formal" and the "informal" city. In fact, this era actually worsened the phenomenon with the deportation of population from the areas of the centre that were "gutted" into the so-called "*Borgate Ufficiali*", "official hamlets". These areas were defined by a noteworthy spatial isolation, far away from the consolidated city and proper infrastructure, in facilities built with dubious building quality [8].

After WWII, the city of Rome saw a bitter struggle for the right to housing, especially in the new neighbourhoods of public residential housing (ERP, *Edilizia Residenziale Pubblica*). These areas served as urbanization centres and often arose next to the historical and official *borgate*, as well as the *baraccamenti*. As described above, next to an organized and public urban planning, the '70s–'80s were defined by unbridled urbanization also in Rome, driven by building contractors (in Rome also called "*palazzinari*", from the *palazzina*, the most common type of housing, with reduced volumes and isolation from the street front), often unscrupulous businessmen connected to the political power of parties from the First Republic [8]. The combination of these two phenomena, with the ERP areas once again as urbanization centres and the private sector expanding at the expenses of the Roman countryside, was flanked by another type of urbanization driven by the growing economic well-being in Italy. Consequently, new building aggregates arose even more distant from the historical centre of the City, starting from a mixture of subdivisions and authorized and unauthorized buildings. This resulted in entire neighbourhoods that were partly illegal and partly legal, often lacking the most basic urban services, and completely disassociated with the established and planned city. The original *baraccamenti* began to empty, but the practical and political practice of fighting for housing, combined with an overall superficial management of the enormous number of homes and apartment buildings, generated widespread cases of more or less politicised squatting of public and private buildings. Within this social and political context, the occupation and squatting of the Bastogi apartment complex took place [3].

In the 1990s immigration took hold of Italy, and the country's major cities saw a sharp population increase as a result. In this case, social stratification also entailed different levels of access to the real estate market in its various forms. Consequently, the "barracks" arose once again, in an official or informal form, this time assuming also a strong ethnic connotation, yet maintaining always its economic and social causes [10, 11].

Answers to this rapid growth in housing demand can essentially be summarized along three lines:

(1) The growth of informal and self-produced settlements, on one hand with the *baraccamenti*, and on the other hand with the construction of further informal *borgate*, in the outskirts of the Roman countryside, as discussed above;
(2) The unbridled urbanization driven by private profit, investing especially in the eastern area of the city;
(3) The public residential housing (ERP, *Edilizia Residenziale Pubblica*).

Each of these three answers further stratified the social classes of the capital city. The *baraccamenti* and self-produced settlements concerned the last and penultimate ones; the second were mainly addressed to the families of the wealthier classes who could access housing at market price; the last was addressed mainly to the working class that had fed the city's economic growth.

1.2 Root Causes of Informal Settlements in Rome

The existence and persistence of urban social marginalization, particularly in Rome, are due to a series of causes with deep historical roots, albeit of different natures:

- Normative and programming, especially related to the implementation of public housing policies, which are rarely accompanied by social inclusion policies;
- Architectural, with striking examples of mistakes, especially in the implementation phase;
- Urban planning, due to a fragmentation of the urban fabric as well as the substantial isolation of entire nuclei of urbanisation;
- Social and economic, specifically due to an extensive deregulation of the real estate market, with consequent speculation, leading to an economic selection of the social composition of the neighbourhoods based on the price of the properties.

The city of Rome, or, more correctly, "*Roma Capitale*" [12], occupies an area of 1287.36 km^2, with a population of 2,855,397 (February 2019), with an average population density of 2218.03 inhabitants/km^2. The municipal territory is as large as the sum of the larger Italian cities (Milan, Naples, Genoa, Catania, Palermo, Florence and Bologna, all together), and larger than the municipal area of New York (1214 km^2, including the waters of the Hudson bay).

In this regard, Rome represents a true anomaly on the international level. The capital has with a quite low population (not even three million residents), characterizing itself as a conurbation, with neighbourhoods that are far from the centre, yet belonging to the municipal administrative area, such as Ostia, more than 14 km from the GRA (great ring road, major highway around Rome) and almost 25 km from the city centre (in comparison, Milan and Pavia are 30 km away, just as Padua and Venice).

There is a direct consequence on the average population density, which is quite low. However, there is also an alternation of almost completely uninhabited areas and highly dense urban areas, with some neighbourhoods with over 15,000 people per square km, mostly in the belt of the so-called "historical periphery". This leads to a vastly dispersed urban fabric, with substantial urban sprawl phenomena, and to a fragmentation in numerous settlements even quite populous, but extremely far from the centre, left disconnected [13].

The low population density and the dispersion of specific housing areas make the organization of public services such as transport (for which, according to current legislation, the municipal authority pays to the provider based on the number of km travelled) and waste collection (with means of transport has to cover enormous distances) extremely complicated and structurally expensive. This applies also to the organization of social and health services [14], especially in a context where the predominant model is hospital care. Only in recent years has there been a spread of the so-called "*Case della Salute*" (literally, "health houses") [15], an organizational form that allows to take care in particular of fragile patients suffering from chronic pathologies, for whom, unless complications—often avoidable—occur, hospitalisation is certainly oversized, in particular in terms of cost compared to a territorial management. To date, in the face of a regional regulation providing one of these structures for each socio-medical district, only seven *Case della Salute* are active in the territory of "*Roma Capitale*" [16].

Another direct consequence certainly concerns the amount of traffic that crosses the city every day, also considering the enormous number of cars circulating in the capital [17]. The problem particularly concerns the city centre, where institutional and administrative activities are concentrated, and therefore a large part of the workforce, since the public employment sector is by far the most representative of the working population [18]. Traffic is primarily caused by the weakness of public transportation, which is clearly insufficient in order to guarantee effective connections among the different parts of the city. Moreover, due to the aforementioned fragmentation of the urban fabric, lack of efficient public transportation is one the main causes found in current studies on increasing volumes of private traffic [19], in a city with still a quite high number of road accidents [20].

This issue of population density is also connected to other problems of the city, with certainly more nuances, albeit also with perhaps more interesting roots. Different density patterns are correlated to the political orientation and to the economic sustainability of local commercial and business activities. These are contexts often characterized by a "segregated" population, due to their social background [21]. The groups also live in stigma and shame with respect to their belonging. Moreover, these elements also emerged several times during research and action activities in Bastogi [3].

Therefore, the study and analysis of data based on a single area of study would not allow—given the complexity of the phenomena in question—for an in-depth understanding of these contexts. Above all, a singular approach would lead only to a limited ability to act, in particular on the part of social and health institutions. The very existence of these areas involves problems relating to accessibility to services, varying from schools to hospitals. However, there are also problems related to crime, which has its roots in the economic deprivation, as well as social and economic problems, as in the case of Bastogi [3].

2 Social Determinants of Urban Health Inequalities

In order to try to reconstruct the multiplicity of factors that can affect health in urban areas, a classic instrument of epidemiology is quite useful: the directed acyclic graphs (DAGs) [22–24]. In DAGs each graphic sign acquires a precise meaning in regulating the causal relationship between the parties. The diagram in Fig. 1 is a DAGs. The development of DAGs may precede a research hypothesis, guiding the development of the consequent statistical analysis, or it may follow it, once significant associations have been highlighted by tests (obviously they are not necessarily random connections, however they can be a prerequisite).

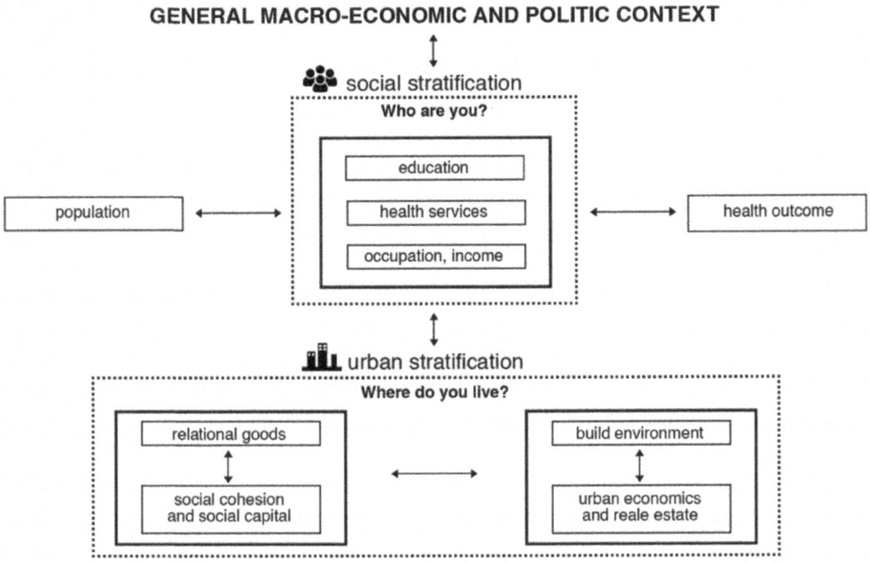

Fig. 1 A proposal of DAG of principal interaction between social determinants of health in urban contexts

There are examples in literature of proposed DAGs regarding urban health, some of which also consider the effect of the urban social ecosystem, or that of the constructed environment as well as macroeconomic dynamics.

The DAG proposed here (Fig. 1) is an attempt to synthesise a conceptual framework within which to move.

The proposed scheme is generally divided into two sectors, which correspond to the principal aspects related to the state of health in an urban environment [25–27]. In detail, we find the personal characteristics of social stratification, namely the social determinants of health (income, education, social-health services). These contribute to the definition of the state of health of a population, also in relation to the socio-economic and political general context, also according to the first scheme defined by Dahlgreen and Withehead in 1991 [28]. Specifically, the arrow connecting the "who you are" section with health outcomes is bidirectional. This is due to the fact the health outcomes themselves, starting from the concept of "health-poverty trap" [29], can in turn socially stratify the population, especially in contexts where social welfare policies do not protect the most fragile groups of the population.

The second section concerns "where you live". These last two groups of factors are strictly interdependent. Dialectically, the urban economy contributes to defining the constructed environment, however the constructed (or "built") environment influences the possibilities of urban economy development. Together, they create a dialogue with those factors most closely linked to sociality and to the ways of living the city, such as relational goods (squares, green spaces, gathering places), social cohesion and social capital (described above and defined as effect mediators from the scheme produced by CSDH) [30]. Finally, relational assets, cohesion and social capital, are obviously linked to one another, and mutually dependent: the availability of relational goods in fact conditions the capacity to develop social cohesion and social capital, which in turn can lead to forms of self-organization capable of autonomously developing physical spaces for aggregation and socialization.

Therefore, according to the proposed scheme, "who you are" moderates the effects of the population on the built environment. Consequently, starting from features such as work, education, possibility of accessing services, and ultimately possibility of action in the context in which it is immersed [31], the environment can have greater or lesser influence on the characteristics of its urban context, modifying its physical structure and socio-economic relationships (and therefore also the health characteristics of the resident population).

Albeit far from creating a thorough study on the vast discussion on the relationship between personal characteristics and context in the definition of the state of health, the proposed scheme is useful in highlighting the research's approach, within a perspective of urban health [32].

3 Analysing Spatial and Social Segregation

There is an extensive body of literature on social inequalities in health in the urban context. In Italy, extremely interesting assessments and results have been obtained from the network of the SLM (Metropolitan Longitudinal Studies) [33–37], epidemiological tools able to integrate heterogeneous but fundamental data sources for the study of social and health dynamics of the urban contexts.

These systems have developed around the evaluation of the impact of social determinants of health, i.e. those social and material dimensions that determine, through direct or indirect casual pathways, the health of people and communities.

The SLM surveys [33] integrate different administrative sources:

- General Population Census. This is the main administrative tool, managed by the National Institute of Statistics (ISTAT), which, every ten years, surveyed the Italian population resident and not (since October 2019 the census survey is on an annual basis and on a sample basis), defining its main dimensions and aspects, such as socio-demographic characteristics, education, employment and, starting from the 15th General Census of 2011, as well as the state and upkeep of buildings and housing. The ISTAT Census also allows for an effective geolocation of the data, taking advantage of the Census Sections, areas that in the urban contexts have the indicative size of a block. These Census Sections can be aggregated into further levels, such as the administrative levels of the larger Municipalities and of the Metropolitan Areas. In particular, in Rome, these are called *Municipi* (15 urban areas administered independently on particular management areas) [38] and *Zone Urbanistiche* (Urbanistic zones, 155 areas divided on topographical, toponymic or urban planning criteria, corresponding in general line to the districts, in the city centre).
- Flow of health information and mortality registers. These are generated starting from the data coming from people's contacts with the National Health Service in its various forms. The Health Information System flows are regulated at national level. They were created for administrative purposes, but have become particularly useful for defining the state of health of the population through the definition of incidence and prevalence of pathologies, evaluation of outcomes and performance of health organizations, as well as for study purposes. The main limitation of this tool is related to a certain territorial variability of the quality of the data, as well as problems linked to the privacy of the patients, even if this last aspect is now managed in the terms established by the European General Data Protection Regulation.
- Register of Municipalities. These are the main sources of administrative information, and allow to obtain constantly updated information on the resident population within the municipal area, identifying its main demographic characteristics and the place of residence.

3.1 Bastogi as a Case-Study of Urban Segregation

The context of Bastogi (also known as ex-Bastogi, or former-Bastogi Building Complex) is a valid example of spatial and social segregation within the area of the Municipality of Rome. Built as a corporate motel [3, 38], occupied to address the necessity for housing for the most disadvantaged popular classes, then taken over by the Municipality and used to deal with the so-called "housing emergency", today the area finds itself in a sort of limbo where formal assignees of public housing, long-standing occupants, new squatters and more or less organized crime all coexist together [3, 39].

In order to study this context, an approach integrating different information sources was used:

- General Census of Population and Housing;
- Health information flows;
- Tailored questionnaires developed by institutional bodies.

Each of these sources ensured that the research offered a different point of view on the context. Moreover, multiple sources led to an understanding of some specific aspects. The integration and harmonization of the sources has also guaranteed the definition and quantification of certain problems, their outcome in terms of access to services, and the identification of possible solutions.

ISTAT, in particular, through the use of the bt.viewer online software [40], identified, from satellite images, areas of interest, and defined the administrative boundaries related to the Census Sections, the basic units of census detection. These images allowed researchers to geolocate not only the data related to the census survey, therefore guaranteeing a rather high level of detail that more or less corresponded to a city block, but also a communication between the health and personal information systems, linking to the code of the section the totally anonymized residents' codes. As already specified, the Census Sections in the Municipality of Rome can in turn be aggregated in the form of *Zone Urbanistiche* (Urban Zones) and *Municipi* (Municipalities).

However, the aspect that needs to be emphasized is the heterogeneity of the denominators of each source. In fact, with approximately 2000 inhabitants estimated by the volunteers of the associations operating there [3], only 1033 were registered in 2011, while on the other hand an average of 1222 inhabitants per year were registered in the municipal registry between 2011 and 2017. This difference is essentially linked to the methodology behind the various sources, as described below.

3.2 General Census

The 15th General Census of Population and Housing of 2011 [41] is the basis used to quantify some aspects related to the socio-demographic characteristics of the population of Bastogi. This is the main institutional instrument in Italy for population assessments, managed by ISTAT and carried out every ten years. It allows for a fairly in-depth evaluation of some aspects relevant to health, previously exposed, such as education, employment, distribution by age classes, quality of buildings. The limitations of this source are mainly related to the way data are collected, for example as regards the aspects connected to the identification of the census population and the acquisition of census information of citizens through a self-compiled questionnaire [41].

The data relating to Bastogi were then compared with those relating to the *Zone Urbanistiche* (Urban Zones) of the XIII *Municipio* (Municipality), the administrative district in which Bastogi falls.

3.3 Institutional Health Data

Evaluation and assessment of health information flows, carried out by the Department of Epidemiology of the Health Service of the Lazio Region, has in particular led to an understanding of the Bastogi population's use of health services, in terms of accesses to the Emergency Room and hospitalisation by using the data relating to the SIO (Hospital Information System) and SIES (Health Emergencies Information System) database.

This was possible through record linkage procedures between the Municipal Registry, with a survey carried out up to December 31st, 2014, which allowed the research team to define the demographic characteristics of the population, as well as the Healthcare Registry of the Lazio Region, by extracting the 2015 data using anonymous unique identification codes, to which the health information was linked.

Once again, in this case the survey unit was the Census Section, and the data were compared with the aggregate of some neighbouring areas (urban zones) of the XIII *Municipio* of "Roma Capitale". The data extracted have been age-standardized with the method of direct standardization with reference to the population under study, allowing in such way the comparison between the different areas.

3.4 Official Health Survey: PASSI

The last source of data is the questionnaire called PASSI (an acronym that can be loosely translated as an assessment of "Progress of Healthcare Services in Italy") [42], a tool used since 2005 by the Italian Local Health Authorities to verify the state of health perceived by the resident population recorded in the healthcare registries. Alongside this instrument, two further brief questionnaires were developed, concerning housing quality and Health Literacy. This survey was managed by the Prevention Department of ASL RM1 (Roma 1 Local Health Authority). In this case, the results were partially compared with the territory of the entire ASL RM1.

4 Results and Discussion

The Census data give us a fairly complete picture of Bastogi (Table 1). This area, compared with the XIII *Municipio* urbanistic zones, has significantly higher percentages of population with low educational qualifications, a higher number of foreigners, as well as a higher unemployment rate. All of the buildings appear in a poor state of maintenance and upkeep. Furthermore, all values are significantly higher than the comparison areas [3].

Regarding the data from the health information flows (Fig. 2), the Bastogi population has higher hospitalisation and Emergency Room accesses compared to the neighbouring areas of the XIII *Municipio*. In particular, rather high rates are found in the younger age groups (20–39) and among the elderly, both with regard to hospitalisations and access to the ER. Regarding access to the Emergency Room, we observed rates more than double for all age groups and both sexes.

From the data relating to the PASSI monitoring system, an overall picture of the health perceived by the population of Bastogi emerges (Table 2), with obvious

Table 1 Distribution of social determinants of health between Bastogi and the surroundings urbanistic zones

	Ex-Bastogi (%)	18F Boccea (%)	18E C. di Boccea (%)	18C Fogaccia (%)	18B Val Cannuta (%)	18D Aurelio Nord (%)	18A Aurelio Sud (%)
Age classes							
<14	20.30	17.50	15.13	14.75	13.65	11.31	12.04
15-39	34.00	31.00	31.00	30.40	25.80	22.40	22.40
40–64	37.56	38.00	36.90	37.90	37.00	36.10	37.30
>65	8.03	13.50	17.00	16.90	23.60	30.10	28.20
Foreign population	18.10	9.01	11.51	10.41	10.18	6.23	7.39
Educational level							
High	2.94	12.07	9.69	10.89	21.26	24.50	30.60
Intermediate	64.67	64.88	64.03	64.39	57.34	57.63	53.16
Low	32.39	23.05	26.29	24.71	21.40	17.87	16.24
Employment							
Employment Rate	79.75	64.30	60.51	61.07	66.48	66.37	68.44
Unemployment Rate	20.25	9.40	11.67	12.16	7.79	8.25	6.87
State of buildings							
Good	0.00	85.98	73.81	94.30	89.77	94.79	95.77
Poor	100.00	14.32	26.19	5.70	10.23	5.21	4.23

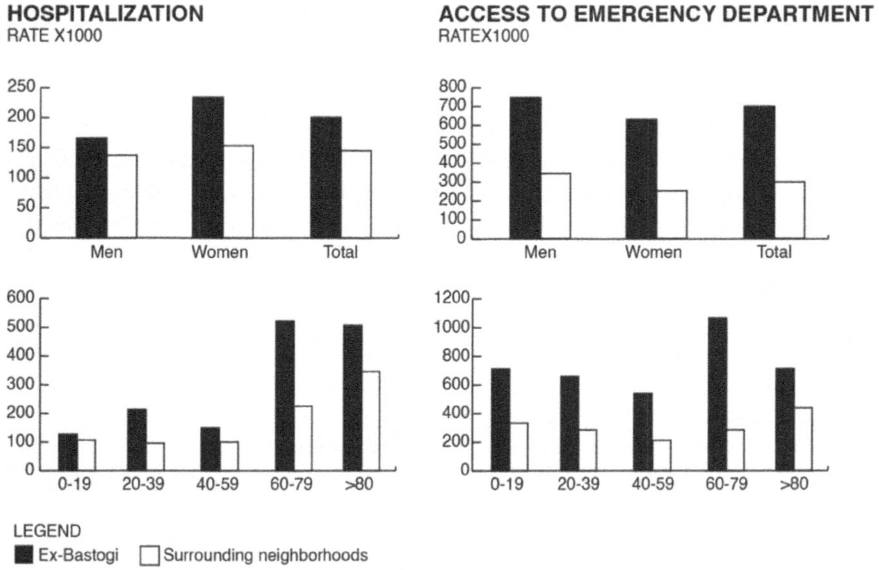

Fig. 2 Results from Regional Informative Health Data, Department of Epidemiology of Regional Health Service, Rome

Table 2 Results from PASSI survey on the self-reported perception of health

	Bastogi (%)	ASL RM1 (%)
How is your health in general?		
Very good—good	60	74.1
Fairly well, not so well, bad	40	25.9
In the last 30 days, for how many days did you not feel good?		
Physical distress	6.1	1.6
Mental distress	7.9	2
In the last 30 days, for how many days was he unable to do your usual activities because of a bad physical or psychological state of health?	3.7	0.7
Which health/medical service in particular took charge of your health problem?		
General Practitioner	12	
Hospital or Emergency Department	67.7	
Territorial Public Health facilities	12.7	
Private Specialists	4.7	
Others	2.9	

criticalities. Specifically, the Bastogi population has a greater number of days with poor health, both physical and psychological, and a greater number of days in which, due to health problems, the population has not been possible to carry out their usual activities. Overall, 40% of respondents assess their health in negative terms (Table 2). Furthermore, although the majority of residents declare that they have their own general practitioner in the vicinity of their place of residence, two-thirds of the interviews state that their health problems are managed in particular by second level services, such as emergency rooms, outpatient clinics and hospitals.

5 Conclusions

The reported results suggest that are fundamental differences between the population living in the Bastogi area and the population of the neighbouring areas. These differences regard not only the social determinants of health distribution, such as low level of education and unemployment, but also self-perception of health and the use of health services, a pattern defined by a greater use of emergency health services in Bastogi when compared to their neighbours.

Moreover, the Bastogi population, although younger than the population of the surrounding areas, have alarming hospitalisation rates, indeed higher in the younger age groups.

Despite the different information sources used, the territory-based assessment of the Bastogi area shows a coherent picture, characterized by a concentration of social and health problems, with which the population copes by using hospital services rather than relying on prevention and primary care. On the one hand, the latter underlines issues in the offer of healthcare service and appropriateness of use, while on the other this aspect suggests that local health services have extensive room for improvement in health promotion and health services orientation, according to urban health principles [43, 44]. The interpretation of Census data—based on the Social Determinant of Health theory—may represent an effective starting point in the definition of possible issue related to the socio-health dimension. The implementation of additional integrated tools capable of communicating different data bases, such as the Permanent Census [45], or the Metropolitan Longitudinal Studies described above, certainly represents a step in the right direction.

References

1. Massey DS, Denton NA (1988) Suburbanization and Segregation in U.S. Metropolitan Areas. Am J Soc 94(3):592–626
2. Mudu P (2006) Patterns of segregation in contemporary Rome. Urban Geogr 27(5):422–440. https://doi.org/10.2747/0272-3638.27.5.422

3. Iorio S, Salvatori LM, Barnocchi A et al (2019) Social inequalities in the metropolitan area of Rome. A multidisciplinary analysis of the urban segregation of the "formerly-Bastogi" compound. Ann Ig 31(3):211–229
4. Benevolo L (1993) La città nella Storia d'Europa. Gius Laterza & Figli, Roma-Bari
5. Capanna A (2005) La casa per tutti. Il primo concorso INA-Casa e la ricostruzione civile del Paese. Rassegna di Architettura e Urbanistica 117:78–85
6. Nardozzi G (2003) The Italian "Economic Miracle". Rivista di storia economica, Rivista fondata da Luigi Einaudi. 2(2003):139–180. https://doi.org/10.1410/9557
7. Secchi B (2005) La città del ventesimo secolo. Editori Laterza, Bari
8. Insolera I (2011) Roma Moderna, da Napoleone I al XXI Secolo. [(1° ed. 1962), Edizione ampliata con la collaborazione di Paolo Berdini, 2011]. Einaudi, Torino
9. Berlinguer G, Della Seta P (1960) Borgate di Roma. Editori Riuniti, Roma
10. Mudu P, Rossini L (2018) Occupations of housing and social centers in Rome: A durable resistance to neoliberalism and institutionalization. In: Lopez M, Angel M (eds) The urban politics of squatters' movements. Palgrave MacMillan, pp 99–120
11. Associazione 21 Luglio. I margini del margine, comunità rom negli insediamenti formali e informali in Italia, rapporto 2018
12. Legge 42/2009, modifica dell'art114 comma 3 della Costituzione, introdotto con la L. Cost.3/2001 di revisione del titolo V parte II. G.U. n.103 del 6 maggio 2009
13. Lelo K (2017) Suburbs and fragmentation patterns: the case of Rome. Eurodiv Paper 44
14. Capolongo S, Rebecchi A, Dettori M et al (2018) Healthy design and urban planning strategies, actions, and policy to achieve salutogenic cities. Int J Environ Res Public Health 15:2698
15. Brambilla A, Maciocco G (2014) Le Case della salute. Recenti Prog Med 105:147–150
16. On Local Health Institution in Rome [Case della Salute nel territorio di Roma Capitale]: http://www.retesalutelazio.it/rete-salute-lazio/it/
17. Vehicles circulating in Rome [Veicoli circolanti a Roma Capitale], Ragioneria Generale—I Direzione "Sistemi informativi di pianificazione e controllo finanziario"—U.O. Statistica, anno 2016
18. Ufficio Statistico Roma (2016) Le Caratteristiche dell'Occupazione a Roma, anni 2008–2015. Ragioneria Generale—I Direzione "Sistemi informativi di pianificazione e controllo finanziario" U.O. Statistica, Dicembre 2016
19. Batty M, Besussi E, Chin N (2003) Traffic, Urban growth and suburban sprawl. Centre for Advanced Spatial Analysis, UCL, Working Paper Series, paper 70
20. Gariazzo C, Stafoggia M, Bruzzone S et al (2018) Association between mobile phone traffic volume and road crash fatalities: a population-based case-crossover study. Accid Anal Prev 115:25–33
21. Tomassi F (2013) Disuguaglianze, beni relazionali ed elezioni nelle periferie di Roma, Rivista di Politica Economica, n. 1–3, pp 403–450
22. Pearce N (1996) Traditional epidemiology, modern epidemiology, and public health. Am J Public Health 86(5):678–683
23. Greenland S, Pearl J, Robins JM (1999) Causal diagrams for epidemiologic research. Epidemiology 10(1):37–48
24. Lederer DJ, Bell SC, Branson RD, Chalmers JD, Marshall R, Maslove DM et al (2019) Control of confounding and reporting of results in causal inference studies. Guidance for authors from editors of respiratory, sleep, and critical care journals. Annals ATS 16(1):22–8
25. Vlahov D, Galea S, Gibble E, Freudenberg N (2005) Perspectives on urban conditions and population health. Cad Saúde Pública 21(3):949–957
26. Fleischer NL, Roux AVD (2008) Using directed acyclic graphs to guide analyses of neighbourhood health effects: an introduction. J Epidemiol Commun Health 62(9):842–846
27. Borrell C, Pons-Vigués M, Morrison J, Díez È (2013) Factors and processes influencing health inequalities in urban areas. J Epidemiol Commun Health 67(5):389–391
28. Dahlgren G, Whitehead M (1991) Policies and strategies to promote social equity in health. Institute for Futures Studies, Stockholm, Sweden

29. Whitehead M, Dahlgren G, Evans T (2001) Equity and health sector reforms: can low-income countries escape the medical poverty trap? The Lancet 358(9284):833–836
30. CSDH (2008) Closing the gap in a generation: health equity through action on the social determinants of health. Final Report of the Commission on Social Determinants of Health. World Health Organization, Geneva
31. Marmot M (2005) Social determinants of health inequalities. Lancet 365:1099–1104. https://doi.org/10.1016/S0140-6736-(05)71146-6
32. D'Alessandro D, Apolloni L, Capasso L (2017) Public health and urban planning: a powerful alliance to be enhanced in Italy. Ann Ig 29(5):453–463. https://doi.org/10.7416/ai.2017.2177
33. Caranci N, Di Girolamo C, Giorgi Rossi P on behalf of the IN-LiMeS Group et al (2018) Cohort profile: the Italian Network of Longitudinal Metropolitan Studies (IN-LiMeS), a multicentre cohort for socioeconomic inequalities in health monitoring. BMJ Open 8:e020572. https://doi.org/10.1136/bmjopen-2017-020572
34. Cacciani L, Bargagli AM, Cesaroni G et al (2015) Education and mortality in the rome longitudinal study. PLOS ONE 10(9):e0137576
35. Cesaroni G, Badaloni C, Romano V et al (2010) Socioeconomic position and health status of people who live near busy roads: the Rome Longitudinal Study (RoLS). Environ Health 9(1):41
36. Agabiti N, Barbieri G, Bardin A et al (2019) Immigrants' health and socioeconomic inequalities of overall population residing in Italy evaluated through the Italian network of longitudinal metropolitan studies. Epidemiol Prev 43(5–6 Suppl 1):1–80
37. Paglione L, Angelici L, Davoli M, Agabiti N, Cesaroni G (2020) Mortality inequalities by occupational status and type of job in men and women: results from the Rome Longitudinal Study. BMJ Open 10(6):e033776
38. Statuto Roma Capitale, Delibera n.8 del 7 marzo 2013, confini stabiliti con Delibera n.11 dell'11 marzo 2013
39. Battisti A, Barnocchi A, Iorio S (2019) Urban regeneration process: the case of a residential complex in a suburb of Rome, Italy. Sustainability 11(21):6122
40. Online software bt.viewer, ISTAT. http://gisportal.istat.it/bt.viewer/
41. 15th General Census ISTAT. https://www.istat.it/it/archivio/189483
42. Progresses of Local Health Units for Health in Italy [Progressi delle Aziende Sanitarie per la Salute in Italia—PASSI], EpiCentro, National Health Institute. https://www.epicentro.iss.it/passi/
43. Corburn J, Cohen AK (2012) Why we need urban health equity indicators: integrating science, policy, and community. PLoS Med 9(8):e1001285. https://doi.org/10.1371/journal.pmed.1001285
44. D'Alessandro D, Arletti S, Azara A, Buffoli M, Capasso L, Cappuccitti A, Casuccio A et al (2017) Strategies for disease prevention and health promotion in urban areas: the Erice 50 Charter. Ann Ig 29:481–493
45. Permanent Census, National Statistic Institute (ISTAT). Available at: https://www.istat.it/it/censimenti-permanenti/popolazione-e-abitazioni

Inhabiting an "Un-common" Space: Health Promotion in the Area of Pescarola, Bologna

Francesca Cacciatore, Rita Maralla, and Martina Riccio

Abstract This article reports on a community-based action-research project initiated in July 2014 by the Centre for International and Intercultural Health. The project aims at promoting health through empowerment and community participation in a low-income suburban area of the city of Bologna (Pescarola). Based on an in-depth analysis of the ethnographic material collected (field notes, interviews, focus groups, meeting transcripts), this article focuses on critical moments of the action-research process, which made us reflect on our role and status in relation to other actors in the field, particularly community members. Specifically, we focus on the opening and development of a community space and on the potential and critical issues inherent to the action-research methods we used, such as community care, creative workshops, and theatre. These methods constitute both answers to the needs that emerged from the initial phase of the research (loneliness and lack of social connections), and strategies to investigate health needs together with the community. Our work shows how, in contexts of marginalisation, the material and symbolic conditions for people's participation in a collective space, and the very presence of a 'community', cannot be assumed, rather they need to be constructed with the people as a central part of the health promoting action.

Keywords Participatory action-research · Health promotion · Community participation · Empowerment · Ethnography · Marginalised urban areas

1 Introduction to the Field: Our Arrival in Pescarola and the Initial Mapping of Local Needs and Resources

Pescarola is a suburb of Bologna, in the Navile neighborhood. Due to a high concentration of low-income housing, Pescarola is an area where multiple conditions of economic deprivation and social vulnerability intersect. Health problems (physical

F. Cacciatore · R. Maralla · M. Riccio (✉)
Centre for International and Intercultural Health, Bologna, Italy
e-mail: csi.aps@inventati.org; martina.riccio2@unibo.it

A. Battisti et al. (eds.), *Urban Health*, Green Energy and Technology,
https://doi.org/10.1007/978-3-030-49446-9_7

disabilities, substance abuse, chronic disease, and mental health issues) are associated with and aggravated by isolation and conflict, both within the community and with local services. From a structural point of view, the ACER[1] Agucchi-Zanardi low-income housing complex within Pescarola is surrounded by large infrastructures, including the airport (500 m away), the high speed rail and the highway, all of which have an impact on the environment and on the health of the population.

As Centre for International and Intercultural Health (CSI),[2] we arrived in Pescarola in July 2014, following a call from Dispositivi PsicoSociali (DPS), an association for social intervention. For years, DPS had operated on the ground, in close collaboration with a local residents committee (Comitato cittadini residenti Agucchi-Zanardi) and a volunteers network (Coordinamento Volontariato Lame—CVL). Together, in 2012, they instituted the "Spazio Comune" (common space), a room for community activities within the ACER housing complex. Through a qualitative and quantitative research done in collaboration with the University of Bologna Department of Sociology,[3] DPS had documented the presence, in the ACER housing complex, of several health-related conditions, deeply connected with the social marginalisation of its inhabitants. As a result, DPS opted for involving CSI, in order to deepen the analysis on health conditions and prompt more proactive interventions and closer proximity to the community from the local health and social services.

In action-research, the conditions of access to the field are a primary and inexhaustible source of knowledge, essential for understanding one's role and position in relation to the different actors involved [1]. In our case, the reflection carried out throughout the years highlighted two central elements which relate to our position on the ground. Firstly, even though our arrival was mediated by actors who were active in the community, it was not responding to a request or need expressed by residents, nor were we called upon by institutions or local services. This led to asking ourselves "to whom are we accountable for what we do?", a question which continues to be a fertile ground for reflection on our ethics and methodology. The second element relates to the fact that we did not choose the site of our action. Since our arrival we asked ourselves, "why Pescarola? How are health conditions and access to services distributed in the rest of the city?". This second question led to the development of a second action-research project, in collaboration with the Local Health Authority and the Municipality, aimed at investigating the distribution of ill-health in the city of Bologna [2].

---

[1] ACER stands for Azienda Casa Emilia-Romagna, the regional Public Housing Agency.

[2] CSI was born in 2006 as a Centre for Research and Studies in the Department of Medicine and Public Health of the University of Bologna. In 2015, a civil society organisation was also founded with the same name (CSI-APS). Currently, the university centre has moved to the Department of History, Culture and Civilization (DiSCi), under the direction of Professor Ivo Quaranta. These are the links to the association's website www.csiaps.org and the university website https://centri.unibo.it/csi/it.

[3] We are referring to the research project "Pescarola is not an island", conducted in 2012, coordinated by Professor Maurizio Bergamaschi and Professor Roberta Paltrinieri from the University of Bologna Department of Sociology. The research was part of the project "Citizens of Pescarola: a suburb becomes a village", promoted by the volunteers network CVL.

With the aim to ensure the continuity of the work that had already been done in the area prior to our arrival, in early 2015 we initiated a structured exchange of information and mutual learning process with the actors involved (DPS, CVL, Comitato Agucchi-Zanardi, Department of Sociology). This self-training process allowed the different groups to present and discuss the theoretical and methodological approaches they were using in their research and/or volunteer work, and led to the creation of a cross-disciplinary common ground in terms of language, analyses and methods. The involvement of community volunteers, experts in the day-to-day reality of the area, allowed us to incorporate in the knowledge generation and sharing process not only scientific theories but also elements of practice and lived experience.

Following a search for financial support, we conducted an analysis of health needs and a mapping of the available resources (end of 2015–2016), using both quantitative approaches (statistical analysis of demographic and health data and of indicators of access to health and social services) and ethnographic and participatory research [3, 4] (participant observation in local activities; interviews with social and health service workers; focus group discussions with volunteers; participatory mapping activities with groups of residents).

Demographic data analysis, between 1996 and 2015, showed how Pescarola, compared to the surrounding areas and to the rest of the city of Bologna), is characterised by a strong demographic decline of the overall population (−12,8%), combined with aging of the population (+10,3% of people over 65 and −7,6% of people between 15 and 29 years old). Many families have more than three members.

The mapping highlighted a separation between the ACER housing complex and other areas of Pescarola. For example, residents of the ACER complex do not frequently access the nearby social spaces, such as the bowls area, the cafe and the elderly club. What surfaced are invisible borders, rooted in the profoundly different life conditions between people who live in the ACER complex and those who live in the surrounding areas. These differences can also be noted from an aesthetic point of view, with the surrounding areas containing parks and small terraced houses. Through participant observation, we also found what had already surfaced from previous research projects conducted in the area and discussed above, which is a strong sense of abandonment and loneliness experienced by many inhabitants, often accompanied by conflictual relationships between neighbors. The citizens committee, the volunteers and local services also highlighted scarce participation in proposed activities and initiatives, or "misleading" participation ("*they only come if there is food to eat and then they leave*").

With regards to health conditions and relationships to public services, the qualitative analysis highlighted a lack of proactive and integrated health, social and educational services. In particular, family doctors working in the area highlighted how the changes in healthcare organisation, which no longer allow adequate time for home visits, have had a strong impact on their knowledge of the territory and of the life conditions of their patients, and how this has affected their ability to fully grasp the scope of problems faced by patients. This often translates into ineffective care, which is accompanied by a high use of medicines (such as antidepressants, anti-anxiety medications and pain killers) and use of the emergency department for non-urgent conditions by many residents from the ACER housing complex. This finding was confirmed by a mixed-method analysis, done at the local Mental Health centre, which highlighted a significant discontinuity in the relationship between family doctors and local mental health and substance addiction services. When anxiety- and depression-related symptoms are managed only by family doctors, this may translate into patients' needs being predominantly geared towards pharmaceutical therapies that are difficult to monitor and often become forms of self-medication, which are not monitored through regular checkups.

In line with the qualitative analysis, an initial quantitative survey on health data of people living in Pescarola illustrated a higher incidence of chronic illnesses (in particular diabetes and heart conditions), and higher access to healthcare services—compared to the rest of Bologna—for causes that could be managed in Primary Health Care [5] at the local level. As previously mentioned, the collected data was also strategic to solicit key health policy makers(primarily the Director of the Department of Public Health and the Director of the Bologna Health District) and to increase our outlook and action towards the city as a whole [2].

In relation to the complex picture that emerged, we decided to move contemporarily on two levels of action-research aimed at improving the health outcomes in the area: (1) establish a direct relationship with the residents of the ACER complex and with local associations and groups, in an empowering approach for the improvement of social capital; (2) sustained advocacy towards the representatives of local institutions, healthcare and social services to support a reorganisation towards an integrated and comprehensive Primary Health Care approach in the area of Pescarola.[4] The focus of this chapter will be on the first level of the action-research. Following the needs assessment, in the beginning of 2017, we decided to activate a weekly space of sharing with the community. This space constitutes both a response to the needs expressed in relation to sense of loneliness, abandonment, and lack of social spaces, and an attempt to continue research regarding health needs together with those who are directly involved in the problems that we are seeking to analyse. Regarding the second level of action-research, we are at present still in a negotiation phase with the involved institutions.

2 "Spazio *Non* Comune" as a Health (Research) Space

> If you have come to help me, you are wasting your time, but if you have come because your liberation is bound to mine, then let us work together.

[4]A strong inspiration in this direction is the "Habitat Micro-Areas, Health and Community Development" programme, which has been active for more than fifteen years in the territory of Trieste and Friuli-Venezia Giulia Region (north-east of Italy). Over the years, we met and exchanged several times with key people involved in that project, which represents a national point of reference for the promotion of health through a community perspective. For a critical sociological reflection on the development of Micro-Areas Programme in the frame of "local active welfare" in Italy see Bifulco et al. [6].

Lila Watson, Aboriginal woman leader

Field notes, October 22nd 2016:

Yesterday was the fourth Friday in a row that I went to the food distribution after the summer [...]. I was with M. [CSI colleague], at around 5 pm we were getting our things to go when a woman came running in, S., she was very agitated, speaking in a tone somewhere between aggressive and submissive, saying these words more or less: "I'm sorry for my lateness, sorry there was the strike, it's not my fault, you can get upset with the transportation services, but if I can't get anything anymore I will go...". She says this mostly to M. and I [...]. I have spoken to S. various times during the food distributions in the past weeks, I like her, we established a minimal level of trust. And so, spontaneously, as soon as she enters, she looks at us and justifies her lateness to us. M. and I are also shocked and look at each other as if to say, "Why are you speaking to us since we are not the volunteers?" [...]. In the meantime a volunteer comes and says "Look, I am the manager here, you have to speak with me. It's okay, anyways, we will give you the box of food anyways", but the woman does not listen. You could tell that she was very stressed and anxious, she kept on saying different things, not listening, until at one point she turned to M. and I and said: "Don't give me that look! Ok, I'll go, but don't give me that look, out of all people, not from you!" I was very upset, she misunderstood, but in that chaos I didn't know how to explain myself to her. In the meantime a volunteer brought her box of food and put it on the table, but the woman was offended and continued to say: "I won't take it, no actually I'll take it and leave it outside, I can do whatever I want with it." [...] Two other volunteers interfered saying, "No, you cannot leave it outside!" and then, "How dare you use that tone!". The woman continued addressing M. and I; "Fine, I'll go, I won't take it, but you cannot look at me like that, don't give me that look..." I couldn't resist any longer and I took her outside to speak with her. She addressed me as if I was one of the volunteers. I told her I am not a volunteer, but I didn't know how else to explain to her what it is that I do there. [...] I managed to convince her to take the box of food, but when we went back inside the volunteers had already dispensed the goods in her box into bags to give to other people. One of them says: "What are you waiting for? It's not there anymore, you gave it up and we will give it to those who wait, if you had really wanted it you would have taken it immediately." [...] A verbal argument starts. The woman says, "You are volunteers, you cannot decide who you give things to, it's the social worker who decides, it is my right to have this". "I don't believe that you are not paid to be here!". "What do you think, that you're the only one who does volunteer work? Do you think you're a better person because you do volunteer work? I do it too, the only difference is that you do it in an office and I do it door to door!". [...] This morning I sent a message to the volunteers to say that I was upset by the incident that happened. One of them responded, "In our activities, it is not uncommon to run into particular subjects. Yesterday it was your turn. Don't worry about it and stay serene." The woman had become a "particular subject". The volunteer activities are an operative branch of social services and reproduce the same aid-based mechanisms based on power. Whatever happens, "the client" can always be blackmailed. The only tool they have on their side is to play the part of the victims, as services expect them to be. [...] And what role did M. and I have? If we hadn't been there would all of that have happened anyways? [...] Our role is not clear at all, neither to us nor to who is there, volunteers and inhabitants both. What right do we have to act as mediators between social services and the inhabitants? And do we really want to do mediation?

This episode was one of the first moments in which our interactions on the field put us in front of the question of what our role is in the area and how we can translate it into concrete actions. In over a year of observation and active participation in existing activities we had in part built relationships with some community members, but no one knew how to consider our work, what requests they could make to us and what our intentions were. This lead to misunderstandings and incidents, such as with S., which could have potentially negative impacts on the trusting relationships that we aimed to build as the necessary basis for any future activities. At the same time, from our point of view, what we were doing was coherent with our vision of health promotion as deeply rooted in community participation [7–9]. The attempt was to build, since the beginning, possible actions together with the different actors in the area, volunteers and mostly residents, and to start from a shared view on health needs.

Referring to health needs, it is important to consider that what is perceived as a need and the way in which it is expressed are greatly influenced by the resources that are available and usually depend on what is offered to the community [10]. From this point of view, the questions that are often formulated and brought to the institutional level are those that people believe will be listened to and taken into account, and do not always reflect and answer to the needs that are actually experienced and perceived. Furthermore, a socio-cultural context pervaded by an individualised and biomedical vision of health [11], together with the disintegration of social relationships and networks in suburban marginalised areas [12, 13], strongly influence the collective consciousness with regards to what needs can be expressed.

For the entire initial phase of observation and participation, we thus sought to keep the field of meaning-making broad (what is health?) and to avoid being identified, and identifying ourselves, in a specific task or role, in order to keep the expression of needs as open as possible. In particular, our main worry was that, since the CSI team includes medical doctors, this may lead to requests for health services and pharmaceutical prescriptions. The expression of needs would then be channeled into an exclusively biomedical view of health. Furthermore, despite our doubts regarding our role on the field, the intent from the beginning was to not substitute medical and social services, but to contribute to improving their efficacy and accessibility.

A central moment that shaped the space of (research on) health which we were to progressively developed over the months, was the focus group discussion that we conducted with the CVL volunteers.[5] Keeping in mind the issues that emerged out of the initial phase of ethnographic research—in particular, the lack of a welcoming space within the ACER residential complex, that is truly open to the people—the idea behind the focus group was to understand the challenges that the volunteers encountered and to evaluate the possibility to support them in order to better face them. The focus group highlighted that a key challenge for volunteers was the relationships with residents, with frequent tensions and conflict due to the reported aggressiveness of residents. When we proposed to reflect together on the strategies that would be helpful for surpassing these difficulties and establishing better relationships with the

[5]Seven members of CSI (two facilitators and five observers) and seven CVL volunteers (involved in food and clothing distribution, after school programs and Italian classes for foreign women) participated in the focus group discussion, centreed on three questions: 1. What lead you to become volunteers in Pescarola? 2. What are the main challenges you have encountered throughout your volunteer experience? 3. Based on the identified challenges, do you believe it is possible to reflect on them with CSI and seek improvement strategies together?

community, the volunteers sustained that the "target" of our actions should not be them, but the residents the ACER housing complex:

> Volunteer #1: […] What you can do to help us?…but the project was created to help the citizens of Pescarola, not us. […]
>
> Volunteer #2: I think the most important thing is what V1 is saying, the interventions should be geared towards the ACER housing complex. […] It depends on how you would manage this, meaning that, based on the studies and the mapping activities that you did, you have to find something that will really activate the people and get them involved. Because that is really the point, activating the people.
>
> V.1: […] What I mean is that this project has been going on for eight months but we really didn't create anything with the community. We studied a lot, at the end we will write our report and that's it […]. From my point of view, the proposal is keep the "Spazio Comune" open for the health issues that are relevant. […]
>
> V.2: V1 emphasised the most important point, because everything must be done for them [the residents], this cannot be forgotten […].
>
> V.3: […] The people that I got to know always have this aid mentality […]. I think it is very difficult to get them involved because they are used to getting and not giving, it's a question of culture and self worth, to give means getting involved and putting yourself out there, and these people are not used to that […].
>
> V.4: We are born as a group in this context to activate citizens into active citizenship, I mean, I bring certain services here that offer certain things so that people can benefit from them, roll up their sleeves, see how it's done, and slowly substitute me and operate themselves, developing these activities themselves, since they are the ones living here. This is the most difficult transition that we find, we found that […] they remain closed in their homes. It's true, the most difficult thing is getting them involved. (Focus group discussion, October 27th 2016).

The focus group discussion shows how volunteer activities are structured through an aid-based relationship and approach, centered on the binary "us" and "them", between those who give and those who receive. At the same time, the volunteers themselves focus on the necessity to involve the population in order to construct effective actions of health promotion, something that seems particularly difficult to achieve through their mode of operating. Based on a participatory action-research approach [14–16], it is important to redefine the relationship between what is perceived as "us" (volunteers, researchers, workers) and "them" (residents, clients), surpassing the rigid definitions of roles and professional boundaries to construct meaningful knowledge that is born from sharing common experiences [17, 18].

In relation to this, and considering what had been expressed by the volunteers in the focus group, in March 2017 we decided—as part of the action-research—to open our own weekly activity within the "Spazio Comune". We named this activity "Spazio *non* Comune" (S*n*C) ("un-common space"), referring both to the fact that the space was not perceived by residents as being open for them (communal), and to convey the idea of a space to co-construct together with residents as an alternative path towards greater participation.

The S*n*C was activated with the following aims:

1. Give a new meaning to the "Spazio Comune" as a welcoming space that puts people and their resources at the centre;

Fig. 1 *One of the first* S*n*C meetings, April 2017

2. Contrast the isolation and loneliness expressed by residents through building peer and mutual support;
3. Help people identify health needs and problems through the sharing of knowledge that comes from the experiences of all participants (Fig. 1).

3 Experimenting "Community Care" and Making the Group: A Path with Obstacles

Now that you have broken through the wall, what will you do with the cell next door?

S. J. Lec

Field notes, April 24th 2017.

Spazio non Comune: it's a Monday afternoon and we are busy organizing a meeting with the residents of Pescarola. That afternoon, like previous ones before, we wanted to try to create a joyous climate of sharing, relationship building and storytelling. This Monday as well would be a test, an experiment, to understand and define how we can better address our work in Pescarola and do this together with the community. M. arrives, she is a 60-year-old woman, one of the most regular and consistent people who come to our space: she is particularly quiet and she is not well. Before the beginning of the meeting she tells to the group that in the morning she had negative thoughts and tried to cut herself on her arm. She shows us light wounds and asks us to medicate them, telling us that she is full of sad and anguishing thoughts. We are all a bit disoriented, we try to give her space, attention and the opportunity to express herself, to make her feel a group that is welcoming and willing to listen. M. takes that space for herself with a lot of strength, almost as if, in that moment, it is her natural right. She says she feels lonely, abandoned, especially now that she has had a surgery, which has weakened her physically. This condition keeps her from doing many things in her daily life, from her walk in the morning, to going out to get coffee or cigarettes, to cleaning her house. She says that she is not able to eat or cook, that she has not cleaned her house in months and that her phone has credit and she has cigarettes only because a nice neighbor sometimes goes out to buy these things for her.

M. is an emblematic case of the many situations of social vulnerability that are present in the ACER housing complex. Stories that often speak about multiple factors of frailty that are not addressed, not even through the interventions of health and social services. In fact, the majority of the people we encountered are, for the most part, already linked to these services. A story like M.'s put us in front of the critical issues that are inherent to the social and health care system, and also represented a challenge for us and our role. The space that we made available was meant to allow people share different experiences of suffering: why did M. come to this place specifically? Does this mean that other spaces are not there and/or are not working for her? What do we do when suffering emerges but in such unexpected and sudden ways? The group discussion brought to the mobilisation of various resources. Some residents made themselves available to cook and deliver food to M. We made contacts with service providers to report the deterioration of M.'s condition and to request the activation of home care services. When services could not intervene (for instance, in helping M. with her house cleaning), we looked for solutions together with her neighbors. We managed to find makeshift solutions to help M. in her suffering, making her feel like there was a small support network around her. But how could we face each single story through this highly demanding approach? How can we address people's needs while keeping the effort manageable within the scope of the project?

M.'s case raised the need, which we had already perceived for some time, to activate a space in which it would be possible to elaborate on suffering, a space different from those traditionally offered by social and health services and helpful for exiting conditions of isolation and loneliness. We imagined a space in which suffering, in the broadest sense possible, could be collectively welcomed and elaborated on, going from being an inadvertent, individual incident that can only be addressed and managed by expert knowledge, to being a condition that is born in a particular kind of relational and social context, inside of which it is possible to find the knowledge and resources needed to confront it.

The experience we decided to draw on[6] was that of "Integrative Community Therapy" (ICT), theorised and experimented in Brasil by the psychiatrist and anthropologist Adalberto Barreto, starting from the 1980s [19]. The activities done with residents thus far had brought up relational and conflictual dynamics, and we feared that this would be an obstacle to implementing ICT. At the same time, we thought that this very instrument could potentially help confront these dynamics in more constructive ways and eventually transform them. In light of these deliberations, we thought to organise sharing and support meetings, following the ICT approach

[6]In that period of time (beginning of 2017), we also had a very enriching exchange with colleagues from Rome, who were involved in a health promotion project in the suburb of Bastogi, where they were also considering to experiment with Community Therapy.

but renaming it "Community Care", in order to stay away from any medicalising language.

We decided to start with thematic groups, addressing health-related aspects, the relationship with social and health services, relationships within the neighborhood and the community: themes that would allow us to gradually approach the deepest dimensions of lived experience and suffering in the community. After the first meeting, we tried to address more intimate and emotional aspects, supporting the sharing and connecting of similar lived experiences. We decided to adopt some of ICT rules, those that would support a trusting and open atmosphere and enable people to come together in constructive and respectful ways: listen without interrupting, do not give advice or judge, speak in first person [19]. Inspired by the emphasis placed in ICT on creating a welcoming atmosphere, crucial for supportive sharing [19], we thought to structure the meetings in two moments. First, a welcoming and an introduction to the activities, sharing some food prepared by organisers and participants. Second, a group setting for sharing experiences in a structured and dedicated way, with the goal of creating a deep and intimate space of discussion that would allow for reciprocal understanding and knowledge of potentially shared themes. The group facilitators were two anthropologists from CSI, both also trained in relational family counselling and who had attended ICT training courses conducted by Barreto himself.

The experiences that emerged from the first meetings were very important and deep: isolation and loneliness; relationships lacking authenticity and solidarity, also because of a widespread sense of frailty and precariousness; discrimination and racism. And the Group facilitation proved to be complex and demanding: it was difficult for people to respect the talking rules and there were often overlapping debates and distractions that hindered full and active listening. This highlighted the lack of experience among participants in sharing space with others. Furthermore, the very lack of other opportunities for relationship building and listening, lead to the space becoming a stage for conflicts and to forcefully expose on others individual "tragedies" (Fig. 2).

Thanks also to the support of an external counsellor and ICT expert, we tried to rethink the space through an in-depth self-reflective process. In order to contrast the function being attributed to the space as a "stage for conflicts", we tried to give every person the space and time they requested in other moments as well (for example, before or after the meetings), to give everyone the sense that they were seen and recognised in their individuality, including through small gestures such as bringing particular music, references to authors or books that had been requested, etc. It was also very important to create new interpretative frameworks, new models to read and attribute meaning to individual experiences [20]: from the condition of passive subjects and victims of human injustice, to persons with profound, intrinsic resources. Many of the activities were conducted with the objective of giving a new view on personal life experiences, moving away from a vision of pity to one that attributes an active and positive role to people.

Another point of reflection was on the function that food can play in conviviality, which remained an unchanged and attractive component over time. We found that this

Fig. 2 S*n*C thematic activity with images on "what does community mean for you?", June 2017

aspect, after the group was consolidated, could be superfluous or even counterproductive, difficult to sustain economically and too burdensome on our time. We also wondered if we were not replicating the aid-based approach that we earlier criticised. To use Batesonian terminology [21], a kind of complementary schismogenesis was being consolidated, a model of interaction according to which the more we sought to be welcoming, the more participants were accommodating to a position of being assisted, thus consolidating an asymmetric relationship. Initially, some participants contributed by bringing something to eat as well, but over time their contributions waned while ours increased. We thus changed the time of the activity, which served a double function: to free ourselves from this aid-based form of welcoming and to ascertain whether people really came for the moments of supportive sharing or not. In fact, even though we changed the time and outlined a moment exclusively dedicated to supportive sharing, the solid core of participants remained. For us this was a very important step as we had suffered from feeling stuck in this incumbency, and probably had difficulties exiting out of it also due to our own biases and our own difficulties in giving ourselves a less protective and supportive role.

In conjunction with the described meetings, we conducted creative workshops (cooking, crafts) that, in our view, had significance in as much as they offered more recreational contexts, which were less emotionally draining. More or less, the same people who participated in the Community Care meetings attended the workshops. This more practical space also became a way for consolidating relationships and valuing everyone's skills. However, even though the workshops came out of a spontaneous initiative of ours together with the participants, we still did not feel fully at ease in this role. Where did our specific competencies go? What about these workshops was significant?

We tried to answer these questions also with the support of interviews with participants. We asked them first and foremost, what they got from their participation in the different activities. Different positions emerged, which were all important for our subsequent reflections. Generally speaking, the Community Care meetings were experienced as pleasant by the majority of participants, but there were also some ambivalent positions. On one side, a lot of value was given to personal sharing with others, and a modality through which people could get to know each other and give space to the parts of themselves that were often silenced, with opportunities for suppressed memories to resurface in a protective space and be seen through a different lens. On the other hand, some participants expressed strong difficulties with the reemerging of experiences of pain and suffering. The observation made by two people struck us in particular. They expressed the difficulties of dealing with these dimensions once they returned home, almost as if the solitude, back at home, made the suffering related to remembering even more acute. This was not only in relation to their own experiences, but also in relation to others' experiences that they identified with, which resonated with them and their emotions. This emerges in some of the interviews when we asked the participants how they felt in our meetings:

> I feel a sensation of regret because I suffered so much. It's recalling suffering, a lot of it, a lot of it… during the day you have other things, other thoughts, other things to face. Recalling the past makes me suffer. (M., August 2018)

> Some stories brought suffering to me and to experience the suffering of the other person. When I see others who are sad, I feel sad too […] I know the weight that some people carry. (G., July 2018)

Bringing the past to the present, bringing to the here and now events and emotions that probably did not always have the chance to be reconstructed into a horizon of newly processed meaning and to find peace with the present situation [22]. Despite our attention on the closing rituals (emotional connection activities among participants), the meetings likely required further elaboration and protection so that returning home could be reflective and not anguishing for the participants.

A strong attraction to the creative workshops and the playfulness and fun they involved emerged along with the feeling that completing something practical offered a sense of satisfaction. The limit that was highlighted here was the lack of purpose. Different people suggested the possibility of obtaining a cash flow from what was made or to use it for decorative purposes in order to give more significance and concreteness to the things that were done together. In relation to this, we developed a program after the summer of 2018. A proposal from a community theatre association (Teatro dei Mignoli), born by chance, lead us to believe that the needs for practicality, playfulness and sharing could be addressed through a theatre workshop.

4 The Body as the Locus of Agency: The Unexpected Outcomes of Theatre

One does not have a body. One is a body.
Kristen Hastrup

In September 2018, in the S*n*C, a theatre workshop began in collaboration with Barbara Baldini, theatre actress and director of "Teatro dei Mignoli". Through play, activation of the senses, movement, reciprocal contact, role plays, and recalling emotions and life stories, the theatre workshop became an effective instrument for generating individual and collective wellbeing. The analysis of the interviews conducted with community members by Flavia Grottanelli, who did her MA thesis at CSI, highlighted how the workshop generated in participants a shared feeling of belonging to the group and to a collective process, a sense of complicity and solidarity, and a strengthening of self-esteem and self-confidence. It also implemented communicative and expressive abilities in participants, activated mechanisms that facilitated social cohesion, improved some relationships between neighbors, and created a community spirit. Consequently, "simple games" and activities can be sources of wellbeing because "if people have a higher degree of freedom and self-determination in their behaviors, they increase control over their health. This capacity […] increases when the social context people live in concretely helps and supports them in this direction. Social relationships, the community, can thus become key allies in changing behaviors towards the promotion of health" [23].

After about three months of weekly activities, the theatre workshop ended with a performance, which was presented to the community in November 2018, during the neighbourhood's usual chestnut roasting party. The possibility to perform in front of the community and neighbours had a beneficial effect on participants as it allowed them to feel like true actors and main characters. As Antonin Artaud suggests, "[…] the action of theatre is beneficial because, in pushing people to see themselves as who they are, it makes masks fall […] and, in revealing their hidden strength to the collective, people are invited to assume a courageous and superior attitude in the face of their destiny, which they would not have otherwise taken on" [24]. For people who often feel invisible, adopting a different role from the one they are usually attributed and interiorise strengthens their self-esteem and allows them to concretely show themselves differently from how they are used to being perceived. The heroic and superior attitude that Artaud suggests derives from the fact that participants/residents surpassed the limits of their own beings, assuming an active role in relation to their collective world, and not just a passive one, thus increasing their personal pride and their trust in themselves. As G., who lives in the neighbourhood and participated in the theatre workshop, highlights: "*the activity I liked the most was the theatre show because it attracted many people and people then asked me, when will they do another one? These things should be done more often! See, this is already an input that people are giving: they enjoyed the show and they want these things to happen more often*" (G., April 2019) (Fig. 3).

Fig. 3 Just after the theatre performance during the neighborhood's chestnut roasting party, November 2018

Being a protagonist becomes a way to imagine oneself as an "agent in the community", as individuals who are desired and desirable, as people who can create, and not only benefit from, recreational, playful and social moments, especially in contexts which, for social and political reasons, often "habituate" people into feeling that they are generic, passive or incapable beings without potential. Furthermore, what is important is the sharing of what Victor Turner defines as "*an* experience" [25], which, from his point of view, departs from the classic experience. "The simple experience is nothing more than bearing and accepting events. *An* experience on the other hand, like a rock in the sand of a Zen garden, emerges out of the uniformity of the hours and the years that pass and creates what Dilthey called the 'structure of experience'" [25]. Performance thus becomes a moment in and of itself, a unique event that detaches itself from the daily flow of things in a non arbitrary way, and contributes to the creation of what Kristen Hastrup defined as "the bubbling experience" [26]; an experience that "undergoes a process, becomes socialised and transformed, for no other reason than the fact that it is assigned an initiation and a completion—a beginning and an end—which cannot be given to the 'simple experience'. This deviation from everyday life and the importance placed on the bubbling experience also cause an additional process, which is the 'reactivation of responsibility'" [26]. This process has a direct consequence, which is the experience itself emerging as the main locus of learning, allowing people to knowingly recognise themselves as capable of action and response, and making themselves increasingly responsible for what happens around them, since they are the "promoters" of what is happening.

The emphasis placed on agency and individual will should not however forget the less rational aspects that affect individuals as well, since, differently from the modern conception of ego intention, agency is not only the result of rational cognitive process located in the mind and separate from the body. Beyond individual intentions and reasons, it is "the most profound reasons, that do not belong to the explicit and empirical order, but to the implicit and receding order of embodied culture" [26] that tend to shift people. It is important to point this out because what theatre elicits is the body in its totality more than the rational mind, consequently the main characters in the theatre workshop should not only be seen as rational people but as "profoundly motivated living bodies" [26], capable of improvised and not always intentional transformations.

In a different way, but with similarly positive consequences, the process of capacitation in people has the potential to overturn roles and the power dynamics that tend to regulate personal relationships. The theatre workshop and the final performance were thus effective instruments for involvement, learning, and development of social and human capital, and they allowed people to retain unique and exclusive knowledge and power which, in some cases, were able to significantly influence the development of individual and group empowerment processes [27].

Regarding the relationships between us, members of CSI, and the residents of Pescarola, the playful-participatory instruments allowed us to continue the sharing of personal life stories through a more pleasant approach, and to continue sustaining the creation of a horizontal context. Sharing the same scenic space and the activities proposed by Barbara positively influenced relationships within the group, which were often characterised by insurmountable differences between "us" (residents of the ACER housing complex) and "you" (members of CSI). Even though this border constantly re-emerges in our relationships to this day, what we are working on is the idea of possibly transforming the concept of "border" into one of "frontier", which is a more fluid terrain, hybrid and permeable to reciprocal contamination.

Due to its positive results, the theatre workshop continued and gave us the possibility to participate in and get accepted for an open call from a research and social intervention cooperative based in Milan. The call topic was on the concept of "inhabiting", and on the material and symbolic meanings it can acquire within specific marginalised areas.

We presented a co-research project that placed the creation of a multimedia theatre performance at the centre (meaning an expressive modality capable of intertwining multimedia, theatre and cinematographic techniques, with autobiographical story telling), with the intention of continuing the experimentation with theatre as an instrument for social cohesion and sharing. From a methodological point of view, the intent has been to initiate a horizontal co-research process, which could be able to involve both us from CSI, and the residents of ACER housing complex, throughout all the different phases: from the initial decision to present a shared research project, to the written proposal, to participation in the selection interviews, to consent-based collective decision-making with regards to what the group wants to do, to sharing the management of the allotted resources, to choosing how, when and in which way to present the outcome of the workshop. The multimedia theatre proposal is in continuity with what was already initiated on two levels: elaborating on the theme of contemporary living in relation to both the historical infrastructural transformations that have occurred in the area and the social relationships within the neighbourhood, and moving the centre of knowledge production and use into the hands of the residents.

As often happens, the construction of a non-hierarchical decision-making process is not straightforward and, in different moments, the desire for horizontal relationships clashed with a reality in which different positions (roles, opportunities and responsibilities) are experienced on both sides as—and in fact are—different and asymmetrical. A recent episode illustrates this well. There was a discussion in the S*n*C on how the allotted money would be used and some participants ironically commented on the desire expressed by a CSI member to receive a part of the money as a compensation for the extra work she was doing for the workshop. A. said, "*for me it's not a problem. This is your project, do what you want, I am in anyways.*" It is clear that the you-us distance determines a line of separation; beyond good intentions, there is a part of the group that has more decision-making power (CSI) and another part of the group that tends to follow the proposals and decisions. For A., the project is not "ours" in a collectively constructed sense, but it is "ours" as a group who is doing research with residents, giving them the possibility to connect with one another. What remains is the question on how to act on the excluding dynamics that are generated and how to create new horizons for authentic and real participation, despite (or perhaps starting with) the different positions, which determine unequal possibilities in taking decisions and actions. The attempt is to not conceal these questions, but to make them the heart of collective reflections and actions.

Regarding the actual theme of contemporary living, as a group we decided to investigate the existing relationship between place, memory and remembrance, placing both lived experiences and daily neighbourhood relationships at the centre of the research. At the same time, influenced by the famous phrase, "Living means being at home anywhere", uttered by Ugo La Pietra in the documentary L'appropriazione della città (1997), we immediately questioned the idea of contemporary living as a merely private practice and reinvented its meaning as an active contamination of public space. By interrogating ourselves on the conditions that make it more or less possible to "be at home anywhere", we investigated living practices as potential acts of contamination of public space, which is "invaded" by the private sphere, but can go back to being a "public square" in which both the I and the we can manifest.

5 Conclusions: On "Community" and "Participation"

> In micro-social action, it would be false to believe that one cannot see further than the bell tower or the tip of their nose. [...] The primordial problem of "implication" [...], if posed, can only be posed in micro-social action, in the real field of the forces that elicit us and on which we can hope to have an effect.
>
> René Lourau

Analysing the nature of connections in consumer societies of liquid modernity, Zygmunt Bauman highlights how "the swarm tends to substitute itself to the group". Differently from the group, within the swarm, each element has to be able to do everything on its own, become independent and autonomous from the others due to the fact that, inside, there are no relationships of cooperation or complementarity. Guided and seduced by objectives that are changing and by interactions that last exclusively in the consumer act, personal relationships become entirely occasional and superficial, "they do not have any influence on the future movements of the swarm and do not project any light on the past of its components" [28]. What Bauman highlights is how much, nowadays, the productive nature of consumerism—intended as desire that must however remain unsatisfied lest the consumer society come to an end—is what pushes individuals to unite; we are a swarm of consumers guided by individualistic and solitary goals. Bauman's reflection, which is primarily connected to the consequences of contemporary consumerism, interrogates us on the nature of interpersonal connections in today's society, on the structural dynamics that make it difficult to create community, intended as a group of people characterised by strong and lasting bonds, by relationships of reciprocity and common objectives.

Regarding our experience in Pescarola, we experimented the local effects of structural processes that strongly limit local action geared at the promotion of community health. We are referring to two issues here. Firstly, the exacerbation of the historical divide between the centre and the suburbs of a city. On an urban level, the economic policies of the last decades have incentivised the duality of "city for the rich" versus "city for the poor", emptying the outskirts of cities of services and areas for meetings and social connection,[7] and feeding processes of social fragmentation and disintegration of community relationships [12, 13]. This does not only undermine the social basis on which suburban areas were constructed, but mostly poses a problem of cohesion and integration in neighbourhoods, making them increasingly more vulnerable.

The principal inequalities that structure social life are crystallised and take shape in the urban space, which experiences increasingly marked lines of separation. In fact, new border lines are drawn (intergenerational, inter-ethnic, and between people of different socioeconomic statuses), which impair relationships between individuals, their "capacities to collaborate" and experience "an exchange in which participants benefit from being together" [13]. The desire for community thus constructs itself on the need to find similar people and involves excluding the other as someone different. Consequently, the community risks becoming a "voluntary ghetto" that feeds mechanisms of segregation and exclusion, which perpetrate and feed themselves over time.

Another aspect is related to the instrumental use of participation. In the face of weakening representative institutions, what is witnessed in many cities—and

[7]Related to Pescarola, indicative of this is the fact that all the now empty and closed spaces under the colonnade within the ACER housing complex were once stores (grocery, stationary store, bar) and constituted meeting places in the memories of the residents. It is also significant that the square inside the complex does not have a name.

Bologna is a national example—is an increasing push for "participatory democracy", expressed through instruments such as participatory budgeting and collaboration deals [29]. What we experienced in Pescarola,[8] is the feeling of moving within pre-established enclosures and in the shadow of economic and political choices which have, in fact, already been made. Furthermore, these kinds of confrontation spaces are often inaccessible to those who, due to their cultural capital, do not fit the social model that wants to be promoted. Instruments born to facilitate collective confrontation and construction of shared decisions (World Café, Open Space Technology) are used as mere "pacification" tactics for conflicts and for facilitating consensus-building [30]. The outcomes are the opposite of what real participation would point to: the de-politicisation of welfare policies that actually have strong social relevance, and the stabilisation and reproduction of neoliberal processes [29].

Within this socio-political context, the S*n*C experience in Pescarola speaks to the possibility of experimenting with (micro) practices of authentic participation, and attempting to construct (an open) community to identify with. To this end, the instruments used (mapping, community care, creative workshops, theatre) have, in different ways, solicited active participation and deep sharing. In particular, the use of the body and theatre gave voice to the emotional and expressive components of action, making the collective space more accessible and usable, leading to an overthrow of roles of knowledge/power, and making us feel, in our asymmetry and differences, part of the same group.

However, there were also considerable critical issues that we encountered. Firstly, despite the numerous and repeated attempts, to this day, the people with whom we collaborate in the construction of activities are a small, though consistent, number, compared to the residents of the ACER housing complex. As CSI, we believe that different factors interact in limiting the involvement of people. Some factors are related to the shape of our action and its internal sustainability. Being there once a week is not sufficient for responding to the characteristics of presence and continuity that a community space should have in order to be a point of reference for people. Furthermore, we believe that being able to keep the space open for longer hours could allow the organisation of different activities and, perhaps, lead to more involvement of new people who have not yet approached it.

Another issue concerns people who approached us in the past and attended the S*n*C meetings, showed visible signs of improvement in their wellbeing and social interactions, but then stepped back from it (at times literally withdrawing in their homes) and, despite repeated attempts to re-engage them, never came back. Our perception is that these people need concrete and consistent support for conducting their daily lives (house cleaning, food shopping, taking care of a sick or disabled family member, going out, paying bills, etc.) and for managing multiple physical issues in order to be in the condition to participate in a collective context. In this sense, community-level actions cannot be detached from individual support aimed at addressing daily problems. In fact, community work as a strategy for the promotion

[8] As CSI, together with the resident committee and the other local associations, we took part in the first Participatory Budget for the area of Pescarola, promoted by the Municipality in 2017.

of health has to be founded on an approach that aims at involving especially those who have fewer personal, social and material resources to act for their own benefit.

The response to this challenge, rooted in both our political strategy (not substituting ourselves to the public healthcare system but acting to improve it) and our material condition (lack of internal sustainability) is to advocate for a reorganisation of public services towards an integrated and comprehensive Primary Health Care approach in the area of Pescarola. In particular, to test a model of ongoing presence of one or more health and social staff that may proactively reach out to the population, particularly the most vulnerable groups, and be a reference and coordination point for health and social needs and for accessing public services.[9] We are thus moving in this direction, fully aware that the path is still long, that different actions are needed at multiple levels, and that the outcome depends on a close synergy between a variety of institutional actors.

References

1. Lapassade G (1993) De l'ethnographie de l'école à la nouvelle recherche-action. Université Paris VIII, Document Dactylographie
2. Bodini C, Gentilini V (2020) Addressing health inequities in the city of Bologna: a mixed-method, multi stakeholder and action-research approach towards health equity. In: Battisti A, Marceca M, Iorio S (eds) Urban health. Participatory action-research models contrasting socioeconomic inequalities in urban context. Springer, Heidelberg (in press)
3. Loewenson R, Laurell AC, Hogstedt C, D'Ambruoso L, Shroff Z (2014) Participatory action research in health systems: a methods reader. TARSC, AHPSR, WHO, IDRC Canada, EQUINET, Harare. Avialable at: http://www.equinetafrica.org/sites/default/files/uploads/documents/PAR%20Methods%20Reader2014%20for%20web.pdf. Last accessed 5 Nov 2019
4. Baum F (2006) Participatory action research. J Epidemiol Commun Health 60(10):854–857
5. World Health Organisation (1978) WHO: International conference on primary health care, Alma-Ata, USSR, 6–12 Sept 1978. Available at: https://www.who.int/publications/almaata_declaration_en.pdf. Last accessed 07 Nov 2019
6. Bifulco L, Bricocoli M, Monteleone R (2008) Activation and local welfare in Italy: trends and issues. Soc Policy Adm 42(2):143–159
7. World Health Organisation (1986) WHO: Ottawa Charter for Health Promotion. First international conference on health promotion, Ottawa, 21 November 1986. Available at: https://www.who.int/healthpromotion/conferences/previous/ottawa/en/. Last accessed 10 Nov 2019
8. Labonté R, Laverack G (2008) Health promotion in action. From local to global empowerment. Palgrave Macmillan, Basingstoke
9. World Health Organisation (2002) WHO Regional Office for Europe: Community Participation in Local Health and Sustainable Development. Approaches and techniques. Available at: http://www.euro.who.int/__data/assets/pdf_file/0013/101065/E78652.pdf. Last accessed 18 Nov 2019
10. Bush M, Dewar T, Fagan K, Gelberd L, Gordon G, McCereins A, McKnight J (1975) Al di là del bisogno: la società è servita. In: Ongaro Basaglia F (ed) Basaglia F. Crimini di pace. Ricerche sugli intellettuali e sui tecnici come addetti all'oppressione. Einaudi, Torino

[9]In the Trieste Micro-Areas Programme, previously mentioned, this health professional is called "referente di microarea" (micro-area manager). A similar example is the "agente comunitário de saúde" (community health agent), a key role in the primary healthcare strategy of the Brasilian national health system [31].

11. Kleinman A, Eisenberg L, Good B (1978) Culture, illness and care. Clinical lessons from anthropologic and cross-cultural research. Ann Intern Med 88:225–251
12. Castel R (2005) Incertezze crescenti. Lavoro, cittadinanza, individuo. Socialmente, Bologna
13. Sennet R (2012) Insieme. Rituali, piaceri, politiche della collaborazione. Feltrinelli, Milano
14. Baum F (2016) Power and glory: applying participatory action research in public health. Gac Sanit 30(6):405–407
15. Elliott WP (2011) Participatory action research. Challenges, complications, and opportunities. Centre for the Study of Co-operatives, Community-University Institute for Social Research, University of Saskatchewan, Canada
16. Montero M (2000) Participation in participatory action research. Ann Rev Crit Psychol 2:131–143
17. Genat B (2009) Building emergent situated knowledges in participatory action research. Act Res 7(1):101–115
18. Larrosa Bondía J (2002) Notas sobre a experiência e o saber da experiência. Revista Brasileira de Educação 19:20–28
19. Barreto A (2018) Una Comunità che cura. Terapia comunitaria integrativa passo a passo. Centro Culturale Studi Storici, Eboli
20. Watzlawick P, Weakland JH, Fisch R (1974) Change: la formazione e la soluzione dei problemi. Astrolabio, Roma
21. Bateson G (1988) Naven. Einaudi, Torino
22. Boscolo L, Bertrando P (1993) I tempi del tempo. Una nuova prospettiva per la consulenza e le terapia sistemica. Bollati Boringhieri, Torino
23. Capra P, Coppo A, Dettoni L, Di Monaco R, Marino M, Pilutti S, Suglia A (2018) Il coinvolgimento della comunità per il contrasto alle disuguaglianze di salute. La governance della comunità. Avilable at: https://www.disuguaglianzedisalute.it/wp-content/uploads/2018/06/policybrief_def.pdf. Last accessed 13 Nov 2019
24. Artaud A (1938) Il teatro e il suo doppio. Dino Audino Editore, Roma
25. Turner VW, Edward MB (1986) The anthropology of experience. University of Illinois Press, Champaign, Illinois, Urban & Chicago
26. Hastrup K (1995) Il corpo motivato. «Locus» e «Agency» nella cultura e nel teatro. Teatro e Storia 10(17):11–36
27. Wallerstein N (2006) What is the evidence on effectiveness of empowerment to improve health? Copenhagen, WHO Regional Office for Europe, Health Evidence Network report. Available at: http://www.euro.who.int/Document/E88086.pdf. Last accessed 15 Nov 2019
28. Bauman Z (2007) Homo consumens. Lo sciame inquieto dei consumatori e la miseria degli esclusi. Edizioni Erickson, Trento
29. Moini G (2012) Teoria critica della partecipazione. Un approccio sociologico. Franco Angeli, Milano
30. Boarelli M (2018) Partecipazione senza potere. In: A che punto è la città? Bologna dalle politiche di "buongoverno" al governo del marketing, Edizioni dell'Asino, Bologna, pp 24–39
31. Bornstein VJ, David HMSL, Araujo JWG (2010) Agentes comunitários de saúde: a reconstrução do conceito de risco no nível local. Interface—Comunicacao, Saude, Educacao 14(32):93–101

Addressing Health Inequities in the City of Bologna: A Mixed-Method, Multi Stakeholder and Action-Research Approach Towards Health Equity

Chiara Bodini and Valeria Gentilini

Abstract This chapter analyses the experience of a multidisciplinary, multiprofessional and interinstitutional research group that carried out an action-research project on health inequities in the city of Bologna, with an approach strongly oriented to making an impact in terms of health policies and outcomes, towards health equity. The group met regularly from February 2017 to October 2019 to design and implement a project in two phases: a first one based on a quantitative analysis of health inequalities, and a second one focused on qualitative research in selected areas of the city. An action-research approach was embedded throughout the project, with periodic evaluations to ensure progress towards the intended results. Although the action-research is still underway, interim results can be documented in terms of activation of local decision-makers and support to the second phase, a step towards a local and tailored approach to tackle health inequities. Our experience shows that addressing the issue of urban health inequities through a mixed method, multi stakeholder and action-research approach may lead to greater integration of research findings and evidence into healthcare policy and practice, towards health equity.

Keywords Health inequities · Action-research · Know-do gap · Ecological approach

1 Introduction

This chapter analyses the experience of a multidisciplinary, multiprofessional and interinstitutional research group that carried out an action-research project on health

C. Bodini (✉) · V. Gentilini
Centre for International and Intercultural Health, Bologna, Italy
e-mail: csi.aps@inventati.org

C. Bodini
University of Bologna, Bologna, Italy

A. Battisti et al. (eds.), *Urban Health*, Green Energy and Technology,
https://doi.org/10.1007/978-3-030-49446-9_8

inequities[1] in the city of Bologna, with an approach strongly oriented to making an impact in terms of health policies and outcomes, towards health equity.

The analysis carried out through the chapter fits in the framework of implementation science that, according to Fogarty International Centre, is "the study of methods to promote the integration of research findings and evidence into healthcare policy and practice". Implementation science is a complex, non-linear process that requires communication with multiple stakeholders and evaluation along the process to ensure that strategies are producing the intended results. In this sense, the field has its roots in the action-research approach [2], which is the methodological framework of our work.

Two collective actors are central to this story. One is the Department of Public Health of the Local Health Authority of Bologna (epidemiology unit), the other is the Centre for International and Intercultural Health (CSI), a multidisciplinary group composed of medical professionals and anthropologists, born in the University of Bologna in 2006 and also linked to a civil society organization by the same name.

In 2014, CSI started a community health action-research project in a marginalized area of the periphery of Bologna [3]. As part of the action-research, quantitative and qualitative data were collected through analysis of databases of the local health and social services, semi-structured in-depth interviews to social and healthcare staff working in the area, participant observation and field diaries [4]. While continuing the actions in the field, a parallel process started in order to bring the social and health disadvantage documented in the area to the attention of the Health District and the Local Health Authority of Bologna. The main motivation in doing so was to show how a mixed method action-research approach could offer a framework to understand the local processes involved in producing health inequities and therefore usefully orient the policies and programs of public services [5].

From the encounter of these two actors, a common story unfolded in which the efforts converged in designing a city-wide action-research that could shed light on existing inequities but also inform policy action to tackle them. Although the action-research is still underway, interim results can be documented in terms of activation of local decision-makers and support to the second phase of the project, a step towards a local and tailored approach to tackle health inequities.

We believe that this story is worth telling and analyzing for two main reasons. The first one is that—as Heath [6] poignantly wrote in a 2010 commentary on the BMJ—"*almost no one needs to be told about this [health inequities] any more or to be asked to look at more graphs or tables of figures. Instead, we need finally to find the collective will to do something about it.*" Indeed, the body of literature on the topic has grown exponentially in the past twenty years, but—quite disappointingly—inequities have also grown in many contexts. As in other fields, the know-do gap is evident and problematic both from the deontological and from the ethical point of view [7]. The second reason is that the existing literature covers mainly inequalities

---

[1]In this chapter, we will use the term "inequalities" when referring to the empirical observation of difference in the distribution of health or health resources, and the term "inequities" when theorizing is concerned with causal processes, agency, and accountability [1].

between countries or between regions/areas within a country. Studies that map the situation at a smaller level, for example in a city, are much less frequent and—yet—they are more informative in terms of orienting (and possibly monitoring) policies at the local level [8].

Our experience shows that it is possible to address the issue of urban health inequities through an approach that allows the integration of research findings and evidence into healthcare policy and practice. Using a mixed methodology, involving multiple stakeholders and adopting an action-research approach have been important for the success of our experience. Moreover, we believe that an added value of our work is the choice to rely on data that are routinely collected by the local health and social institutions, in order to facilitate the systematic analysis of inequalities and enable the replication and dissemination of the approach.

2 A Review of the Literature on Health Inequalities

A large body of literature shows how the social, political and cultural context shapes the distribution of health and disease within society. According to the social determination of health approach, health and disease are not merely biological aspects and are not randomly distributed among the population; on the contrary, they reflect broader socio-cultural, political and economic dynamics [9].

Several epidemiological studies have shown how lower socioeconomic classes systematically have higher incidence of mortality and morbidity, and how worse health outcomes linked to barriers in accessing healthcare services particularly concern the population groups that are most vulnerable and discriminated against [10–14]. The study of health inequalities began in the UK in the 1980s, with two historical publications: the "Black Report" and "The Health Divide" [15, 16]. Both documented the presence of statistically significant differences in health status among social classes within the UK. In Italy, the first report on health inequalities dates back to 1994, however the debate remained until recently rather confined to the academic and technical environment [17].

In the last decade, social inequities in health became a relevant topic in European public health, as the body of literature that shows their pervasiveness continues to grow: inequalities are found between individuals with different levels of education or income, between different population groups and between different geographical areas [18, 19]. In 2005, the World Health Organization (WHO) established a Commission on the Social Determinants of Health, that in 2008 published the seminal report "Closing the Gap in a Generation", addressing the impact on health outcomes of the social determinants of health and of inequities, as well as the actions needed to tackle them [7].

As we have mentioned, health inequalities have been traced across different geographical areas, both between countries and within countries, including between different areas of the same city [7, 20, 21]. Studies of the latter type have shown an environmental impact on mortality and morbidity that can be attributed partly to a different composition of the population and partly to modest but sustained effects of the neighbourhood deprivation, that remain visible after adjusting for individual socioeconomic status [22].

In Italy and abroad, the level of geographical variability in health attributable to the area has been studied through ecological studies based on aggregated population data, rooted in the hypothesis that physical or socioeconomic characteristics of an area can impact the health status of the resident population [23]. Initially, the relevant literature included three types of explanations for geographical variations in health: compositional (focusing on the characteristics of individuals concentrated in particular places), contextual (focusing on the opportunity structures in the local physical and social environment), and collective (focusing on the socio-cultural and historical features of communities including shared norms, traditions, values, and interests) [24]. However, more recent studies criticize this differentiation arguing that separating these interconnected components does not enable the evaluation of the complexity of the dynamics that affect a territory and the health of its residents [25].

Other authors have focused more on the structural dimension of the processes and politics that cause a disadvantage in the health of specific neighbourhoods (e.g. the impact of housing or labour policies, the distribution of public services, etc.). These studies call for a clear understanding of causes and impacts (the unequal distribution of health across neighbourhoods as the outcome of unjust power structures), by selecting units of analysis that are coherent with the research question and by including in the research framework the relationships between local structures and policies and the processes at the regional, national and international level [26].

The literature also reports on the limits of ecological studies. On the one hand, this type of research does not allow for the consideration of the social interaction among residents, the interrelations between individuals and context, the spatial dynamics among neighbouring areas and the structural dimension of the processes and policies that cause disadvantage at the local level [27, 28]. On the other hand, it does not account for a lifecourse perspective on health and disease, which is particularly relevant when studying chronic conditions [29, 30].

In conclusion, a multiplicity of intertwined neighborhood factors affect multiple health outcomes through a set of interrelated mechanisms, the strength and importance of which may vary across individuals. Evidence as of today shows that the most effective interventions in small areas are those that address multiple aspects at a time, and that are able to generate change at different levels by altering the functioning of the systems that create spatial inequities (for instance, measures that tackle simultaneously housing policies, public transportation, accessibility of public spaces and services; policies that promote a population mix in terms of socioeconomic level thus reducing segregation by economic class) [31].

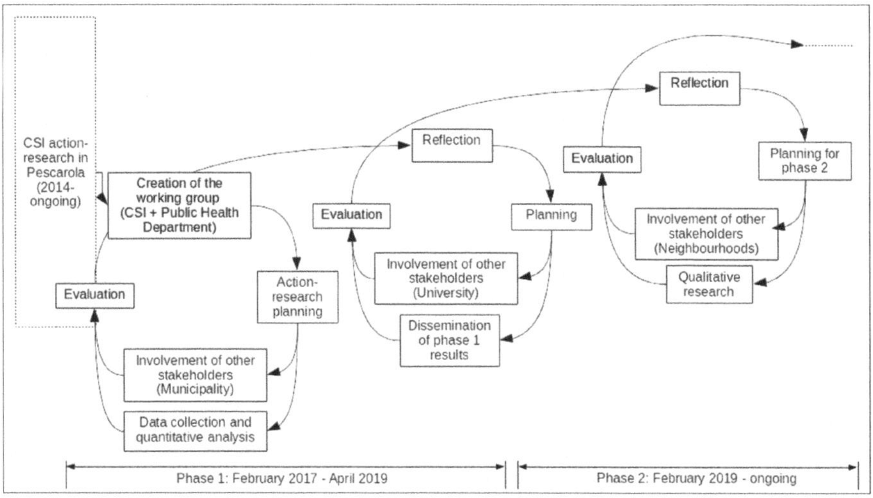

Fig. 1 Action-research cycles and phases of the project

3 Methods

An interdisciplinary, interprofessional and interinstitutional working group was constituted based on the initiative of CSI which coincided with the interest and availability of the Department of Public Health of the Local Health Authority of Bologna (epidemiology unit).

The group met regularly from February 2017 to October 2019 to design and implement a project aiming to document and tackle health inequities in the city of Bologna. The project was structured in two phases: a first one based on a quantitative analysis of health inequalities, and a second one focused on qualitative research in selected areas of the city. Throughout the project, results were presented to and discussed with relevant stakeholders.

An action-research approach was embedded throughout the project, with periodic evaluations along the process to ensure the progress towards the intended results (see Fig. 1). According to this approach, the process is the method, and its intermediate products are described in detail in the results section.

4 Results

4.1 Creation of the Working Group

Following a successful presentation of the Pescarola experience to the Director of the Bologna Health District, in 2017 a working group was formed, including CSI and the

Department of Public Health of the Local Health Authority of Bologna (epidemiology unit). The group was mixed in terms of disciplines (public health, medical anthropology, epidemiology and statistics), institutional belonging (local health authority, university, third sector), experience (senior service managers, junior public sector employees, public health residents, PhD students). On specific occasions, experts in other fields (sociology) and/or representatives of other institutions (Municipality of Bologna) were invited, with a double aim to incorporate different views and expand the ownership of the project.

Thanks to a new budget line introduced by the National Plan for Prevention 2014–18 [32], and implemented by the Regional plan 2015–19 [33], a study was designed with four objectives:

1. Document existing geographical inequalities, in terms of health outcomes and use of healthcare services, in the city of Bologna.
2. In the areas with lower health outcomes, document through a mixed method approach the local determinants involved.
3. Involve local decision and policymakers and residents in discussing policy interventions towards health equity.
4. Evaluate the feasibility and cost-effectiveness of systematically analyzing the data routinely collected by the healthcare services in order to monitor health inequalities over time and evaluate the impact of policies designed to achieve health equity.

4.2 Phase 1: Mapping Health Inequalities

The first phase of the project, which realized objective n. 1, was concluded in April 2019 (a separate paper will be published with the results of this phase) after obtaining ethical approval from the Ethical Committee of the Local Health Authority of Bologna.

While discussing the choice of indicators for the statistical analysis, as well as the unit of analysis, the following issues were carefully considered:

1. data accessibility (including issues of privacy that severely limit the possibility of cross-linking individual data);
2. data availability (routine data collection by healthcare services; existing social and demographic databases for cross-link);
3. evidence of correlation between small area socio-demographic indicators and differential distribution of ill health;
4. size of the unit of analysis (manageable in terms of allowing the qualitative follow up, while considering the statistical significance of the events we wanted to observe);
5. results presentation (mapping as a tool to visualize inequalities throughout the city).

Table 1 List of indicators

Health outcomes	Use of public healthcare services
1. Prevalence of diabetes	6. Access to the emergency department (ED)
2. Cumulative incidence of acute myocardial infarction	7. Access to the ED for non urgent conditions
3. Cumulative incidence of stroke	8. Multiple drug prescription[a]
4. Frailty index[b]	9. Multiple access to outpatient clinics[c]
5. Cumulative incidence of cancer (all types)	10. Admission to hospital
	11. Participation in colorectal cancer screening program
	12. Participation in breast cancer screening program

[a]Individuals taking in one year (2015) three or more different classes of medicines (excluding antibiotics)
[b]Forecasting model that, using a set of social and health variables, attributes to individuals a frailty level, expressed as a probability of death or urgent admission to the hospital in the following year
[c]Individuals that accessed a public or contracted outpatient clinic more than 10 times in a year (2015)

With respect to points n. 1 and 2, a strong preference was given to indicators that are easily accessible and routinely available within health and social services. This in order to minimise associated costs and maximise the possibility of (a) systematically analysing the data in terms of health equity (objective n. 4), and (b) replicating the study in other health districts of the province of Bologna.

Based on these considerations, a set of 12 indicators was chosen (see Table 1) and analysed using an ecological approach (across the 90 statistical areas of the city of Bologna) for the period 2011–15 (an update to 2018 data is ongoing).

Indicators n. 6–10 are interpreted as negative outcomes: people access the ED more frequently, particularly for non urgent conditions, as they may face barriers in accessing primary care services. Similarly, taking multiple medications and accessing several times out- and in-patient services often indicate chronic conditions that are not well managed across the healthcare system. On the other hand, indicators n. 11 and 12 are considered as positive outcomes, as the two screening programs for colorectal and breast cancer are large population interventions offered proactively and for free to the target population.

Results show the presence of significant differences in terms of disease burden and service use between the areas in the North, East and West periphery of the city compared to the centre and South of the city. These differences mirror the urban

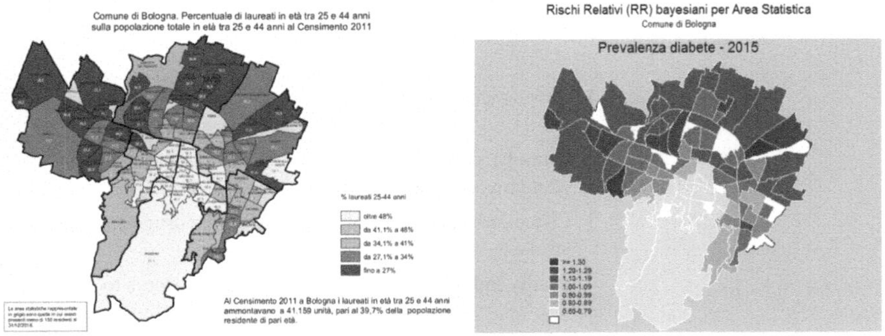

Fig. 2 Left—Percentage of graduates between 25 and 44 years of age over the total population in the same age group in 2011 (*Source* Statistical Office of the Municipality of Bologna); Right—Prevalence of diabetes in 2015 (Bayesian relative risk analysis per statistical area of the city of Bologna)

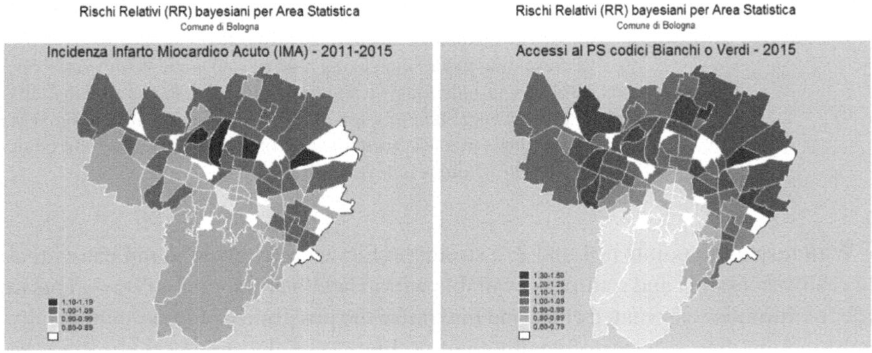

Fig. 3 Left: Cumulative incidence of Acute Myocardial Infarction (IMA) in 2011–2015; Right: Non-urgent admissions to the Emergency Department in 2015 (Bayesian relative risk analysis per statistical area of the city of Bologna)

distribution of wealth/deprivation, measured through different indicators (educational level, income, presence of immigrant population). These findings are exemplified in the two maps below, showing respectively the distribution of the percentage of graduates and the prevalence of diabetes across the statistical areas of the city of Bologna (see Fig. 2).

In particular, the burden of disease was higher in the North, East and West periphery of the city, while the use of public (or contracted) healthcare services shows an opposite gradient: the (richer) areas of the centre and the South appear to consume less healthcare services compared to the Northern, Eastern and Western peripheries (see Fig. 3).[2] Based on the considerations stated above, this can be inter-

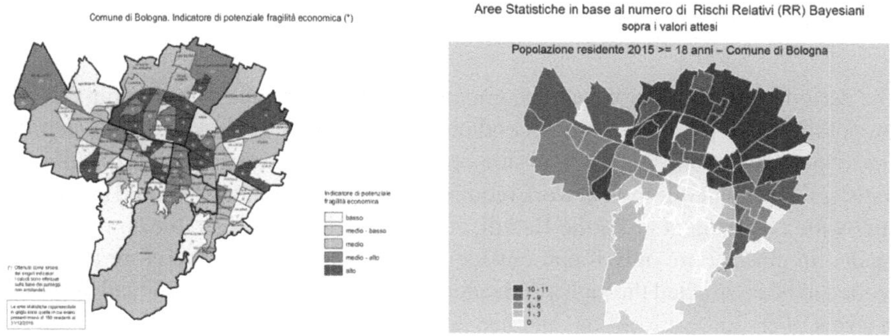

Fig. 4 Left: Indicator of potential economic vulnerability (*Source* Statistical Office of the Municipality of Bologna). Right: Distribution of frequencies of Bayesian relative risks above the city average across the statistical areas of the city of Bologna

preted both in terms of higher burden of disease in the most deprived areas, but also as a lack of appropriate access to primary care services in those areas. In fact, a timely and effective access to primary care would likely reduce the need for multiple access to the ED, multiple drug prescription and frequent accesses to in- and out-patient services.

Results also show a high degree of concentration of the worst health outcomes and healthcare access indicators in some areas of the city, which are also areas where there is a high presence of public housing; these highly unequal areas are clustered in some neighbourhoods of the city (see Fig. 4).

4.3 *Involving Local Decision-Makers*

During 2019, the maps summarising the findings of phase 1 were presented to all relevant local authorities (objective n. 3), including the City Councillor for Health and Welfare, the head manager of the Welfare and Community Wellbeing area of the Municipality, the Director of the city Social Services, the Presidents of the six neighbourhoods of the City of Bologna, the Director General of the Local Health Authority and the Director of the Bologna Health District. They have also been presented in different local and national seminars on health inequities and urban health. According to objectives n. 2 and 3 of the project, the aim of such wide and targeted dissemination was not just to inform the competent authorities and raise awareness on the issue, but also to highlight the need to progress to a second phase of qualitative analysis of the local determinants responsible for the re-production of inequities, in order to inform policies oriented towards health equity.

[2]As our data include only the use of public or contracted healthcare services, there may be a quota of use of private services that we do not trace, and that—if accounted for—would reduce the documented difference in access to healthcare between poorer and richer areas of the city.

4.4 *Progressing Towards Phase 2*

The period of dissemination was accompanied by a high degree of uncertainty about the possibility to progress to the second phase of the project (objective n. 2), mainly due to the unavailability of funds to support the qualitative research. In fact, while the statistical and epidemiological work required for the phase 1 analysis could be carried out by the Department of Public Health, and covered by its budget, the competences needed in phase 2 are only found outside the health system and therefore the work needed to be contracted through a dedicated budget. This required a political decision in terms of resource allocation, and had administrative implications that limited the possibilities that could be pursued (for example, the Local Health Authority could not directly contract CSI as a civil society organisation).

The deadlock was overcome when, in July 2018, the university branch of CSI reopened in the Department of History and Cultures, after a period of inactivity (following the retirement of the former Director). Through an inter-institutional agreement, the possibility to co-finance a research grant emerged as a way to support phase 2. Thanks to the concomitant institution of a Memorandum of Understanding for Health Promotion, Education and Prevention signed by the Municipality of Bologna, the Local Health Authority, the S.Orsola teaching hospital, the University of Bologna and the regional School Office, a bureaucratic path was opened and the research grant established.

As we write this paper, the second phase of the project has been officially launched with a formal meeting involving the Presidents of the six neighbourhoods of the city of Bologna, which will be involved in the identification of the areas for the qualitative research (scheduled to start in January 2020—see Fig. 1).

5 Discussion

Based on a review of the existing documentation on the project, including many accounts of the reflections within the working group and in the research group at CSI, in this section we discuss three aspects that were key for the success of our experience: the choice of a mixed-method approach, the involvement of multiple stakeholders and framing the project as an action-research. We then review the limitations of our work.

5.1 *Methodology, Methodologies*

Since the very beginning, the study has been conceived and developed with a mixed-method approach, as both observations coming from the field (Pescarola) and discussion of statistical theoretical models and hypothesis have contributed to the definition of the research question. However, the balance and relationship among quantitative and qualitative approaches to knowledge generation have often been object of discussion. After the decision was taken to start with a quantitative analysis of health inequalities, the discussion shifted towards the meaning of such analysis, and if and how a statistical approach, based on the power of large numbers, could at each stage of its development interact with the perspective of the local actors and lead towards greater (health) equity.

According to Borghi and Giullari [34], for decades we have witnessed a change in the relationship between knowledge, experience and decision-making in both the public and the private sectors. When dealing with complex issues and social phenomena, decision-makers rely more and more on abstract standardised knowledge, often quantified and reworded by technical experts according to scientific language in the attempt to legitimise its neutrality and objectivity. This has several social implications, including the separation between the targets of knowledge generation (decision-makers, public service operators, citizens) and the issue or problem that needs to be addressed [34]. According to Hibou [35], abstract and standardized knowledge gives rise to indifference, separation and de-politicisation between the people, deprived of the subjective and experiential component of their knowledge, and politics and government. The knowledge that cannot be translated into abstract and standardised formats is delegitimised for different reasons, including the power asymmetries involving those who produce it [35].

In our study, we decided to rely on the power of large numbers for the first phase of analysis, as we could access indicators that were relatively easy to process by the Department of Public Health and covered a sufficient number of cases, therefore granting the possibility of achieving a statistical significance in the areas. However, the study design was informed by the findings from the mixed-method action-research in Pescarola. Moreover, we ensured a close link between the quantitative data collection and analysis and the planning of the second phase of the study, through making some relevant choices:

- Map the territory through an ecological approach, in order to include the entire population and guide the following field intervention. In this respect, a limitation was the impossibility to include in the study those who are not in the population register, such as undocumented migrants, university students, precarious workers.
- Select indicators that could shed light on priority health issues, to be further explored in the second phase with a specific focus on their local determinants (urban characteristics of the area, relationships between residents and primary healthcare services, formal and informal resources and their accessibility, etc.).
- Handle with care the concept of statistical significance when discussing the vulnerability of each area. While from a technical point of view only statistically significant indicators had to be included for the selection of the areas with the worst health outcomes and healthcare access indicators, we made the decision not to strictly follow this criterium as it would have led to the exclusion of areas that—based on different sources—did present a high degree of vulnerability. We therefore decided to include also some indicators that showed a clear disadvantage,

although not statistically significant, based on the rationale that we were unsure that a purely quantitative approach could lead to a correct identification of the priority areas for intervention, and we felt safer to be more inclusive in this first stage.

- Rely on tools and analysis produced by the Municipality, in particular a mapping of social and demographic indicators across the statistical areas of the city of Bologna. The rationale for this was on the one hand to take advantage of an existing and detailed study, but even more so to open a direct communication with different actors within the Municipality using data they were familiar with. This translated into a closer connection between the different actors involved, strategic in view of phase two, but also implied some limitations. In particular, several indicators used by the Municipality do not correspond to those used in the literature on health inequalities, and the unit of analysis based on statistical areas does not have an attached social or urbanistic meaning.

The different disciplinary, theoretical and professional background among components of the research group translated into different views being exchanged in the construction of the project, that sometimes caused delays in the process as they needed to be thoroughly addressed in order to proceed. CSI's role has often been to help the group to keep the focus on the full spectrum of objectives of the project (from knowledge to action). In fact, to the different roles corresponded different practices and attitudes towards data collection and knowledge generation, ranging from those more oriented towards the verification of hypothesis and the generation of new knowledge, to those who saw their role as being more operational and oriented to support the functioning of healthcare services.

Intertwined with this one, another difference emerged between two epistemological positions: one founded on a positivistic view of the researcher as being neutral and detached from the object of the research, and another one that sees the role of the researcher as positioned within the context and inevitably and subjectively linked to it. The latter position informs the action-research approach, grounded on the idea that engaging with the experiences of those involved in a problem is the first step towards enabling them to address it. Following this idea, it is very important that there is a connection between policies and the information base on which they rely [36], and between the experiences that people have of a problem they face and the research process that is part of policy making. In this light, giving voice to the plurality of experience and knowledge within the decision-making process implies to include not only the information that is considered as being more relevant, but also that which has been excluded but concerns directly the beneficiaries of the policy or intervention [37].

Finally, attention was given to the choice of a set of indicators describing access to healthcare services, backed by two considerations. The first one was based on the literature review, which shows that a better use of healthcare services, framed as the best possible use in the interest of the patient, is linked to the socio-economic position [38, 39]. The second one was related to the overall design of the study, and in particular to the expected result in terms of a change in health policies and outcomes. This required the formulation of a specific "theory of change", which is the causal pathway that links the interventions with the outcome [40]. Based on a shared analysis within the group, the Local Health Authority emerged as the actor that could be more easily reached through the action-research and influenced in terms of a change in policies, aimed to achieve greater health equity. In fact, an appropriate use of healthcare services has been an objective of the Local Health Authority for several years, and is included in the Regional Plan for Prevention 2015–2019 [33]. Documenting how the use of healthcare services in the city of Bologna differs across geographical areas and how it is linked to socio-economic conditions appeared in this light to serve a dual purpose. On the one hand, to make a link with the debate on the cost-efficacy of healthcare services, and on the other to support a transformation towards services based on Primary Health Care, an approach that sees in the interaction between individuals, communities and their territory a successful strategy to tackle health inequities [7].

5.2 *Involving Multiple Stakeholders*

Multi-stakeholder approaches have become very common in public health policy-making, less in public health research. However, the early engagement of decision-makers in research is a good practice towards addressing and reducing the know-do gap [41], considered by WHO as "*one of the most important challenges for public health*" [42].

Through our experience, it has been important to work for the progressive engagement of multiple stakeholders (Department of Public Health of the Local Health Authority, University, Municipality of Bologna in both its technical and political offices), while at the same time keeping an explicit analysis of the levels of implication and power involved, and how they came into play in the action-research and towards its goals.

In fact, at the micro level of relations within the working group, at the meso level of institutional relations, and at the macro level of city policies and politics, differences in interests and power shaped the direction of the action-research. Keeping them visible, shared and explicit through the action-research was key in using them instrumentally and with strategic awareness.

Analysis of implications As we have described, the research group was heterogeneous in terms of disciplinary background, profession, role and experience of its components. We will focus here on the difference in professional roles, particularly between medical doctors and statisticians employed by the Local Health Authority (epidemiology unit) and the members of CSI, whose work for the group was not remunerated. In addition, a pivotal role was played by a former manager of the Bologna Health District, retired and participating on a volunteer basis.

While sharing a common concern for the topic of health inequities and an ethical tension towards acting on it, the different professional roles corresponded to different motivations, obligations and interests in undertaking the research. It was important to clarify this level of different implications in order to prevent conflict and make choices that could respond to the different needs and maximise the strengths of the group across its diversity.

For instance, a research on health inequalities was a budget objective for the Director and the staff of the epidemiology unit (thanks to a new budget line introduced by the National Plan for Prevention 2014–18, and implemented by the Regional plan 2015–19). This was an asset because it provided the work needed to produce the statistical analysis. However, the budget objective did not include aspects of knowledge translation and impact on outcomes, which was something introduced by the CSI group.

On the other hand, CSI's participation was not motivated by an economic incentive. Indeed CSI researchers were prepared to do some voluntary work in order to achieve the goal of accompanying local institutions towards a greater awareness and capacity to act on health inequities. The extent of this voluntarism was however conditional upon progress being achieved towards an action-oriented approach, and accompanied by a constant effort to mobilise resources along the process to at least partially support the work.

As mentioned above, a pivotal role among two different interests was played by a retired manager of the Bologna Health District, very respected and still influential within the Local Health Authority but no longer subject to institutional obligations. His participation in the project was formally framed as a volunteer contribution, through an agreement with the epidemiology unit.

It is relevant to observe how a person who had served for decades in decision-making positions within the health system, returned to it in a different role to see his capacity less limited by the logics, structures and constraints of the institution. It is also relevant to see how a significant amount of volunteer work was needed/instrumental in moving from "yet another research" on health inequalities to a more ambitious project that aims at impacting on health policies and outcomes. Such work, exceeding institutional budget and boundaries, was needed in order to move beyond the institutional framing of health inequalities to bring in the political element of the transformations needed to tackle them.

Institutional analysis Moving from a micro to a meso level of analysis, we can observe the differential distribution of power among the institutional actors involved in the action-research, and how this impacted on the development of the project.

Within the working group, the power differential between the Department of Public Health and CSI was initially very high. Before the involvement of the University, CSI as a civil society organisation could only play a rather informal, behind-the-scenes role, yet quite instrumental in advancing the action-research as described above.

Despite several efforts from participants in the working group, including appeals to the Director General of the Local Health Authority, search for opportunities within the institutional budget for research and innovation, and a joint project proposal submitted to a local banking foundation (which was not financed), it was impossible for almost two years to formalise and support the collaboration. Besides the implications in terms of unpaid work, mentioned above, this also represented a weakness in the process, creating a dependency from the institutional dynamics of the Local Health Authority and threatening to interrupt the project (as both the workforce and the expertise for phase 2 of the action-research were not available within the institution itself).

When a second, powerful institutional actor came into play, the Department of History and Cultures of the University of Bologna, the dynamic changed and it was easier to conceive and implement a collaboration. The mutual recognition between public institutions, together with the existence of a Memorandum of Understanding regulating their interactions on health promotion activities, greatly accelerated the process of formalising a collaboration and co-financing a research-grant.

It is important to note that the involvement of the University did not interrupt the continuity of the action-research process as it had been conceived and carried out within the working group. This was made possible by the ongoing engagement of CSI, which ensured a close link between the process and the University engagement.

Analysis of political opportunities Finally, at the macro-level of city policies and politics, the working group had to engage with the Municipality of Bologna. While there had been contacts during phase 1 with both the statistical offices and the managers of the Welfare and Community Wellbeing area of the Municipality, for phase 2 of the action-research the challenge was to interact with the political level. This was needed in order to ensure the level of engagement of local stakeholders required to decide the areas to prioritise for the qualitative research, access the field, share and discuss the emerging results and ensure the link with local policy-making. A challenge in this step is linked to the fact that the city governance is shared between the central government (Mayor, Councillors and Municipal Council) and the six neighbourhoods, which have their local President and Council (that may represent different parties compared to the city political majority).

The presentation of the project raised great interest at the level of city politics, from the Councillor for Health and Welfare downwards. Nevertheless, the path towards the formalisation of such (almost) unconditional endorsement took more than one year, through shifting political winds, complex inter-institutional bureaucracy, excessive workload and insufficient staff within public offices.

While the endorsement of the project by the Municipality is seen as a success, there are risks associated in terms of appropriation of the project and possible deviation from its aims. Appropriation may be positive in terms of ownership, translating into a greater engagement of the institutions both in the research phase and, even more crucially, in implementing changes based on the research findings. On the other hand, there may be a risk if the project is formally adopted without a real commitment to the results it may deliver (which may also be in contrast with the administration's policies).

A deviation from the project's aims may occur when different rationales, the technical and the political, enter into play. For instance, while the decision within the working group was to priorities for phase 2 the areas with the worst health outcomes and healthcare access indicators, the Municipality introduced as a criterium the fact that the qualitative research had to involve all six neighbourhoods. We were faced with two different ideas of equity (social and political), and the power differential oriented the decision towards the condition posed by the Municipality.

While the working group shares a vision of "engaged science" as a way of producing knowledge that may result in social change towards greater (health) equity, the boundary between this and a form of "coopted science", which serves the interest of the existing power, is particularly subtle and slippery. The power differential is crucial in determining the direction of these interactions, and is something to be carefully considered, evaluated and strategised along the process.

5.3 Action-Research as a Navigation Tool

As we mentioned several times across the paper, the whole project was broadly framed around an action-research dynamic, with repeated cycles of action and reflection (see Fig. 1).

Action-research is a field, more than a methodology, founded in the late 1930s by Kurt Lewin, whose thought and practice is summarised by the quote "*no action without research, no research without action*" [43]. Lewin criticized the lack of integration of science and practice and argued for a pragmatic epistemological approach that combined social theory, experimental or quasi-experimental methods, and practice perspectives that could be used for local decision making and contribute to generalizable knowledge [2]. According to Loewenson, participatory action-research (PAR) seeks to understand and improve the world by changing it, i.e. by developing, implementing, and reflecting on actions as part of the research and knowledge generation process [44].

The working group acted as a PAR group in the sense of collectively discussing the problem (how to approach a study on health inequities in a way that may lead to concrete results in terms of health policies and outcomes, towards health equity), designing strategies and actions to address it (two-phase action-research process), producing action and collectively evaluating it in order to assess the progress towards the desired outcomes.

This approach was particularly valuable in terms of tempering the power differentials within the working group, allowing to integrate inputs from all participants and to take advantage of the group diversity for mutual learning and better interpretation of both data and results of actions.

Moreover, it allowed to constantly link the actions and their evaluation with all the objectives of the project. This proved to be very useful while deciding the indicators for phase 1 data collection, keeping in mind that their main goal was not to describe a situation, but to provide analytical tools that could inform action.

Thirdly, the action-research approach was central to devising new strategies to progress where the external conditions changed and/or the assumptions we made at the beginning were not met (for instance, the impossibility for the Local Health Authority to support the work of a civil society organisation and the need/opportunity to seek the engagement of the University).

Finally, by including in the reflection both the knowledge generated through the data collection, and the experience of putting it at work into action, the group was able to consciously evaluate all the potential biases or limitations deriving from the interaction between the technical approach to data and the political path towards their transfer to action. Each time, the pros and cons of according priority to one side or the other were carefully evaluated, and awareness was increased through the choices that were made.

5.4 Limitations

Our experience has some limitations. The action-research design, while allowing for a high degree of flexibility that enables ongoing adjustments to accommodate changes in context, also entails some uncertainty due to the fact that the design remains always open. This exposes the project to possible delays, deviations, and even complete stops. The time needed to care for the process, and the uncertainty concerning its duration, are increasingly difficult to sustain, particularly in the public sector, where resources are scarce following years of cuts and underfinancing. In order to compensate for this, as described the project relied on a considerable amount of unpaid work. While personal and collective motivation are positive resources to rely upon, they are also volatile and their fluctuation may threaten the sustainability of the project.

A second consideration, following from the one above, is that the originality of the experience and its links with the personal commitment of different actors may limit its replication in other contexts. Being aware of this, we have reported throughout the paper several contextual elements in order to provide the background needed to fully understand the choices that have been made. However, we acknowledge that—given the specific set of constraints and opportunities that we faced—similar approaches in other contexts may require different choices. In this sense, the action-research framework is probably the most exportable aspect of our experience, and the progress towards phase two the most encouraging result. However, the need remains for a strong mandate, coming either from the institutions or from the community, for such an experience to unfold.

In this respect, a relative absence of the community is the final limitation that we want to highlight. While the third objective of the project is to "*involve local decision and policymakers and residents in discussing policy interventions towards health equity*", only the former have been engaged so far. Active involvement of residents is however planned during phase two.

6 Conclusion

In the past two and a half years, we have carried out an action-research project that—starting from an epidemiological mapping of health inequalities across the city of Bologna—has now led to a second phase of qualitative analysis in selected areas, in tight connection with the local policy and decision-making processes.

In order to achieve this result, we have mainly relied on resources that are routinely available within public services, particularly in terms of data and statistical capacity. We have also had the opportunity to draw on unconventional resources, such as the availability and motivation of volunteer contributors, in different roles and positions.

We believe that our experience demonstrates the added value that working across disciplines, roles and institutions may bring to the complex field of health inequities, when approached with the aim of moving from knowledge to action. We also believe that the choice to rely on data that are routinely available may open an interesting route for the replication of our experience in other contexts, and possibly for its use to monitor the impact of interventions aimed at reducing health inequities.

Finally, we would like to argue that action-research is an approach with the potential to reduce the know-do gap in public health. However, applying it in a multi-stakeholder setting requires some pragmatism in order to align different values, cultures and attitudes, particularly the independence of researchers (which may lead to self-referentiality), the focus on everyday operations of public service professionals, and the quest for consensus of policymakers.

Acknowledgements We wish to acknowledge the contribution of Gabriele Cavazza and Chiara Di Girolamo, who carefully reviewed the paper and gave us very relevant indications for its improvement. We would also like to acknowledge the contribution of the whole working group who participated in the action-research project, and particularly Paolo Pandolfi, Vincenza Perlangeli, Paolo Marzaroli, Muriel Musti, Lorenzo Pizzi, Martina Riccio and Ilaria Camplone. It is thanks to our collective work that we have been able to write this paper.

References

1. Krieger N (2011) Epidemiology and the people's health: theory and context. Oxford University Press, Oxford
2. Estabrooks PA, Brownson RC, Pronk NP (2018) Dissemination and implementation science for public health professionals: an overview and call to action. Preventing Chronic Diseases 15
3. Cacciatore F, Maralla R, Riccio M (2020) Inhabiting an "un-common" space: health promotion in the area of Pescarola, Bologna. In: Battisti A, Marceca M, Iorio S (eds) Urban health. Participatory action-research models contrasting socioeconomic inequalities in urban context. Springer, Heidelberg (in press)
4. Centro di Salute Internazionale e Interculturale (CSI)—Associazione di Promozione Sociale (2017) La comunità che cura: una ricerca-azione per promuovere salute e partecipazione nella zona di Pescarola. Report annuale Fondazione del Monte. Available at: http://csiaps.org/wpcsi/wp-content/uploads/2015/07/Una-comunit%C3%A0-che-cura.pdf. Last accessed 18 Nov 2019

5. Gentilini V (2018) L'equità nel diritto alla salute: il contrasto alle disuguaglianze nella città di Bologna. Un approccio interdisciplinare. Scuola di Specializzazione in Igiene e Medicina Preventiva, Alma Mater Studiorum-Università di Bologna
6. Heath I (2010) Crocodile tears for health inequality. BMJ 340:c2970–c2970
7. World Health Organisation (2008) WHO. Closing the gap in a generation: health equity through action on the social determinants of health. WHO, Geneva
8. Barr B, Higgerson J, Whitehead M (2017) Investigating the impact of the English health inequalities strategy: time trend analysis. BMJ 358:j3310
9. da Rocha PR, David HMSL (2015) Determination or determinants? A debate based on the theory on the social production of health. Revista da Escola de Enfermagem da USP 49(1):129–135
10. Acheson D (1998) Independent inquiry into inequalities in health: report. HM Stationery Office, London
11. Marmot MG, McDowall ME (1986) Mortality decline and widening social inequalities. Lancet 2:274–276
12. Marmot MG, Wilkinson R (eds) (2005) Social determinants of health. Oxford University Press, Oxford
13. Osservatorio italiano sulla salute globale (OISG) (2006) A caro prezzo: le diseguaglianze nella salute: 2° rapporto dell'Osservatorio italiano sulla salute globale. Edizioni ETS, Pisa
14. Wilkinson RG (1996) Unhealthy societies: the afflictions of inequality. Routledge, New York
15. Black Sir D (1982) Inequalities in health: the Black report
16. Whitehead M (1987) The Health divide: inequalities in health in the 1980's. A review commissioned and published by the Health Education Council, London
17. Costa G, Faggiano F (eds) (1994) L'equità nella salute in Italia: rapporto sulle diseguaglianze sociali in sanità. Franco Angeli, Milano
18. Di Girolamo C et al (2019) Progress in reducing inequalities in cardiovascular disease mortality in Europe. Heart. https://doi.org/10.1136/heartjnl-2019-315129
19. Mackenbach JP et al (2018) Trends in health inequalities in 27 European countries. PNAS 115:6440–6445
20. Costa G et al (2016) 40 anni di salute a Torino. Spunti per leggere i bisogni e i risultati delle politiche. Inferenze, Milano
21. Petrelli A et al (2019) Atlante italiano delle disuguaglianze di mortalità per livello di istruzione [Italian Atlas of mortality inequalities by education level]. Epidemiol Prevenzione 43(1):15–16
22. Pickett KE, Pearl M (2001) Multilevel analyses of neighbourhood socioeconomic context and health outcomes: a critical review. J Epidemiol Community Health 55(2):111–122
23. Marinacci C et al (2004) The role of individual and contextual socioeconomic circumstances on mortality: analysis of time variations in a city of north west Italy. J Epidemiol Community Health 58(3):199–207
24. Macintyre S (1997) What are spatial effects and how can we measure them? In: Dale A (ed) Exploiting national survey data: the role of locality and spatial effects. Faculty of Economic and Social Studies, University of Manchester, Manchester, pp 1–17
25. Forrest R, Kearns A (1999) Joined-up places?: social cohesion and neighbourhood regeneration. YPS for the Joseph Rowntree Foundation
26. Riley AR (2017) Neighborhood disadvantage, residential segregation, and beyond—lessons for studying structural racism and health. J Racial Ethnic Health Disparities 5(2):357–365
27. Bernard P et al (2007) Health inequalities and place: a theoretical conception of neighbourhood. Soc Sci Med 65(9):1839–1852
28. Macintyre S, Ellaway A, Cummins S (2002) Place effects on health: how can we conceptualise, operationalise and measure them? Soc Sci Med 55(1):125–139
29. Hayward MD et al (2000) The significance of socioeconomic status in explaining the racial gap in chronic health conditions. American Sociological Review, pp 910–930
30. Kivimäki M et al (2018) Neighbourhood socioeconomic disadvantage, risk factors, and diabetes from childhood to middle age in the Young Finns Study: a cohort study. The Lancet Public Health 3(8):365–373

31. Diez Roux AV (2016) Neighborhoods and health: what do we know? What should we do? Am J Public Health 106(3):430
32. Ministero della Salute (2014) Piano Nazionale di Prevenzione 2014–2018. Available at: http://www.salute.gov.it/imgs/C_17_pubblicazioni_2285_allegato.pdf. Last accessed 18 Nov 2019
33. Regione Emilia Romagna (2015) Costruire Salute, Piano della Prevenzione della Regione Emilia Romagna 2015–2019. Available at: https://salute.regione.emilia-romagna.it/prp/piano-regionale. Last accessed 18 Nov 18
34. Borghi V, Giullari B (2015) Trasformazioni delle basi informative e immaginazione sociologica. Rassegna Italiana di Sociologia 56(3–4):379–404
35. Hibou B (2012) La bureaucratisation du monde à l'ère néolibérale. La découverte, Paris
36. Sen A (1990) Justice: means versus freedom. Philos Public Aff 19(2):111–121
37. Sen A (1999) Development as freedom. Oxford University Press, Oxford, p 56
38. Löfqvist T et al (2014) Inequalities in avoidable hospitalisation by area income and the role of individual characteristics: a population-based register study in Stockholm County, Sweden. BMJ Qual Saf 23(3):206–214
39. Van Doorslaer E, Masseria C, Koolman X (2006) Inequalities in access to medical care by income in developed countries. Cmaj 174(2):177–183
40. Clark H, Taplin D (2012) Theory of change basics: a primer on theory of change. Actknowledge, New York
41. Grimshaw JM, Eccles MP, Lavis JN, Hill SJ, Squires JE (2012) Knowledge translation of research findings. Implement Sci 7:50
42. World Health Organisation (2005) WHO. Bridging the "Know–Do" Gap. Meeting on Knowledge Translation in Global Health. WHO, Geneva. Available at: https://www.measureevaluation.org/resources/training/capacity-building-resources/high-impact-research-training-curricula/bridging-the-know-do-gap.pdf. Last accessed 18 Nov 2019
43. Adelman C (1993) Kurt Lewin and the origins of action research. Educ Act Res 1(1):7–24
44. Loewenson R et al (2014) Participatory action research in health systems: a methods reader. TARSC, AHPSR, WHO, IDRC Canada, Equinet

The Ascoli Piceno Case: The CCUHRE Project

Rosalba D'Onofrio and Elio Trusiani

Abstract Regenerating the existing city and placing health at the centre of policies, plans, and projects represents an effective response to contrast the effects of climate change that impact cities and the health of inhabitants. Convinced of this need/opportunity are the World Health Organization (WHO), eminent international researchers, and public administration representatives in many European cities. Urban planning is called to play a key role in adapting cities to climate change and at the same time to improve citizens' health and quality of life. To do this, it is necessary to review the tools for gathering knowledge and assessment, involve local communities, and welcome the support of new IoT (Internet of Things) technologies finally centred on people. CCHURE aims to define an interdisciplinary method to evaluate the effects of climate change on health and direct policies and projects for adaptation/mitigation through health-based solutions and with the support of IoT technologies and mobile crowdsensing techniques. The research project aims to reach these objectives through the contribution of many scientific disciplines, interaction with the local municipality, local health agencies, and citizen involvement.

Keywords Urban health · Incremental and adaptive urban planning · Climate change · Community planning · Community sensing

Premise

This essay on the Monticelli Quarter in Ascoli Piceno first requires some historical and cultural notes referring to its background and the state of the art in the relevant literature, because it is precisely these two points that have provided the motivation for the research and the input for experimentation. The link with the town planning of the Modernist Movement, current design experiences, technological innovations to support healthy cities, and the need to renew knowledge-building urban-planning tools represent part of the research itself and constantly provide material for updating and repositioning the method in the experimental phase. In this sense, the approach

R. D'Onofrio (✉) · E. Trusiani
School of Architecture and Design, University of Camerino, Ascoli Piceno, Italy
e-mail: rosalba.donofrio@unicam.it

E. Trusiani
e-mail: elio.trusiani@unicam.it

A. Battisti et al. (eds.), *Urban Health*, Green Energy and Technology,
https://doi.org/10.1007/978-3-030-49446-9_9

adopted serves as a path of reference, one that is flexible to allow for integrations, adjustments, and continuous remodelling according to a health-based approach, as addressed below; it falls within the field of incremental, adaptive planning. For these reasons, the brief treatment in Sects. 1 and 2 constitutes an 'active' part of the research itself and, as the research progresses, a primary source for fine-tuning the methodological and technical/design aspects for the Monticelli Quarter, from the Climate and Health Profile to Climate and Health Actions, from the Climate Health Lab to the IoT (Internet of Things), from governance to design checklists.

1 Urban Planning and Health. Work in Progress

Rosalba D'Onofrio, Ilaria Odoguardi and Elio Trusiani

Abstract The acceleration of urban drift of the world's population, ageing in western countries, the increasingly unequal distribution of riches, and the impacts of climate change all lead to the need to recover and update the tie between urban planning and health that was interrupted over the course of the twentieth century. Urban planning is a key component in defining a model of a healthy, equitable city, as many scientific studies have demonstrated in recent decades. However, it is not always easy to glimpse the positive results of this link in the policies and plans promoted by cities. Traditional approaches persist wherein health is addressed a simplistic way according to a linear cause-and-effect procedure that tends to isolate individual variables, simplifying the complexity of the urban system and its effects on health. The keystone may be more adaptive and co-evolutionary urban planning that refers to a flexible regulatory framework, uses bottom-up skills that learn from errors, encourages residents' self-organization, and educates the different players in cooperation. A dual level of investigation and design may be hypothesized: a regulatory framework inspired by a top-down approach and practical adaptive and associative solutions corresponding to daily practice of a society and environment that is undergoing perennial transformation. In Europe, the project in Barcelona, 'Urban Environment and Health', moves in this direction.

Keywords Urban health · Incremental and adaptive urban planning · Climate change · Community planning · Urban regeneration

R. D'Onofrio · I. Odoguardi (✉) · E. Trusiani
School of Architecture and Design, University of Camerino, Ascoli Piceno, Italy
e-mail: ilaria.odoguardi@unicam.it

1.1 A Relationship from Afar

The connections between 'town planning' and health date to the origins of the discipline of urban planning in the nineteenth century. The idea of dividing industrial cities into zones to separate non-hygienic uses and pollution from places in which people lived was an important public-health initiative that revealed a clear connection between community health, the environment, and city organization.

Key factors such as hygiene, atmospheric pollution, and overcrowding became the foundation for movements and models of ideal cities such as the 'garden city' theorized by Ebenezer Howard in 1902 in *Garden Cities of Tomorrow.* These self-sufficient cities contained interconnected residential nuclei surrounded by green areas that were to services, shops, production zones, and administrative areas.

Throughout the twentieth century, the initial health-city connection vanished and urban planning began to concentrate on themes regarding 'efficient and functional cities', causing a disciplinary reflection on the health-city relationship to disappear for a long time [1].

For some years now, the situation has changed. The acceleration of urbanization processes (more than 85% of the world's population will live in urban areas by the end of the twenty-first century), the ageing population in western countries, the increasing imbalance in wealth distribution (not only in developing countries), and the impacts of climate change are waiting for answers that also consider the health and well-being of people, as evidenced by the increase in chronic disease, obesity, and stress and the incidence of social pathologies such as isolation and a feeling of exclusion [2]. The signs of renewed interest in the link between urban planning and health can be seen in many fields, beginning with research.

As sustained by the European Academies Science Advisory Council (EASAC), evidence abounds regarding the negative and direct impacts of climate change on health [3], starting with atmospheric pollution and moving through high temperatures to the combined effects of high temperatures and air pollution. Atmospheric pollution is tied to illnesses such as asthma, pulmonary development deficit, the development of allergies in children, etc. The urban heat island effect has been tied to death and discomfort of the most vulnerable populations (children and elderly people). The combined effects of pollution and the heat island have been tied to an increased risk of high blood pressure, coronary disease, etc. There are also indirect relationships to consider, such as the reduction in cognitive and physical performance due to high temperatures; cardiovascular events, injuries, etc., due to flooding; increases in infectious disease; water and food-borne diseases, etc.

Other research has studied the associations between the presence of greenery in living environments, the improvement of mental health, and the reduction of mortality [4]; the promotion of physical activity in a mixed urban environment that is easily pedestrian-accessible and the reduced risk of obesity and diabetes [5, 6].

Many researchers also recognize the potential of urban planning to mitigate or moderate the growing risks for health of the urban heat island effect [7], as well as notably reducing health costs [8].

In parallel with these lines of research, there is growing interest in the link between equity, health, and the city. The environmental risks in urban areas affect low-income people above all, who are more exposed to noise and pollution. Even for the richest cities, differences in health can be seen within a single city where there are many differences in terms of life expectancy and rates of disease attributable to the urban environment [9–11].

All this research, and even more, highlights the need for disciplines to come together. Health workers themselves recognize that public health is largely determined beyond the health sector; that socioeconomic factors, education, and culture, the city's physical characteristics, environmental factors, etc., have a greater impact on health and quality of life than the health sector itself and that the role that urban planning can play in improving health is very important [12, 13].

The recognition of health as a process involving different subjects and aspects and the role of urban planning and design lies at the basis of the 'requirements of engagement' set out by the WHO European Healthy Cities Network (WHO/EHCN). This global network of cities is dedicated primarily to promoting health in urban environments.

Since its founding in 1986, the European Healthy Cities Network (currently encompassing more than 1400 cities) has evolved through a series of work programmes called *phases*. In Phase VI (2014–2018), participating cities applied the themes of the 'Healthy 2020'[1] strategy to the local community based on four primary actions: investing in health throughout one's lifetime (life-course approach) and empowering people; tackling major public health challenges; strengthening people-centred health systems and public health capacity; and creating resilient communities and supportive environments [14]. Some recurring themes include community resilience, healthy environments, urban planning and design according to healthy criteria, transport that favours healthy lifestyles, climate change, interventions on housing, and urban regeneration.

All these aspects are central to urban planning, which is called to respond to the new needs of urban communities, which are increasingly aware that health and well-being are inextricably tied to the state of the living environment.

1.2 The Need/Opportunity for Incremental and Adaptive Urban Planning

Urban planning is a key component in defining a model of the equitable city as it has a non-secondary influence in promoting a healthy lifestyle. While scientific evidence on the relationship between health and the living environment is becoming

[1] Health 2020 is a strategic political framework for the twenty-first century that explicitly recognizes the influence of the urban environment on health and the role of healthy cities and national networks for carrying forward the objectives and themes of this European strategy. Health 2020 recognizes the emblematic role of local governments' leadership in developing health.

increasingly important and convergent, it is not always easy to connect this evidence to policies promoted by the cities, and there have been numerous related failures.

Jason Corburn, in his 2009 book *Toward the Healthy City: People, Places, and the Politics of Urban Planning*, twenty years after the founding of the European Healthy Cities Network, highlighted some limits. These include the inability, despite the declared objectives, to influence urban plans for cities, to counteract the iniquities present and perpetuated in the plans, the lack of a clear theoretical approach, and consistent strategies to guide the changes in the name of citizen well-being and health [15]. With the passing years and growing experience in the field, the critical aspects have partially been overcome, but there is still a long way to go. A report compiled a few years ago [16] showed that in proceeding through the first five phases of the programme's implementation (we are currently in Phase VII), we have achieved some appreciable results. In particular, there has been a progressive shift from small-scale projects limited in time and dedicated mainly to promoting healthy lifestyles, to more extended policies and programmes that regard questions of urban sustainability, urban planning, and equity. Cities are increasingly less interested in short-term, demonstrative interventions and more interested in long-term structural policies. They have begun to interrelate the different interventions, questioning the results obtained from the different policies implemented in relation to the social determinants of health, governance, and equity.

There is still a lot to do. In particular, the report highlighted the persistence of traditional approaches that address the theme of health is a simplistic way according to a linear cause-and-effect procedure that tends to isolate individual variables in a reductionist manner [17]. This approach has unsatisfactory consequences for urban planning.

For example, in an attempt to provide an overview of the evidential strength of the impacts of the built and natural environment on health, the guide entitled 'Spatial planning for health: An evidence resource for planning and designing healthier places' by Public Health England [18] is based on an umbrella method that centres on 5 topics: neighbourhood design, housing, healthier food environment, natural and sustainable environment, transport. It associates planning principles, the health impact, and health-related outcomes to inform policies and design actions.

While of great use in that it clarifies and does not discount some connections between the physical structure of the city and implications for health based on the most recent scientific studies, this work cautions against considering that successful practices in one context can always be transferred to another context, reiterating that the subjective and individual nature of the built and natural environment make it difficult to develop evidence-based approaches that can be universally applied.

It is therefore necessary, in so many words, to flee from the tendency to address the theme of health in a simplistic, static manner following a linear cause-and-effect procedure that tends to isolate individual variables, inevitably simplifying the complexity [13, 17].

This is why the recent renewed proposal for the 'garden city' model, transformed into a 'healthy city'[2] model may be cause for concern. This is due not only to a series of motives tied to the ineffectiveness or even acceleration that these models may entail in terms of health inequalities, but also to the consideration that no model can represent the complex network of dynamic processes through which the various health determinants make their effects felt [19, 20]. Assuming a degree of control in urban planning to create urban environments that promote health and well-being is therefore rather unrealistic.

On the other hand, some authors support an approach that recognizes the complexity of health and cities [20–22], challenging the idea of stability, linearity, and regularity that guides evidence-based policies and emphasizing the limits of the capacity to foresee, plan, and control the behaviour of social systems. These authors express the need to change the approach for more adaptive, co-evolutionary planning [23].

Corburn invites us to promote evolution towards a healthy and equitable urban-planning framework, an evolution from excessive dependence on scientific rationality to the co-production of knowledge and new measurement and monitoring networks; from physical determinism to a relational vision of places, whose meanings and interactions are viewed as crucial in understanding how the urban environment models its human well-being. There are those who suggest learning a little at a time from experiences in the field (learn by doing), proposing small projects supported by local contextual information, selecting those that are shown to be effective, learning from errors, encouraging city residents' self-organization, constantly modifying the approach, and adapting to an urban and social system that is continuously changing [13].

Both approaches lead to a very different vision of the traditional role of urban planning. The planning process cannot be seen as a sequential process or well-structured political cycle, but rather as a series of events pursued over time, in which the public decision-maker is one participant.

In a 2017 article in *Eco Web Town,* 'Urbanistica del progetto urbano: ambiguità e ipocrisie' [Planning the urban project: ambiguities and hypocrisies], Pier Carlo Palermo wrote of the scenarios that are projected on the horizon for the discipline of urban-planning, which he summarizes with three slogans: 'continuing as we are', 'longing for orthodoxy', and 'taking risks' [24]. He suggests making a possible analogy with three scenarios of 'health-based' urban planning. According to the author, the first scenario regards the acceptance of the constituent interests; in the case of the health/city relationship, this may mean continuing with a silo approach and small cosmetic interventions. The second scenario, 'longing for orthodoxy', means accepting a nostalgic reliance on the models of the past, identifying a model with strong public control that is still based on the 'traditional method of planning', i.e.

[2]The first step in the 'Healthy New Towns' programme launched by the National Health Service (NHS) in 2015 was to identify ten representative sites throughout England to explore in what way the development of new cities/quarters may create communities that are healthier and better connected to integrated, high-quality services. The Healthy New Towns guidance leaflet, which discusses ten principles to creating healthy towns, was recently produced and distributed.

on rigid, minute systems of rules that are always applicable. This model is probably similar to Health Impact Assessments (HIA) and revival models of the garden city. The third scenario, 'taking risks', means renouncing presumed certainties to run the risk of a practice that is simpler from the organizational and management perspective but yet more politically responsible (because it is consciously discretional with respect to certain families of decisions). The practice is also more design-based, not only with respect to regulations or visions, but is capable of directly contributing to the quality of the effective transformations. This latter scenario may imply a double level of investigation and project for 'health based' urban planning: a regulatory framework inspired by a top-down approach regarding rules and guidelines that can provide general responses to conflicts and social/environmental impacts on health; and practical adaptive and associative practices corresponding to the daily practice of society and a dynamic environment [25].

The keystone may be a regulatory framework that develops flexible application through space and time based on supplementary bottom-up contextual information. According to the location and social context (variable), some general rules could be interpreted more or less rigorously based on commitment and bottom-up competence to implement better spatial solutions.

This third scenario is the most convincing, as demonstrated by some current experimentation, especially in North America, that relies on the very close involvement of civil society, which is empowered with respect to living spaces in the city and becomes a promoter of planning initiatives.

In these contexts, experimentation in the field is very often assisted by guidelines and tools that are tasked with providing indications about designs, not ironclad rules, to technical offices and designers. In these experiences, it is the context that guides the interventions, avoiding simplistic, ineffective generalizations. The approach tested in the United States and Canada in particular, constitutes an interesting comparison for European cities to avoid running into easy generalizations, especially where, for example, too much reliance is placed on HIAs as a tool to validate plans and projects and not, instead, as a tool to support decision-makers. Great importance is attributed to training technicians, politicians, and the local community to guarantee the creation of a more equitable city.

Acting in this way, the traditional top-down planning approach would be adapted to specific situations and changing circumstances and open to community commitment and the knowledge of non-experts. Proactive bottom-up actions to create a healthier environment would also be facilitated. The local community would be able to identify the conflicts of environmental health, analyse them, organize debates and consultations and even propose solutions. It would be able to exert pressure on the city government to resolve the problem and would subsequently be able to collaborate constructively to find a solution. In this way, each community would be able to follow its own path towards a healthier environment [20].

The Experience of Barcelona

In Europe, the project for the city of Barcelona, 'Urban Environment and Health', is one of the most important, falling directly in line with the principles/needs expressed in the previous section. Launched in 2010 by the Provincial Council, this project aims to create urban environments that encourage people to live healthily, and reduce health disparities; it falls under the framework of the Table for Urban Improvement (or TxMU, its Catalan acronym). The TxMU [26] is an instrument of coordination and transverse work to support municipalities promoted by the Department of Planning and Sustainability of the Barcelona Provincial Council. It facilitates the formulation of comprehensive intervention projects in neighbourhoods and urban areas that require special attention due to the presence of various problems (demographic, urban, socioeconomic, etc.) that generate—or can generate—a spiral effect regarding segregation and social exclusion if action is not taken.

The 'Urban Environment and Health' project has developed two initial lines of action to improve and increase awareness of those working in health and the city. The first relates to training courses on 'healthy urban environments' to address local technicians from different disciplines and areas of work dealing with the design, management and maintenance of a healthy urban environment for everyone. The second is the 'Urban Environment and Health Guide'. This is an online product that aims to create urban environments where people are encouraged to live healthily. It also envisages the environmental minimization of factors that can pose a risk for the health of people.

In order to guarantee an approach that integrates the policies, the guide also sets out some specific objectives:

1. Fostering cooperation among various Barcelona Provincial Council departments by pooling work and knowledge
2. Enhancing assistance to municipal councils in carrying out comprehensive intervention projects in neighbourhoods which are the focus of significant urban, social, economic, and environmental problems
3. Enriching the content of comprehensive intervention projects by coordinating, cooperating, and pooling various sectoral policies
4. Promoting cross-disciplinary work and intra-administrative cooperation in municipal councils.

The guide[3] is structured into five areas of action: information and participation, urban planning, public space, amenities and housing. Through a total of 75 different files it explains how to design, maintain and use those public areas to promote health and prevent them from becoming a risk for health.

Specifically, in order to reach the health objectives in every step of planning and design in the urban environment, the guidelines relate the characteristics of the physical environment in which people live with some indicators of health. It refers to experiences in which the recommendations proposed by the guide or similar characteristics were applied and it provides technical documentation for support through a search engine.

Among the initiatives developed by the city in line with this integrated approach (TxMU) and with attention for the themes of health, the 'Planes de Barrios' stand

[3]https://www.diba.cat/en/web/entorn-urba-i-salut/Planificacio-urbana.

out. This municipal initiative launches social, economic and urban actions to improve the neighbourhoods that need it most. These plans establish a new way of working between the public administration and the quarters, which is based on creativity and effectiveness of neighbourhood action supported by the capacity and resources of the municipal council, which relies on the support of the Urban Environment and Health Guide.

The established actions also include those aimed at reactivating the local economy through projects for social and integral economics for training and work insertion; activities aimed at supporting social rights with projects for community participation and reinforcement; and activities aimed at improving health through prevention projects, favouring physical activity and improving lifestyles, creating strategies to favour accessibility to neighbourhood resources. The 'Planes de Barrios' involve a total of 16 districts divided into three areas—Besòs, Montaña-Colinas, and Litoral—and is designed especially as a tool to combat the increase of social inequality in the city and to address the deficiencies and problems of each territory in a global, transverse way through shared strategies and local cooperation.

2 Renewal of Cognitive and Assessment Tools for the Urban Project. Construction of a Method Attentive to the Themes of Health

Rosalba D'Onofrio and Elio Trusiani

Abstract The researchers that study the impact of the built environment on health find themselves proposing solutions to a complex social problem that requires its different dimensions to be understood and which often requires multiple methods (quantitative and qualitative). A strategy for integration using mixed methods may contribute to reinforcing the capacity of urban planning to acquire new knowledge about the multi-dimensional nature of the relationship between the built environment and health, allowing for better city planning and design. In Europe and around the world, some interesting experiences are beginning to develop in this direction. These projects overcome the quantitative analysis long used by the discipline and do not simply propose renewed unconditioned trust in digital technologies of the smart city, aiming to combine the advanced technology of big data and sensors with a bottom-up approach that directly involves citizens in interpreting and assessing their living environments, and empowering them at the same time. Among these experiences, the 'Bristol Approach', which deals with balancing bottom-up and top-down approaches in regenerating the city of Bristol, gives citizens the responsibility of selecting problems and finding solutions. The 'Quantified Community' in New York, a network of urban neighbourhoods aims to collect, measure, and analyse data about the physical

R. D'Onofrio · E. Trusiani
School of Architecture and Design, University of Camerino, Ascoli Piceno, Italy

and environmental conditions and human behaviour to better understand how the built environment influences individual and social well-being.

Keywords Mixed knowledge and town planning · Urban health · Community planning · Digital technologies · Community sensing

2.1 *The Healthy Cities Approach: The Role of Knowledge*

Gabriele Pasqui, in *Urbanistica oggi. Piccolo lessico critico* [Urban planning today. A small critical lexicon], writes of the need for urban planning to place renewed attention on the quality of living spaces and to recover the original meaning of the discipline as design for the quality of and well-being in the urban environment [27].

This invitation refers to the need to update knowledge and reinforce the tools for interpreting and assessing the contemporary city and environmental emergencies, carefully using and not just tolerating the information that comes from traditional and non-traditional sectors, such as digital technologies, which the discipline may use today. This is the context of innovation in which urban planning favourable to health acts. In recovering the original meaning of the discipline as a project of quality and well-being, it is open to the comparison of expert, communicative knowledge, experiential and local knowledge, and mixed knowledge.

Communicative knowledge

Today, in terms of both health and economics, we are paying for the effects of a lack of dialogue and scarce integration between policies that show varying degrees of interest in health and well-being in urban areas and betray an estrangement between the different scientific disciplines that inspire these policies. These disciplines may come together only in the name of reciprocal interest, to be verified in practice and not just in theory.

But not only expert knowledge is needed. In *Toward the Healthy City*, Jason Corburn pauses on the importance of local and experiential knowledge, defined as 'intelligence about the context' that the community possesses due to its daily affective contact with the places. At times this intelligence may disagree with the knowledge/needs of administrators and the community of experts. This interaction/clash should give rise to a 'co-production of knowledge' that ensures that technical problems are not disconnected from the social context and that a plurality of participants in the process is also actively committed and contributes to making legitimate, shared decisions that empower everyone regarding the issue of health. According to Coburn, using expert and community knowledge would increase the possibility of finding effective solutions and improve citizens' trust in and the credibility of public institutions.

By adopting an approach that is open to interaction and community expertise, it is also possible to avoid the mistake of building a deterministically defined framework in the physical design of the city. Such a framework would risk dealing with abstract solutions, if these solutions, as the fruit of 'technical expertise' alone, are not related to the history of the places and the community.

The 'vision of places', on the contrary, leads to awareness of how cities are complex systems that cannot be improved with isolated, permanent solutions, but for which multiple adaptive, open solutions would instead be advanced, to be implemented and/or modified by holders of different skills. Corburn defines this method of intervention as '...un unfinished symphony, an extended piece of music with more than one movement, played by groups with different expertise, but all aiming to harmoniously construct a sound that is greater than the sum of its parts'.

The 'democratization' of urban knowledge about 'warm' themes such as health and well-being forces not only a revision of urban planners' traditional cognitive models, forcing them to modify protocols with which knowledge about the plan is built. It also forces them to forge new tools for the plan's construction, giving rise to innovation represented by community planning practices or even more innovative forms, all to be tested, which result from open-source urbanism [28].

Mixed knowledge

Researchers who study the impact of the built environment on health find themselves proposing solutions to a complex social problem that needs to be understood in its different dimensions and which very often requires multiple methods of knowledge (quantitative and qualitative) [29].

While qualitative methods are considered more appropriate for studying sensitive, unexplored questions [30], at times the intuitions gathered from these data inform the selection of quantitative data [31], which notoriously represent the 'structural' characteristics of social life and the 'environmental' characteristics of the place. A strategy of integration using mixed methods to build a healthy city may contribute to reinforcing the capacity of urban planning to acquire new knowledge about the multidimensional nature of the relationship between the built environment and health. In turn, this would allow the determinants of health to be identified and the social and cultural factors that may influence the population's acceptance of a given project to be understood.

The quantitative analysis long used by the urban-planning discipline and the ascent of scientific and technical solutions to planning problems have led to the acceptance of a global rational model of the decision-making process at the expense of political and contextual realities. The most important expression of this model is represented by 'smart cities', an idea full of unkept promises that has often generated confusion and distrust about the potential applications of technology in cities.

Indeed, the smart city model tends to concentrate on connecting physical infrastructures with information technology and the omnipresent Internet of Things [32, 33], again placing all hope in the efficiency of digital solutions to make the city efficient, without an adequate analysis of the local context or the social, political, and cultural realities of the place. In recent years, however, this has been revisited.

Francesca Bria and Evgeny Morozov in their book *Ripensare la Smart City* [Rethinking the Smart City], speak of 'citizens' technological sovereignty', that is, citizens' capacity to participate and have a say in how the technological infrastructures that surround them operate and what goals to pursue, through the use of free, open software and open digital architectures [34]. With this new philosophy, the City of Barcelona, which is addressed in the book, has for some time adopted a system of participatory democracy through the *Dedicim* platform. Citizens are informed about the proposals and projects that are implemented and the requests and needs that ought to be heard, in constant interaction with the local government and a mutual exchange of ideas and possible solutions.

The need to involve the local community and allow residents to better understand and, ultimately, to identify the problems and needs of the places in which they live and their impact on health and to use their knowledge and desires to improve the quality of the places, is a necessary condition for those who deal with urban design, especially amid a full climate crisis. The need for available data to understand environmental phenomena and to study possible measures to mitigate and adapt to climate changes that impact people's health impels us to identify possible forms of citizen involvement, with the added objective of raising awareness about problems. The challenge is to use new methods to collect, combine, and analyse data to allow for better urban planning and design and, finally, to have a positive impact on the quality of life of those who live in the city.

In Europe and around the world, some interesting experiences are beginning to develop in this direction. Some of these experiences have a strong mediation quality; others instead are structured within city government decision-making processes.

Pertaining to the first category is 'smart kite' experience in Beijing, which was created by a group of design students at Carnegie Mellon University and Harvard to map atmospheric pollution in the city and to increase residents' awareness. The kites glow in the dark and reveal carbon monoxide and particulates. The levels of pollution are reflected by changes in the colour of the LED lights. The project has led to numerous seminars to teach people how to assemble and use their own smart kites [35].

In the following section, two experiences falling under the second category are presented. The first regards the City of Bristol, the second is New York City.

Community Sensing Experiences

The world is becoming ever smarter. It is cheaper and simpler than ever to use sensors and big data to create a rich, detailed framework of how our cities live, move, and breathe. It is also true, however, that solutions for 'smart cities' often do not manage to solve problems that are really important to people. Recent examples of bottom-up initiatives, such as monitoring the radiation at Fukushima or the air quality in Amsterdam see citizens dedicated in different ways to gathering data; however, objective difficulties are also seen. People often lack the necessary skills to work with technology and often have trouble making sense of the collected data [36]; crowdsensed data have often raised problems of accuracy, privacy, and security [37, 38].

Promoting the sustainability of ground-based surveying projects goes beyond the design of surveying technologies. What is needed is an approach that resonates with people to reach a shared goal, promoting the design of capacities and technical abilities as well as a sense of shared responsibility about the intervention [39]. Numerous methods are used to design participatory data-collection campaigns. A large part of research, however, concentrates on the technical aspects of the systems rather than on aspects regarding the informed, conscious involvement of citizens.

The Bristol Approach to Citizen Sensing (https://www.bristolapproach.org/) aims to resolve this problem: placing people and communities at the centre of innovation to guarantee that new technologies respond to the needs and priorities of those who use them.

Bristol has a long history of innovation, civil action, and creativity. In 2017 the city was recognized as the main 'smart city' in the United Kingdom. It is also to the Knowle West Media Centre (KWMC), an artistic and charity organization that supports people making positive changes in their lives and in the community using the power of digital technologies and the arts.

Working with Ideas for Change, a society for innovation, and the Bristol City Council, KWMC developed 'The Bristol Approach'. This project allows citizens to work together to map problems in the city, choose priorities, and build solutions using the technology of sensors and the data collected with them. 'Citizen Sensing' is based on authorizing people to build, use, or even act as sensors, identifying and collecting data that will help them to use technology for the social good [40]. A series of events and seminars has been organized, working with artists to interact face-to-face with the people. Rather than imposing technological solutions on citizens to solve problems in the city, the Bristol Approach provides a series of tools and a way of working that helps different groups—from businesses to schools to community organizations—to address urgent problems in the community. A range of sensors are used, usually a mix of new and older technologies, integrated with broader resources and know-how that already exist in the community.

More than 700 people have been involved in more than 45 events. Three sets of prototypes have been designed and tested for citizens to detect data on the humidity in homes, food waste, and mental health.

In the pilot project 'Dampbusters', citizens suffering from humidity and mildew in their homes followed a series of practical workshops and seminars with the university, businesses such as ARUP, specialists in open data, representatives of the city council, and some health experts, as well as artists, architects, investors, and real-estate associations. The scope was to develop a 'humidity muffling' system that included:

- Temperature and humidity sensors
- Digital interfaces to make sense of the data
- Mapping tools to visualize the severity of the problem
- Volunteer citizens to test the data-acquisition devices in their homes.

Plastic 'frogboxes' were created that contain a temperature and humidity sensor connected to a computer that collected and saved the data every five minutes. The residents that volunteered to test these devices for a certain period also received diaries to keep track of their daily activities such as showering or cooking. Combined with the data from the sensors, these personal records helped people to understand and better interpret the data collected and potentially to adopt measures to manage the humidity conditions in their homes.

Bristol's approach to Citizen Sensing helps to address social exclusion, poverty, and environmental problems, providing disadvantaged communities the opportunity to develop new knowledge, digital skills, open-source tools, and innovative strategies for interdisciplinary co-design methods. The Bristol Approach is concerned with balancing bottom-up and top-down approaches to city planning, using strategies for engagement such as art and personal knowledge, and giving citizens the responsibility of selecting problems and finding smart city solutions [41].

The second experience is the Quantified Community (QC) in New York City, a network of urban neighbourhoods that collect, measure, and analyse data on physical and environmental conditions and human behaviour to better understand how neighbourhoods and the built environment influence individual and social well-being.

This initiative was launched by the NYU Center for Urban Science and Progress (CUSP). The project initially looked at three neighbourhoods in New York City: Hudson Yards, Lower Manhattan, and Red Hook in Brooklyn. In these neighbourhoods, quality-of-life measurements were collected with high spatial and temporal resolution and analysed, integrated with a citizen-science initiative that involved local residents in collecting the data and solving problems in the urban environment.

The method relied on a system to collect, measure, and analyse data about environmental conditions and human behaviours to better understand how the built environment influences individual and social well-being [42]. The approach is also different from the Smart City, as in this case the neighbourhood is seen as the ideal scale to study the city and the target of planning based on data and projects.

The work carried out in Red Hook, a low-income neighbourhood, presented the possibility of using low-cost sensors to collect data with citizen contribution. A platform of urban sensing was developed, the QC Urban QoL Sensor, an 'array' of low-cost, reliable sensors to measure and track environmental conditions localized down to the individual street, block, or building. The devices measure air quality, noise, light levels, numbers of pedestrians, temperature, air pressure, humidity, etc.

In this way, citizens joined in the process of identifying the problem, which allowed them to help develop hypotheses to test. Secondly, the participatory surveying created an opportunity for residents to provide data that could favour the understanding of their own neighbourhood. Through the QC initiative, the 'CommunitySense' activity was initiated, which uses physical web devices to allow smartphone users to interact with the sensors. In addition, an interactive web-based survey was developed to measure the difference between subjective and objective measures of quality of life (e.g. heat) to understand how the perception of environmental conditions varies from person to person and from neighbourhood to neighbourhood. Thirdly, the community's commitment was important for improving the decision-making process, building trust in the local communities, and minimizing the risk of a potential abuse of sensitive data.

The experience in NYC demonstrates that each neighbourhood offers a very different context for studying a city. In time, the possibility of comparing the different neighbourhoods through indicators of quality of life, public health, services, and mobility will provide a unique platform to study the dynamics of each quarter in the long term, allowing for comparative analysis of the quality of the neighbourhoods, land use, etc. This approach contributes to modifying the governance of decision-making processes, providing a tool that is useful for encouraging new innovations, quickly assessing their effects, and adopting the ideas that are shown to be effective.

3 Ongoing Experimentation in a Rationalist Suburb: The Monticelli Quarter of Ascoli Piceno

Elio Trusiani, Rosalba D'Onofrio, Roberta Cocci Grifoni, Mariano Pierantozzi, Enrica Petrucci, Ilaria Odoguardi, Graziano Enzo Marchesani, Corrado Sgrò and Chiara Camaioni

Abstract The 'Climate Change and Urban Health Resilience' (CCHURE) project aims to define a method to assess the effects that climate change produce on urban health in order to guide adaptation/mitigation policies with the contribution from researchers in many scientific disciplines, municipalities, and local health agencies, and with citizen involvement. To do this, it uses new IoT technologies and proposes community involvement in designing shared scenarios for development to support public administrations when making decisions. The method proposed is organized in two main phases: building a methodology to investigate the relationships between the impacts of climate change and the health/well-being of inhabitants on the urban scale of the neighbourhood; and proposing a methodology for public administrations to select scenarios for adaptation to/mitigation of the effects of climate change, through the use of real-time analytics and data feedback mechanisms and non-instrumental interaction with local communities. The method is currently being applied to the rationalist quarter of Monticelli in Ascoli Piceno (Italy). The project activities completed to date have dealt with building the Climate and Health Profile (CHP) and identifying the Climate-Health Actions. The subsequent steps will entail public consultation and focus groups with citizens to investigate the problems in the quarter and select possible solutions, as well as building the Climate Health Lab (CHL). This platform will be implemented with citizen contributions through the use of mobile crowdsensing techniques, which will allow smart-phone users to interact with IoT devices.

Keywords Urban health · Climate change effects · Climate and health profile · Climate and health actions · IoT technologies · Mobile crowdsensing techniques

---

E. Trusiani · R. D'Onofrio · R. C. Grifoni · M. Pierantozzi · E. Petrucci · I. Odoguardi · G. E. Marchesani · C. Sgrò · C. Camaioni
School of Architecture and Design, University of Camerino, Ascoli Piceno, Italy

3.1 The CCHURE Project—Climate Change and Urban Health Resilience

Regenerating the existing city and placing health at the centre of policies, plans, and projects represents an effect response to contrast the effects of climate change that impact cities and the health of inhabitants. Convinced of this need/opportunity are the World Health Organization (WHO), eminent international researchers, and public administration representatives in many European cities. However, a consolidated 'silo approach', which is common to the sectors of scientific research and public administration, does not permit the definition of common objectives, especially in small to medium-sized cities, or the formulation of integrated design proposals. CCHURE[4] aims to define a transdisciplinary method to evaluate the effects that climate change has on urban health, to direct policies for adaptation/mitigation through the contribution of many scientific disciplines, interaction with municipalities and local health agencies, and the involvement of local communities.

This will be done with the support of new IoT (Internet of Things) technologies and mobile crowdsensing techniques in order to expand knowledge to measure/assess the effects of climate change on health, involve communities in designing shared plans for development, empower them when dealing with urban health and well-being, and support public administrations in making decisions.

The innovation of CCHURE lies in the possibility of initiating a system of knowledge shared between the public administration, scientific community, and local community to assess projects and plans to mitigate and adapt to climate change and to choose the most advantageous in terms of their effects on health. The objectives of CCUHRE entail:

- Favouring the frontline participation of interested populations to confer validity and concreteness on the evaluation of policies and plans for adaptation to and mitigation of climate change, maximizing the impact of the solutions identified;
- Going beyond the concept of 'urban planning and design' according to a top-down approach, towards 'human-centred design' focused on knowledge of individual behaviour and collaboration with the local community, with a reliance on contributions from various disciplines and the use of modern IoT technologies.

[4]CCHURE is a research project funded in 2018 by the University of Camerino. The members of the group are researchers from different subject areas at the University along with some Italian and international researchers. Research UNIT 1: Rosalba D'Onofrio; Michele Talia; Chiara Camaioni; Ilaria Odoguardi. Research UNIT 2: Iolanda Grappasonni; Costa Giuseppe; Piera Di Martino; Tatiana Guarnier; Barbara Fenni. Research UNIT 3: Diletta Romana Cacciagrano; Leonardo Mostarda; Fabio Pagnotta; Gian Marco Mazzante; Graziano Enzo Marchesani; Franco Raimondi; Marta Magagnini. Research UNIT 4: Roberto Ruggiero; Roberta Cocci Grifoni; Francesca Giofrè; Zoran Djukanovic; Luca Bradini; Maria Federica Ottone; Mariano Pierantozzi; Ingrid Gomes Braga. Research UNIT 5: Elio Trusiani; Enrica Petrucci; Gerardo Doti; George Zillante; Katharine Bartsch; Maurizio Piccioni; Remo Appignanesi; Benedetta Raffaella Ruggeri; Lina Maria Calandra; Andrew Rundle.

Citizens become the suppliers and assessors of data regarding health and well-being, the simulators and evaluators of scenarios for mitigation and adaptation, actively joining in the design of their living environments. This will favour:

- Dialogue among the public administration, citizens, and researchers
- Citizens' participation in and awareness regarding city governance/decision-making
- Understanding of the need/opportunity to adopt an integrated, transdisciplinary approach, the only one capable of responding to the complexity of the effects of climate on health in urban areas
- The fundamental role of the 'urban project' in ensuring 'equitable' access to health.

It is therefore necessary to interact and to establish collaborative relationships between citizens and the public administration by sharing information and ensuring:

- Quality control of the data collected (which should be made known to the interested parties (https://sites.google.com/unicam.it/cchure/home) and made available on an appropriate level of aggregation;
- Assessments of mitigation and adaptation scenarios that should occur through direct interaction between experts, technicians in the public administration, and citizens.

This collaborative process should increase the project's credit, guaranteeing more effective knowledge that can overcome the 'smart-city approach' itself, all focused on technology, to emphasize a collective approach to resolving problems from a human-centred perspective.

Experimentation of the proposed method relates to a quarter of the city of Ascoli Piceno: the Monticelli Quarter.

3.2 Proposed Method

The proposed method in the CCHURE research project is organized into two main phases:

(1) Building a method to investigate the relationships between the impacts of climate change and the health/well-being of inhabitants on the urban scale of the neighbourhood, which contributes to selecting actions and combinations of actions for mitigation and adaptation with citizens' active role. The outputs are:

    (a) The Climate and Health Profile (CHP). To construct the neighbourhood CHP, reference will be made to qualitative/quantitative indicators that assess the effects of climate change on the health and well-being of the population. These indicators will be selected based on existing public health data, the products of international research, and with the contribution of inhabitants by administering questionnaires and activating focus groups.

(b) Climate and Health Actions (CHA). Actions and combinations of actions will be selected for adaptation and mitigation, already present in international best practices with reference to the 'fundamental themes' of urban design—land use, mobility, housing, open spaces, and meeting spaces, the natural environment—and some themes of technological design—temporary use and flexibility, etc.

(2) Proposing a method for public administrations to select scenarios for adaptation to/mitigation of the effects of climate change through the use of real-time analytics and data-feedback mechanisms and non-instrumental interaction with local communities. The output is:

(a) Climate Health Lab (CHL). A platform of sensors and automation technologies (Urban Internet of Things, IoT) will be constructed to provide real-time information/measurement of the physical/environmental conditions of the neighbourhood and its inhabitants. This platform will be implemented with citizen contributions through the use of mobile crowdsensing techniques, which will allow smartphone users to interact with IoT devices.

With the CHL, it will be possible to:

- Analyse and assess the difference between subjective and objective measurements of quality-of-life indicators to understand how the perception of different environmental conditions varies across the neighbourhood
- Verify and compare, with the help of researchers, technicians, and citizens, the 'health' performance of the scenarios identified and their evolution in time, thereby assisting public administrations in the decision-making process.

4 The Territory of Experimentation

Description of the Monticelli Quarter

The Monticelli Quarter (Fig. 1), planned by Leonardo Benevolo, is one of the most populous areas in the city of Ascoli Piceno, with about 10,000 inhabitants. It is located just a few kilometres from the historical centre and was planned in view of substantial demographic growth. It was presented as a 'new' neighbourhood aimed at representing important urban development for the city of Ascoli Piceno, incarnating the dream of modernity and self-sufficiency. Its history is tied to the history of the city of Ascoli Piceno and its urban development outside the historical city centre.[5]

The history of the Plan of Ascoli Piceno (1963–72) represents one of Benevolo's first experiences in the field of urban planning. His operational strategy is realized

[5]At the beginning of the 1900s, Ascoli Piceno was affected by the 'Piano Regolatore Edilizio e di Risanamento e fognature cittadine' [Building and Regeneration and City Sewer Regulatory Plan]. To activate urban-planning law no. 1150 of 1942, the first regulatory plan was adopted in 1954 to govern development outside the historical centre; the ineffectiveness of the plan, however, was soon revealed. For this reason a modification to the regulatory plan began to be prepared in 1968, which was entrusted to Leonardo Benevolo.

Fig. 1 Aerial view of the quarter

through public urbanization of the land, expanding the residential city through independent quarters, close in form to the expressive search of rationalism, the increase of infrastructures, fundamental for connection among the various parts of the city, and the regeneration of the fabric of the periphery, as well as renewing the historical centre [43]. He suggested a city with linear development (Fig. 2a, b) along an east-west axis and defined a broad area of city expansion into a zone that had still not been urbanized: Monticelli.

Up to the 1970s, Monticelli was an agricultural area. Then, after the earthquake in 1972, some ‘emergency’ buildings began to rise, including two skyscrapers in the eastern part around which, in the span of a few years, consistent urbanization had consolidated. In the original project, Benevolo identified a hierarchy of areas with different functions. These were served by a system of infrastructure based on different levels of use: roads for quick decentralized passage (towards the bank of the Tronto River), central roads for internal mobility, and secondary roads orthogonal to the central axis.

Pedestrian paths were designed in the northern part (in the east and west), equipped with green spaces and collective services for the quarter.

Implementation of the plan over the years, long and complex, slowly led to a quarter containing mainly public residential housing, with the hospital, a supermarket, offices, various types of shops, two churches, and, until a short time ago, a fast-food restaurant.

Today, for most residents of Ascoli Piceno, Monticelli is simply a dormitory, a quarter situated between a road axis and the Tronto River, a small town in and of itself with respect to the rest of the city. The quarter is characterized by widespread degradation: building degradation, a difficult mobility system, scarcity of equipped

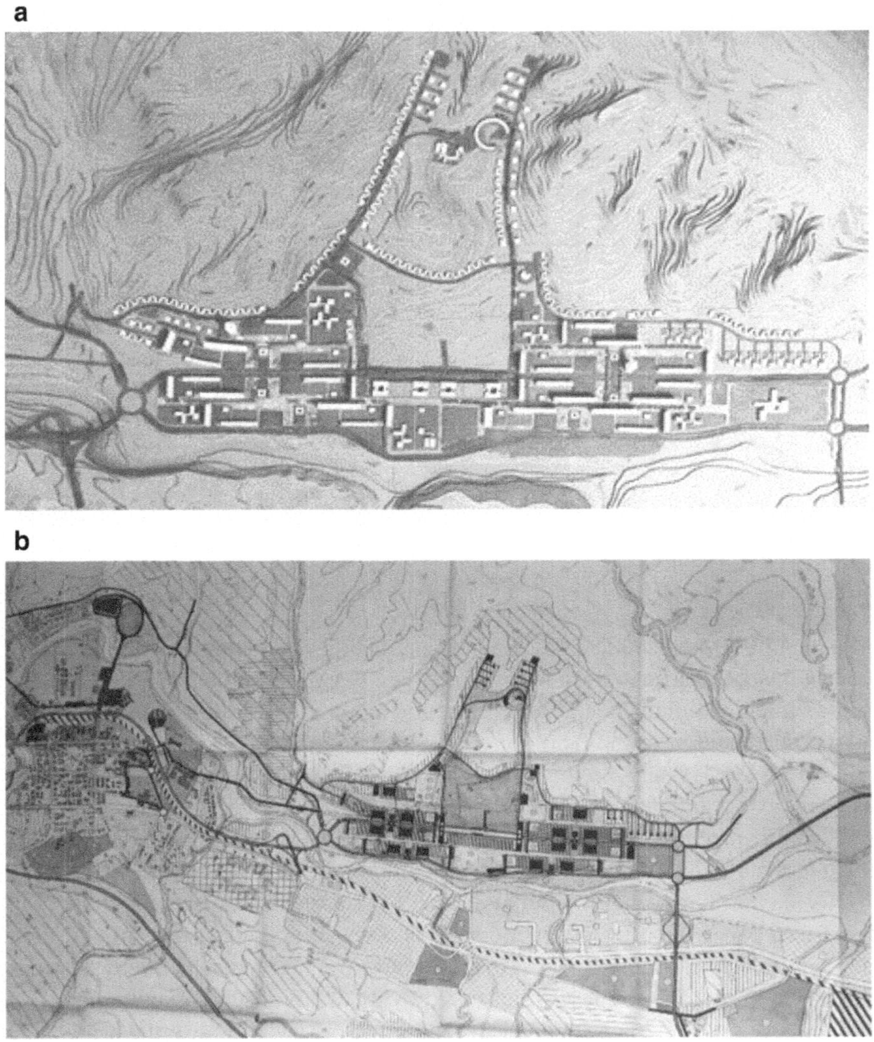

Fig. 2 a Model of the project. b Extract from the local plan

green spaces, insufficient centres of social and public/private service aggregations, etc. It is configured as a settlement in and of itself, in which the main road, secondary streets, open spaces or clearings, and bike paths within the built area do not connect the parts and serve no purpose as social or urban glue. They are testament only to the crushing of physical and spatial relationships in the city, corresponding to a weakening of the social and cultural fabric, which in turn reduces the ties needed to connect people with the places (Fig. 3).

Over time, the system of infrastructure (Fig. 4), evidence of the modernist stamp of the quarter, has seen a succession of point-like interventions such as the new

Fig. 3 Settlement types

Fig. 4 View of the central axis

roundabouts and small widespread maintenance; these have not, however, resolved the existing critical aspects. Moreover, all the interventions made in recent years lack quality and management. The quarter is still characterized today by a system of east-west passage where the real protagonists of the urban scene are the main roadways, which are dangerous and chaotic, the bike path to the south, which is disconnected from the urban fabric to the north, and the recent pedestrian paths to the northern, upper part of the quarter, which are completely abandoned and dangerous. The pedestrian crossings—subways—are perceived by the population as unsafe due to a lack of management, lighting, and integration with the context. The main axis of the quarter is identified only by its quick accessibility, which has led to the loss of interaction between the places and the subjects passing through. This does not allow the urban fabric or its relationships with the context to be read clearly, a context that shows degradation, abandonment, separation, and social isolation.

All this denotes a feeling of insecurity in the community, which frequents only some places of aggregation [44]. The city news reports stories of drug addiction, aggression, and accidents due to dangerous cross traffic—both on the central axis and the internal streets—smog, and noise. Despite this, there are signs of liveliness and action by the local population in the presence of sports associations, social gardens, and a very busy senior centre. This degradation has called the attention of the public administration, which since 2001 has presented a proposal to develop an innovative programme of urban regeneration (Ministry of Infrastructure and Transport Decree no. 2522 of 27-12-2001) to be realized precisely in the Monticelli Quarter. In 2016, under the national project for the urban regeneration of Italian peripheral areas, 'Bando Periferie' [Periphery Announcement], Ascoli Piceno obtained substantial financing to make a series of integrated interventions in the quarter. These include initiatives for sustainable mobility, actions to improve the social and economic conditions of inhabitants, and projects to improve the urban decor and environmental conditions in the area.

Why Monticelli? Why the Neighbourhood Scale?

The urban project of the quarter is inspired by the theoretical and design principles of the rationalist neighbourhood. These can still be read perfectly today, even where the original design was modified and/or where some parts were never completed. The clear separation of functions, a characteristic of modernist movement, are exemplified in Monticelli, albeit in a conclusive, self-referential design, making it possible to trace both the failures of this model and also the unexpected and currently implicit design potential of the model itself.

This makes Monticelli a field of experimentation in design where a critical reflection can begin, together the local community, that brings into play the criteria of urban planning and design of rationalist movement, in particular, of self-sufficient quarters and their analytical/design elements (roads, distances, open spaces, functional zoning, standards, etc.). Today they may be read critically and interpreted in their current unexpected potential in terms of resilience, quality of life, and urban health. In this sense, the urban layout of quarters based on modernist movement may become a favoured field of experimentation capable of responding to design innovations in the urban space such as climate change, environmental security, and urban health. The possibility of intervening on these spaces while protecting their historical/modernist urban-planning footprint may confer a design role on the same urban system. Roads and paths of different sizes and hierarchies, open and green spaces, volumes and spaces, either existing or perhaps never completed, offer the necessary potential and dimensional characteristics to become analytical/design elements again in a project for urban regeneration where the renewed relationship between health and urban planning is the dominant topic. All of this includes one substantial aspect: the participation of the community as co-designer/co-planner and not just as present/future users of anonymous neighbourhood.

In addition to its physical structure and social connotation described above, it is precisely the 'size of the quarter' that contributed to the choice of Monticelli for this experimentation. In fact, as evidenced by the best international practices, the quarter seems to be the most suitable place for experimentation to initiate processes of urban regeneration where the urban planning/health binomial becomes a winning aspect with the community's contribution. In the quarter it is possible to begin and test urban policies adopted by the public administrations.

In this sense, we recall the experiences of Rotterdam and Copenhagen. These two cities evince two design scales of reference for Healthy Cities: the strategic scale of urban policies, where the topics of the healthy city are found in a transverse manner, and the local neighbourhood scale, where favourable conditions for experimentation seem to be concentrated. Based on the examples illustrated, the term *neighbourhood* seems to be returning to the centre of urban planning. It can be considered an experimental unit for the healthy city where a design core between the determinants of health and the quality of public space in the city can be sought without falling back on and/or seconding hygiene or welfare trends, as recommended by Patrizia Gabellini, and even less by arriving at deterministic solutions by following pre-packaged paths [45]. It is good to recall that for a long time, the concept of *quarter* contributed to the growth of intense community life, which meant evident sharing of experiences and conditions which developed a community with identity and social recognition, relationships of reciprocity, relation, and solidarity. Today, the social/demographic situation is undergoing constant change and the idea of *community* is continuously brought into play by exogenous historical/social factors of a temporary and transitional nature. The quarter seems to express the basic potential to be able to activate experimentation in integrating the determinants of health and the network of mobility and access, the creation and diversification of widespread green areas, the activation of participatory forms of co-design, co-production, and co-responsibility, the innovation of public spaces starting with instances of securing areas, the redesign of technological networks in response to climate change, activating responsible participation processes, and the creation of consensus for shared responsibility. In other words, these criteria lie at the basis of theories of the healthy city.

International experiences also return the checklist system as a guide both for planning and for verifying the design. This entails a grid of actions/options that respond to the health/urban planning binomial, and what might constitute a useful reference in the design phase. In England, for example, the experiences show checklists organized around themes of healthy living, active movement, a healthy environment, and 'lively' neighbourhoods. Community, housing, environment, and integrated transport with urban-planning policies already provide a framework of reference within which to work and trace paths in line with the determinants of health. This is an approach that can help designers and decision-makers understand the implications for health, local plans, and interventions for transformation.[6] Checklists aim to combine the requirements and fundamental norms that influence health and well-being, providing support for decision-makers. One example is London's Plan[7] (July 2011), which foresees reports to complement general norms, using precisely the neighbourhood scale to implement and actualize the primary questions of urban health: 'Code for Sustainable Homes', 'Lifetime Homes and Lifetime Neighbourhoods', 'Building for Life', and 'Secured by Design' from 2012, are just some of the examples worth mentioning. The checklist is usually divided into topics and it focuses on problems of health and well-being in relation to local strategies for health and well-being. In many cases there is a strong focus on questions related to obesity and diseases linked to physical inactivity and inadequate food, air and noise pollution, road safety, social isolation, etc. [46].

Another example in the literature that validates the choice of the quarter as an excellent field for experimentation is the recent work by Ann Forsyth, Emily Salomon, and Laura Smead: *Creating Healthy Neighbourhoods*. In this text, the authors provide eight principles to reason for integrated health and city planning. Briefly, these are: (1) Importance: assess how health matters in this place; (2) Balance: make healthier places by balancing physical changes with other interventions to appeal to different kinds of people; (3) Vulnerability: plan and design for those with the most health vulnerabilities and fewest resources for making healthy choices; (4) Layout: foster multiple dimensions of health through overall neighbourhood layout; (5) Access: provide options for getting around and increasing geographic access; (6) Connection: create opportunities for people to interact with each other in positive ways; (7) Protection: reduce harmful exposures at a neighbourhood level through a combination of wider policies and regulations along with local actions; (8) Implementation: coordinate diverse actions over time [47].

---

[6]In the English case, it is worth recalling the UK National Planning Policy Framework (March 2012). This represents a collaborative approach between health and planning according to which local authorities accountable to city government should consider questions related to public health and collaborate with health organizations to understand the state of health and the needs of the local population in order to improve health and well-being. In this sense, the framework promotes a checklist to support those responsible for development proposals or planning, professionals in public and environmental health, forums of community groups, and local associations in order to contribute to involving the community and improving the proposed solutions.

[7]The plan provides a meaningful framework for integrating health and territorial planning. It aims to improve health and address health inequalities. The checklist refers to the policies and standards of London's plan and the standards of quality and design, which are also inserted in complementary reports.

The neighbourhood dimension, recourse to checklists that combine the fundamental requirements and standards that influence health and well-being with reference to plans and projects, reference to directions and guidelines that could be of assistance in formulating design proposals—in that they facilitate discussion among the different sectors of public administration, designers, local communities, and stakeholders—together can constitute a *modus operandi* for experimentation and refinement to construct cities oriented towards the health and well-being of their inhabitants.

In view of the present literature and consistent operational experience, at least in some geographical areas of the planet, the Monticelli Quarter seems to have all the physical/spatial and social characteristics necessary to be able to face the challenge of change under new terms and with new tools. We recall that for this purpose, the challenge lies in regenerating the existing city rather than designing residential areas from scratch.[8] Indeed, it is in the design challenge of urban regeneration for the existing city in peripheral areas, both marginalized and not, that the strongest change and most innovative challenge lies for a conceptual and design-based repositioning of the urban-planning discipline itself.

4.1 *Completed Activities, Work in Progress, Partial Results*

With the method outlined in Sect. 3.2 and the historical and current urban-planning profile of the Monticelli Quarter, the activities carried out to date in the research project, aimed at building the Climate and Health Profile (CHP) and identifying the climate-health actions, are based on:

(a) The social dimension: this relates to on-site actions that have seen the participation of the community and the main social and institutional players present in the quarter
(b) The technical/institutional dimension: this relates to actions regarding the technical/knowledge-building characteristics of the quarter carried out by the City of Ascoli Piceno in the field with direct surveys, on-site verifications, and interviews (Fig. 5).

With regard to the first point, several indicators have been chosen to construct the Climate and Health Profile (CHP) and the consequent Climate-Health Actions to assess the quality of life of the families. These indicators were organized in a questionnaire, which was distributed to families with the support of the primary school in the quarter. It is organized into 9 topics: demographic data, the area where the family lives, safety, accessibility to services, social cohesion in the quarter, daily

[8]In many cases, the new designs are interesting real-estate operations that, updated with new green technologies and the help of IoT, propose past settlement models in addition to the existing city, with the consequent land consumption and access available only to some social classes. This modality has not solved the real problems in the existing city or lead to design and decision-making innovations for public administrations.

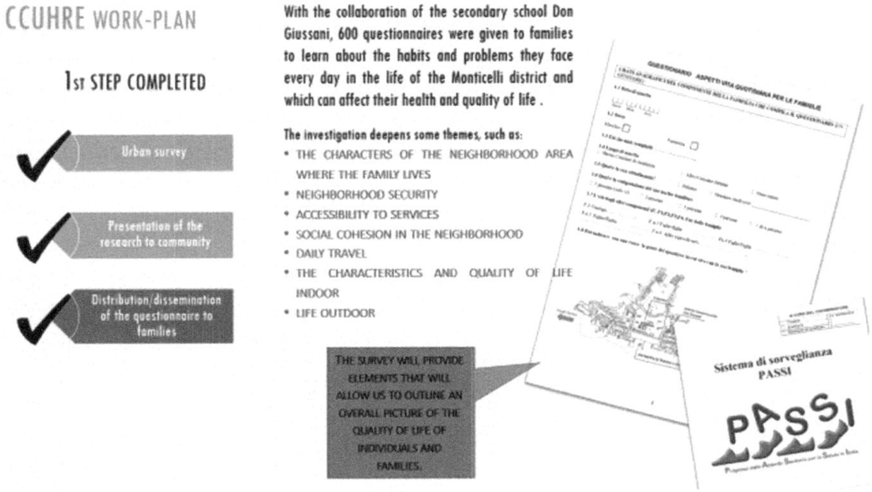

Fig. 5 Work phases – Step 1

movements, characteristics of the home, quality of life in the home, and outdoors. So far, a band of average age between 30 and 55 years has been captured for a sample of about 250 people. The distribution of the questionnaire via Internet will take place shortly. At the same time, in collaboration with ASUR (the regional health authority), distribution of the PASSI (Progress of Health Services for Health in Italy)[9] questionnaire has begun. This questionnaire collects information about the lifestyle and behavioural risk factors of the adult population (18–69 years) in relation to the occurrence of chronic non-communicable diseases such as smoking, physical activity, obesity, overweight, cardiovascular risk, state of physical/mental well-being, and other aspects tied to quality of life that are strictly correlated with health. The results are currently being processed by ASUR.

In reference to the climate investigations to be related with the health of citizens, these regarded the information deriving from the SECAP plan (Sustainable Energy and Climate Action Plan) recently drafted by the city administration with reference to the city climate analysis and the risk and vulnerability analysis. The latter investigation revealed that the city of Ascoli Piceno has urban concentrations that require particular attention in terms of thermal stress (heat waves). Together with the progressive ageing of the population, which is very accentuated in the Monticelli Quarter, heat waves may increase the number of deaths and pathologies among the elderly population. Other impacts have been identified in the availability of water in the civil sector, with the need for more prudent management of domestic water consumption, and hydrogeological risk tied to intensified precipitation. To investigate the first of

[9]Promoted and financed by 2006 by the Italian Ministry of Health, the questionnaire aims to completely monitor the state of health of the population. The results of the questionnaire are currently being processed by ASUR.

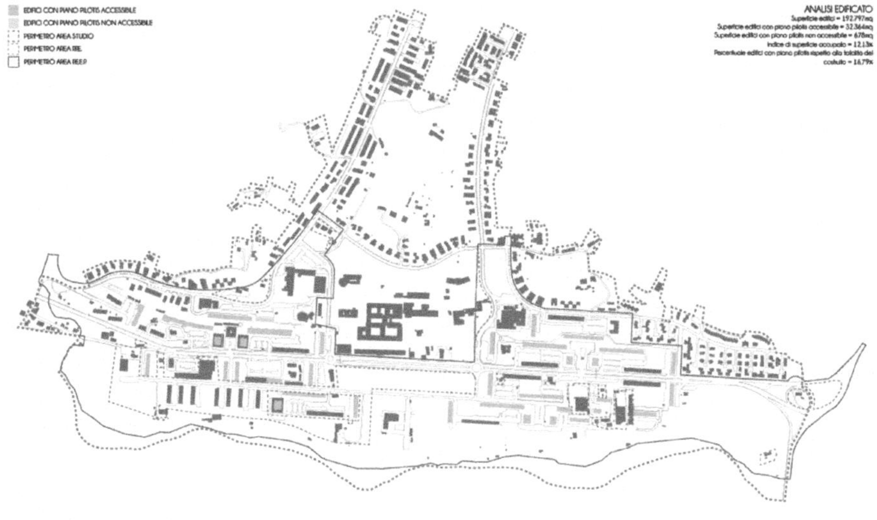

Fig. 6 Building plan with accessible or closed pilotì floor

these critical aspects (heat waves), an ENVI-met simulation is currently being developed. Its goal in the first phase (diagnostic level) is to know precisely the continuous state of the urban climate with a fine temporal and spatial resolution. This is useful for later running numerical simulations for 'urban diagnosis' and to design 'urban strategies'.

With regard to the second point, i.e. the technical/cognitive dimension, a critical reading of the quarter was made by analysing existing planning tools and the state of the places in the quarter (Fig. 6). This dual reading made use of local, general, and implemental urban-planning tools along with current data that provide a snapshot of the current state in relation to demographic data, standard urban planning, land use, services, green areas, commercial areas, roads, housing, etc. The analysis, in close contact with the City of Ascoli Piceno and developed on a GIS basis in order to interact directly with the city itself, has led to the construction of themed maps and, by relating the data that emerged, the ability to interpret current situations and dynamics.

The investigations can be read in either a general or disaggregated way according to the macro areas identified by the questionnaire enabling a double reading and interpretation of the data (Fig. 7).

In view of the completed activities, the partial results emerging from the work considering the social and technical/cognitive dimensions can be synthesized in the following emerging questions: traffic, air pollution, noise, inadequate street lighting, degradation of the road surface, and exclusive reliance on cars for daily activities such as going to work and school or making daily purchases. In this scope, it is necessary to underline that 65.6% of families highlight a problem of night time safety on the roads, and 59.1% note the lack of public lighting. Along with this, we find

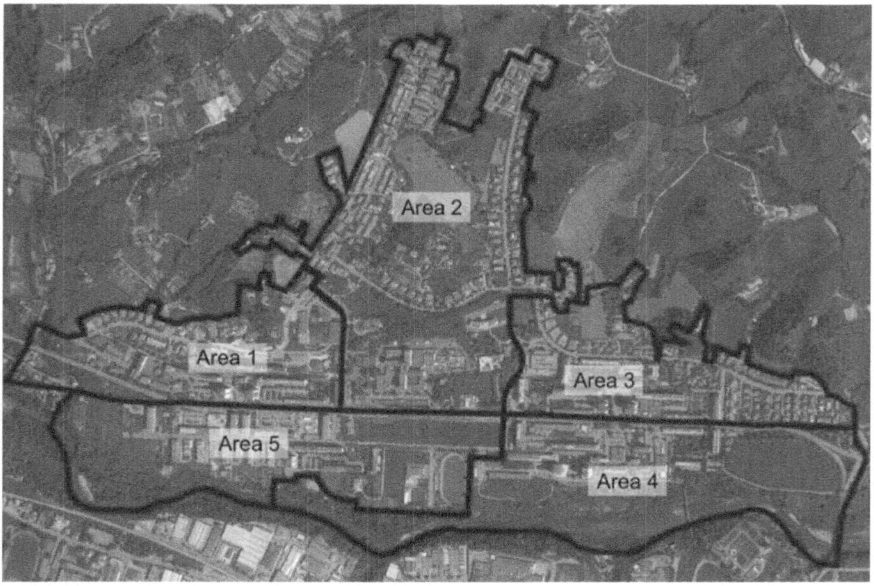

Fig. 7 Macro areas

percentages of insecurity[10] tied to the intensity and speed of vehicular traffic, which is attested to by 30.5% of respondents, while the sense of insecurity due to small crimes is around 16.0% for those interviewed. It also should be noted that 48.1% mention the lack of public surveillance. On the other hand, accessibility to services was judged to be good, from public offices to schools to commercial activities, though naturally through the almost exclusive use of private vehicles. This is a quarter where green areas can be reached on food in less than 15 min for 98% of respondents; and bike paths can be reached on bike in less than 5 min for 89.3% of respondents. An awareness of a notable sense of social cohesion within the quarter also emerges.

Specifically, for some individual themes and related macro areas, it is possible at the moment to outline the following profile:

Topic: zone where the family lives

- Macro area 1: with respect to the general data, the traffic datum emerges noticeably higher with respect to what is registered overall; poor road conditions; great public

[10]Disorientation and insecurity also emerged from a 'collaborative mapping platform' experiment called 'Furia Map', initiated in 2015 within the Urban Design Laboratory (R. D'Onofrio, E. Trusiani [48]) in the School of Architecture and Design at the University of Camerino. This experimentation is carried out in the quarter following an open-source urban-planning approach with contributions from residents. About 40 students were divided into 8 groups pertaining to 8 themes of investigation: uses of spaces, landmarks, heroes, citizens, memory, image, safety, lights-sounds, and colours. The students collected interviews, videos, and photos to create an animated map, accessible at Cityopensource.net, to allow for a continuously updated reading of the quarter.

transport, optimal presence and use of green areas and the presence of bike paths; the sample is divided equally regarding criminality and filth in the streets.
- Macro area 2: the problem of traffic is substantially lower and air pollution is also less; difficulty regarding public transport increases, the judgement about lighting improves, the use of bike paths is lower than the general data.
- Macro area 3: substantial confirmation of the general data, the presence of pollution is higher than the general data, the use of bike paths is less.
- Macro area 4: higher level of traffic, pollution, and noise; optimal public transport; presence and optimal use of green areas and the presence of bike paths.
- Macro area 5: less care of the streets; lower air quality; higher level of criminality; less road maintenance, better use of green areas and bike paths; some difficulty with public services.

Topic: safety

- Macro area 1: greater insecurity on the street at night, confirmation of the general data related to the lack of public lighting and the lack of public surveillance, the intensity and speed of traffic.
- Macro area 2: the people in this zone feel more secure than what emerges from the general data.
- Macro area 3: confirmation of the general data.
- Macro area 4: greater insecurity on the street at night, confirmation of the causes identified in the general data: lack of public lighting and public surveillance; increased sense of danger due to the intensity and speed of traffic.
- Macro area 5: confirmation and increase in the trends found in the general data.

Topic: accessibility to services

- Macro area 1: substantial confirmation of the general data with some additional difficulty in reaching services.
- Macro area 2: confirmation of the general data with some slight additional difficulty in reaching some services and commercial activities.
- Macro area 3: confirmation of the general data.
- Macro area 4: confirmation of the general data.
- Macro area 5: greater difficulty in reaching general services; the schools, however, can be reached easily.

Topic: social cohesion of the quarter

- Macro area 1: confirmation of the general data with an improvement in social interaction; decreased commitment to improving the quality of life in the quarter and safety.
- Macro area 2: confirmation of the general data.
- Macro area 3: decreased satisfaction with the quarter, even if the number of people they say they know well increases.

- Macro area 4: confirmation of the general data but increased commitment to improving the quality of life in the quarter and satisfaction in the quarter.
- Macro area 5: increased satisfaction with the quarter, increased involvement of people in activities to improve the quality of life in the quarter and feeling at ease.

Topic: housing characteristics

- Macro area 1: buildings in the plain; mainly exposed to the north and south; divided sample with respect to wind exposure; for 75% of respondents there are no green areas nearby.
- Macro area 2: presence of very trafficked streets and green areas; hillside buildings for 68% of respondents; the condition of rare wind exposure prevails.
- Macro area 3: confirmation of the general data but greater presence of green areas.
- Macro area 4: confirmation of the general data except the presence of trafficked streets (higher percentage) and green areas, for which the sample is divided.
- Macro area 5: confirmation of the general data.

As already mentioned, this phase will shortly be followed by online administration of the questionnaire. It should be underlined that the work completed and the results of the online survey will then be compared with the results and ongoing processing of the PASSI questionnaire, which will instead render complete monitoring of the state of health of the population. The comparison and interrelation of the data will be fundamental in building the Climate-Health Actions and related evolutionary scenarios.

5 Conclusions

The partial results mentioned above constitute the endpoint of an initial phase of work, which is substantial and difficult to initiate because it addressed all the social, political, administrative/health, and cultural components of the city. The next planned steps regard:

- Activation of a webpage to establish public consultation with citizens to identify problems in the quarter and select shared solutions to a common problem (Fig. 8);
- Activation of focus groups to investigate the results of the questionnaires and identify other possible problems in the quarter that impact the well-being and health of inhabitants. The Climate and Health Profile (CHP) will be defined at the end of this phase;
- Construction of the Climate Health Lab (CHL). This step foresees the construction of a platform of sensors and automation technologies (Urban Internet of Things, IoT), which will provide real-time information/measurement of the physical/environmental conditions of the neighbourhood and its inhabitants. This platform will be implemented with citizen contributions through the use of mobile

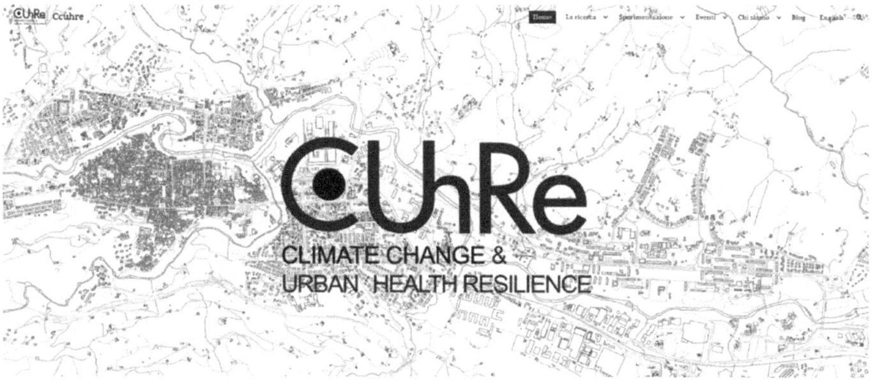

Fig. 8 Web site CCUHRE

crowdsensing techniques, which will allow smart-phone users to interact with IoT devices.

With citizen contributions and based on the results of the ENVI-met simulation, some specific places in the quarter will be chosen to locate sensors to detect the main criticalities from the climate point of view (those detected by the sensors and those perceived by the inhabitants), which are closely correlated with the questions of well-being and environmental comfort within the quarter. This entails a fundamental phase of the research project because it represents the first step in the future interaction of climate data, IoT, community, urban space, urban-planning tools, administration, and the development of scenarios to support decision-making.

These phases, which regard the central and final phases of the research project, are designed to systematize what emerges from exploration in the field of the social, technical/operational, and experimental dimensions and will lead to the development of evolutionary scenarios to support decision-making by the public administration. This result aims to bring together theoretical research and experimental practice through the involvement of favoured institutional actors, citizens, and the interdisciplinary nature of the skills implemented.

References

1. Thompson S (2007) 'A planner's perspective on the health impacts of urban settings. Public Health Bull 18(9–10):157–160
2. Talia M (2019) Salute e equità sono questioni urbanistiche, città bene comune. Casa della cultura. http://casadellacultura.it/883/salute-e-equit-agrave-sono-questioni-urbanistiche. Last accessed 12 Nov 2019
3. EASAC (2019) The imperative of climate action to protect human health in Europe. EASAC policy report 38. https://easac.eu/publications/details/the-imperative-of-climate-action-to-protect-human-health-in-europe/. Last accessed 12 Nov 2019

4. Lee ACK, Maheswaran R (2011) The health benefits of urban green spaces: a review of the evidence. J Public Health 33(2):212–222
5. Durand CP, Andalib M, Dunton GF, Wolch J, Pentz MA (2011) A systematic review of built environment factors related to physical activity and obesity risk: implications for smart growth urban planning. Obes Rev 12(5):e173–182
6. Giles-Corti B, Gunn L, Hooper P, Boulange C, Zapata Diomedi B, Pettit C, Foster S (2019) Integrating human health into urban and transport planning. Springer, Cham
7. Tan J, Zheng Y, Tang X, Guo C, Li L, Song G, Zhen X, Yuan D, Kalkstein A, Li F, Chen H (2010) The urban heat island and its impact on heat waves and human health in Shanghai. Int J Biometeorol 54(1):75–84. https://www.researchgate.net/publication/26787109_The_urban_heat_island_and_its_impact_on_heat_waves_and_human_health_in_Shanghai. Last accessed 12 Nov 2019
8. Zapata-Diomedi B, Gunn L, Giles-Corti B, Shiell A, Veerman JL (2018) A method for the inclusion of physical activity-related health benefits in cost-benefit analysis of built environment initiatives. Prev Med 106:224–230
9. Costa G, Bassi M, Gensini GF (2016) L'equità nella salute in Italia. Secondo rapporto sulle disuguaglianze sociali in sanità. F Angeli, Milan
10. Kohlhuber M, Mielck A, Weiland SK, Bolte G (2006) Social inequality in perceived environmental exposures in relation to housing conditions in Germany. Environ Res 101:246–255
11. Marmot M (2016) The health gap: the challenge of an unequal world. Bloomsbury Publishing PLC
12. Barton H, Grant M (2006) A health map for the local human habitat. J R Soc Promot Health 126(6):252–253
13. Rydin Y, Bleahu A, Davies M, Davila JD, Friel S, De Grandis G et al (2012) Shaping cities for health: Complexity and the planning of urban environments in the 21st century. The Lancet 379(9831):2079–2108
14. WHO OFFICE EUROPE (2013) Health and the environment in the who European Region. Creating resilient communities and supportive environments. http://www.euro.who.int/__data/assets/pdf_file/0005/215645/HEALTH-AND-THE-ENVIRONMENT-IN-THE-WHO-EUROPEAN-REGION-Creating-resilientcommunities-and-supportive-environments.pdf?ua=1. Last accessed 7 Jun 2020
15. Corburn J (2009) Toward the healthy city: people, places and the politics of urban planning. MIT Press, Cambridge
16. de Leeuw E, Green G, Tsouros A, Devlin J (2015) Healthy cities phase V evaluation: Further synthesizing realism. Health Promot Int 30(suppl 1):i118–i125
17. de Leeuw E (2011) Do healthy cities work? A logic of method for assessing impact and outcomes of healthy cities. J Urb Health 89(2):217–231
18. Public Health England (2017) Spatial planning for health: an evidence resource for planning and designing healthier places. https://www.gov.uk/government/publications/spatial-planning-for-health-evidence-review. Last accessed 12 Nov 2019
19. Evans RG, Stoddart GL (2003) Consuming research, producing policy? Am J Public Health 93(3):371–379
20. Glouberman S, Gemar M, Campsie P, Miller G, Armstrong J, Newman C, Siotis A, Grof P (2006) A framework for improving health in cities: a discussion paper. J Urban Health: Bull N Y Acad Med 83(2):325–338
21. Galea S, Vlahov D (2005) Urban health: evidence, challenges, and directions. Ann Rev Public Health 26(1)
22. Corburn J (2005) Urban planning and health disparities: implications for research and practice. Plann Pract Res 20(2):111–126
23. Boelens L (2009) The urban connection: an actor-relational approach to urban planning. 010-Publishers, Rotterdam 1 Jan 2009
24. Palermo PC (2017) Urbanistica del progetto urbano: ambiguità e ipocrisie. Eco Web Town 15. http://www.ecowebtown.it/n_15/

25. Verbeek T (2014) Reconnecting urban planning and public health: an exploration of a more adaptive approach. Annual Congress: from control to co-evolution. In: Proceedings. Presented at the Annual Congress: from control to co-evolution (AESOP—2014 Conference Paper January 2014. https://www.researchgate.net/publication/288668035_Reconnecting_urban_planning_and_public_health_an_exploration_of_a_more_adaptive_approach. Last accessed 12 Nov 2019
26. Barcelona D (2011) La Taula per a la Millora Urbana (TxMU). La iniciativa de treball transversal al servei de la regeneraciò urbana. Last accessed 19 Nov 2019
27. Pasqui G (2017) Urbanistica oggi. Piccolo lessico critico. Donzelli, Rome
28. Sassen S (2011) Open source urbanism. Domus, 29 June 2011
29. Steinmetz-Wooda M, Pluyeb P, Ross NA (2019) The planning and reporting of mixed methods studies on the built environment and health. Prev Med 126(2019)
30. Creswell JW (2003) Research design: Qualitative, quantitative, and mixed methods approaches, 2nd edn. Sage, Thousand Oaks, CA
31. Coyle J, Williams B (2000) An exploration of the epistemological intricacies of using qualitative data to develop a quantitative measure of user views of health care. J Adv Nurs 31(5)
32. Gluhak A, Krco S, Nati M, Pfisterer D, Mitton N, Razafindralambo T (2011) A survey on facilities for experimental internet of things research. IEEE Commun Mag Inst Electr Electron Eng 49(11):58–67. https://hal.inria.fr/inria-00630092/document. Last accessed 12 Nov 2019
33. Gubbi J et al (2013) Internet of Things (IoT): a vision, architectural elements, and future directions. Futur Gener Comput Syst 29(7):1645–1660
34. Bria F, Morozov E (2018) Ripensare la smart city. Codice, Milan
35. Balestrini M, Diez T, Pólvora A, Nascimento S (2019) Mapping participatory sensing and community-led environmental monitoring initiatives, making sense H2020 CAPS Project. Study Publications Office of the European Union, Luxembourg, https://op.europa.eu/en/publication-detail/-/publication/21a45749-316b-11e8-b5fe-01aa75ed71a1. Last accessed 12 Nov 2019
36. Balestrini M, Diez T, Marshall P, Gluhak A, Rogers Y (2015) IoT community technologies: leaving users to their own devices or orchestration of engagement? EAI Endors Trans Internet Things 1(1)
37. Ganti RK, Ye F, Lei H (2011) Mobile crowdsensing: current state and future challenges. IEEE Commun Mag 49(11):32–39. Last accessed 12 Nov 2019. http://www.ece.stonybrook.edu/~fanye/papers/IEEE-Com-Mag-11.pdf
38. Snyder EG, Watkins TH, Solomon PA, Thoma ED, Williams RW, Hagler GS, Preuss PW (2013) The changing paradigm of air pollution monitoring. Environ Sci Technol 47(20):11369–11377
39. Crabtree A, Chamberlain A, Davies M, Glover K, Reeves S, Rodden T, Tolmie P, Jones M (2013) Doing innovation in the wild. In: Proceedings of the biannual conference of the Italian Chapter of SIGCHI, ACM (2013), 25
40. Balestrini M, Rogers Y, Hassan C, Creus J, King M, Marshall P (2017) A city in common: a framework to orchestrate large-scale citizen engagement around urban issues. Proceedings of the 2017 CHI conference on human factors in computing systems, CHI '17. ACM, New York, NY, USA, pp 2282–2294
41. Cardullo P, Di Feliciantonio C, Kitchin R (2019) The right to the smart city. Emerald Publishing Limited
42. Kontokosta C, Johnson N, Schloss A (2016) The quantified community at red hook: urban sensing and citizen science in low-income neighborhoods. In: Proceedings of the 2016 Bloomberg data for good exchange. Last accessed 12 Nov 2019. https://pdfs.semanticscholar.org/28fb/2dc22e4fd29b181f3e8d5e5e002da38569b8.pdf
43. Benevolo L (1957) Ascoli Piceno – Editoriale Domus no. 8
44. Petrucci E, D'Onofrio R, Trusiani E, Odoguardi I (2018) Strada Facendo: riflessioni sul Sistema delle relazioni nel quartiere Monticelli di Ascoli Piceno. In: Capano F, Pascariello MI, Visone M (2018) La Città Altra/The other city. Storia e immagine della diversità urbana: luoghi e paesaggi dei privilegi e del benessere, dell'isolamento, del disagio, della multiculturalità. Federico II University Press

45. D'Onofrio R, Trusiani E (2017) Città, salute e benessere. Nuovi percorsi per l'urbanistica. F Angeli, Milan
46. NHS London Healthy Urban Development Unit (2015) Healthy urban planning checklist. www.healthyurbandevelopment.nhs.uk. Last accessed 12 Nov 2019
47. Forsyth A, Salomon E, Smead L (2017) Creating healthy neighborhoods: evidence-based planning and design strategies. Routledge
48. D'Onofrio R, Trusiani E (2018) Urban Planning for healthy European cities. Springer Brief, Cham, Switzerland

Participatory Local Welfare in Trieste: A Laboratory for Local Welfare Activities

Flavio Paoletti and Alessandro Dario Greco

Abstract "Welfare" is often defined as "the set of public policies aimed at improving the living conditions of citizens". The "welfare state" is today unsustainable considering the number of requests and the resources that countries have at their disposal. The problem must be overcome by changing to a welfare model that is able to regenerate the resources that are already available, giving responsibility to the people who receive help in order to increase the performance of social policy interventions for the benefit of the entire community. As seen in the vast scientific literature in the field of health and healthcare, well-being is not the mere product of individual genetic factors. Wellness also stems from social determinants of health such as education, the home environment, as well as a person's job, income, social network and accessibility to services. Trieste's rather unique demographic distribution makes the city a natural laboratory of what will quite likely be the Italian demographic situation in ten years' time. However, this is not the city's only distinctive trait. In September 2015, the ASUITs [Integrated University Healthcare Companies of Trieste] implemented a systematic set of actions and interventions in order to maximize transparency towards stakeholders and ensure increasingly effective and efficient management. This approach was defined by effective participation at all levels of the organization and oriented to the pursuit of strategic objectives. This initiative gave birth to the "Company Catalogue" of Projects and Participatory Local Welfare Interventions and Actions.

Keywords Participatory local welfare · Social policy · Determinants of health

1 Welfare. A Brief Introduction

Welfare is generally defined as "the set of public policies aimed at improving the living conditions of citizens". Moreover, the expression "welfare state", which came into use in Great Britain following the WWII, is generally translated into Italian as a

F. Paoletti (✉) · A. D. Greco
Azienda Sanitaria Universitaria Giuliano Isontina, Trieste, Italy
e-mail: flavio.paoletti@gmail.com

A. Battisti et al. (eds.), *Urban Health*, Green Energy and Technology,
https://doi.org/10.1007/978-3-030-49446-9_10

Stato Assistenziale (which, however, has a negative nuance) or Stato Sociale, literally meaning "Social State". Unsustainable if we consider the number of requests and resources that the States have at their disposal, this concept must be overcome by passing from a welfare model based nearly exclusively on a State that collects and distributes resources through the tax system and monetary exchange, to a system that can regenerate the resources that are already available. Moreover, the system should also empower the people who receive help, in order to increase the performance of social policy actions for the benefit of the entire community [1].

The reference framework for welfare in Europe was developed in the context of the Health 2020 strategy proposed by the WHO European Region, made up of 53 Member States. This area covers about nine hundred million people living in a wide variety of social, economic, political and cultural contexts. Even if the European Region has certainly the highest human development index among all the WHO [2] Regions many inequalities in health between states and populations persist [3].

The recent WHO health report in Europe [4] states that the main indicators of health—such as infant mortality and general death rates—continue to improve, although significant differences still persist between the different European states. The goals of Health 2020, adopted by the WHO European Regional Committee in 2012, aim to reduce the gap among the health determinants of the 53 states of the European Region by supporting the actions of governments and societies to significantly improve the health and well-being of populations. Furthermore, this strategy is also designed to reduce inequalities, strengthen public health, guarantee health systems focused on the needs of the individual that are universal, fair, sustainable, and of high quality. To this end, two main objectives and four transversal priorities have been identified.

The first two aim to:

- Improve health and reduce social inequalities;
- Strengthen leadership and participatory governance for health.

The four transversal priorities aim to:

- Invest in health through a Life-course approach that works to strengthen each citizen;
- Combat the discomforts of communicable and non-communicable diseases in Europe;
- Strengthen healthcare systems and public health capacities, including readiness and the ability to respond to emergencies;
- Create supportive environments and resilient communities.

In order to monitor the impact of the Health 2020 strategy, a monitoring framework was approved by the WHO European Regional Committee in 2013, divided into areas, objectives, quantifications and core indicators, as shown in Table 1.

This strategy is applied in the new vision of the health variables previously outlined by Dalgren and Whitehead in 1991, emphasizing not only health determinants, but above all, the social determinants. This viewpoint is also found in the vast scientific literature in the field of health and healthcare, which has repeatedly pointed out that

Table 1 Health 2020 monitoring framework

Area	Target	Quantification	Core indicators
Burden of disease and risk factors	Reduce premature mortality in Europe	Reduction of premature mortality	Premature mortality, tobacco use, alcohol consumption, overweight/obesity
		Elimination of vaccine-preventable diseases	Vaccination coverage for measles/rubella and polio
		Reduction of mortality from external causes	Mortality rate from external causes
Healthy people, well-being and determinants	Increase life expectancy in Europe	Increase in life expectancy	Life expectancy at birth
	Reduce inequities in Europe	Reduction in the gaps in health status associated with social determinants	Infant mortality, life expectancy at birth, proportion of children not enrolled in primary school, unemployment rate, (sub)national policy addressing health inequities, GINI coefficient (income distribution)
	Enhance the wellbeing of the European population	To be set	Life satisfaction, social support, population with improved sanitation facilities, GINI coefficient (income distribution) unemployment rate, proportion of children not enrolled in primary school
Processes, governance and health systems	Universal coverage and right to health	Moving towards universal coverage	Private households' out-of-pocket payments on health, vaccination coverage for measles/rubella and polio, total health expenditure
	National targets or goals set by Member States	Establishment of processes for the purpose of setting national targets	Establishment of process for target-setting, national policies aligned with Health 2020

Fig. 1 The main determinants of health—Dahlgren, G. Whitehead, M.: Policies and strategies to promote social equity in health. Background document to WHO—Strategy paper for Europe. Arbetsrapport 2007:14, Institute for Futures Studies

good health is not only the mere product of individual genetic factors (which certainly influence it, albeit marginally), but also affirms the importance of social determinants of health such as education, the home and the work environment, as well as income, social networks and accessibility to services, as shown in Fig. 1.

Based on the classification above, health determinants can be divided into distal and proximal. Distal are those socio-economic factors that influence health, despite the fact that they are not directly connected to the individual's clinical picture. Therefore, we are dealing with education and training, access to the labour market and the economic situation of families (i.e. those general determinants that can explain most health variabilities of populations).

Unhealthy lifestyles—meaning non-health determinants that constitute the main preventable risk factors such as tobacco consumption, obesity, poor diet, lack of physical activity and risky behaviour in alcohol consumption—represent proximal determinants of health as they are directly connected to the onset of a disease and condition its prognosis. In turn, proximal determinants are conditioned by the distal determinants. It is widely recognized that unhealthy lifestyles are not so much the outcome of a free, informed and responsible choice, but rather the search for an adaptation to chronic stress that leads to compensatory behaviour [5].

Several years after the adoption of the Health 2020 strategy, Europe has gone beyond the objectives of annual reduction of 1.5% of premature mortality due to cardiovascular diseases, cancer, diabetes mellitus and chronic respiratory diseases, recently recording an average drop of 2% per year.

Zsuzsanna Jakab, Regional Director of WHO Europe stated: "The latest report on health in Europe shows that most European countries have taken significant steps towards achieving the key objectives set by Health 2020, thus contributing to the achievement of sustainable development goals related to the health of the 2030 agenda; progress, however, is uneven, both within and between countries, between the sexes and between generations, and lifestyle risk factors are an important concern as they can slow down or even reverse life expectancy gains if unchecked".

Moreover, certain numerical gaps among the values of the indicators regarding the social determinants of health (infant mortality, life expectancy at birth, enrolment in primary schools and unemployment) have also decreased, following a positive trend that began in 2010. The main issue remains the consumption of alcohol and tobacco (Europe has the highest rates in the world) and obesity, hindering progress in some countries [4].

Furthermore, the European Union is also committed to correcting the most noteworthy social imbalances. The EU's financial instrument for this purpose is the European Social Fund (ESF), adopted in 1961, whose purpose is to promote the creation of jobs and improve the possibility of employment for workers in order to support professional and geographical mobility.

Financial aid alone can never solve all the problems caused by economic recession or by regional underdevelopment. Above all, the dynamic effects of growth must encourage social progress. This goes hand in hand with legislation that can guarantee a solid set of minimum rights. Some of these rights are enshrined in treaties (e.g. the right of women and men to equal pay for equal work). Others are set out in directives concerning the protection of workers (health and safety at work) and essential safety standards.

The European Council adopted the Community Charter of Basic Social Rights, setting out the rights that all workers in the EU should enjoy: free movement; fair pay; improved working conditions; social protection; the right to form associations and to undertake collective bargaining; the right to vocational training; equal treatment of women and men; worker information, consultation and participation; health protection and safety in the workplace; protection for children, the elderly and the disabled [6].

1.1 The Situation in Italy

The aforementioned inequalities in the state of health also persist within Italy. The geography of health shows a noteworthy difference between the North and South, to the detriment of the latter. Socially-determined inequalities are considered unnecessary and avoidable, due to the fact that they are based on some form of discrimination—as members of a specific group (for example the elderly, women, people who are part of an ethnic group, residents of a specific geographical area), these people are prevented from reaching their health potential [7].

On average, in Italy the levels of health achieved are quite high and growing over time, reflected in the general increase in the well-being of the population. However, in recent years, as a result of the prolonged phase of economic recession that has hit the country, as well as the resulting social imbalances, new challenges have emerged.

Inequalities, not always historically determined, have expanded and new emergencies have arisen. Alongside traditional territorial differentiations, in particular between the Southern and Central-Northern areas of the country, the differentials have transversally affected social groups, generations, old and new citizenship, gender conditions and the different groups and communities of foreign ethnicity living in Italy.

As an answer to part of these problems, the Italian Parliament already approved the law n. 328, or the "Law for the implementation of the integrated system of social interventions and services", based on the principles of subsidiarity, cooperation, effectiveness, efficiency and cost-effectiveness, homogeneity, financial and asset coverage, affirming that "The [Italian] Republic guarantees people and families an integrated system of interventions and social services, promotes interventions to guarantee the quality of life, equal opportunities non-discrimination and rights of citizenship, prevents and eliminates or reduces the conditions of disability of need and individual and family hardship resulting from inadequacy of income, social difficulty and conditions of non-autonomy consistent with Articles 2, 3 and 38 of the Constitution".

These actions must be systematically assessed based on their results in terms of quality, performance effectiveness and gender impact. Furthermore, these verifications must also pay particular attention to the coordination with health and education programs, as well as active training, start-up policies and work reintegration. In addition, these actions must be programmed in such a way as to promote the development of the community's resources at local level through innovative forms of collaboration for the development of self-help interventions, while also encouraging reciprocity among citizens in the context of community living.

Consequently, it is quite clear that we need to rethink the organization of services by calibrating these programs and actions to the emerging and submerged rights and needs of citizens, producing unexpected results. This could lead to the creation of a new type of welfare with significant repercussions on the health of the individual and community, as well as social integration and savings and/or reallocation of social and health resources, towards an effective application of these actions and programs throughout Italy. This is the true goal of Law 328/2000.

However, today's society is too polarized around a scientific and technological belief centred around hospitals that respond only to the needs that are purely clinical. This part of the population suffers from acute pathologies and traumas, or the exacerbation of chronic diseases. The challenge is to refocus aid on objectives that are much closer to the needs of a wider population, reconstructing solidarity, developing the concept of support not only vertically, but above all horizontally, while also widening the governance and planning of players from tertiary sectors. Moreover, these actions must also include associations, social cooperation, self-help and family resources in a context of development of local, municipal and community welfare [8].

This type of structured welfare has the task of incorporating the individual characteristics and resources of users, networks and social and community ties. Needs have therefore changed, giving rise to new needs that will differentiate, requiring a reorganization of the offer and reference paradigms. Services often fail to change at the same speed as demand and the risk of not meeting socio-demographic and epidemiological changes and leaving the rights and needs of the population unsatisfied. The consequences are often confusion and unresolved issues.

The final aim of a new design of services should be the recognition of the rights of the person, albeit increasingly vulnerable and fragile. For the continuation of the promotion of social solidarity, the law specifically underlines the need for involvement and active participation of all local actors: institutions, third-sector, voluntary service, citizens and citizens in single or associated form.

More and more, these changes require a review of the previous organizational systems, which should not concern, albeit essential, solely the legal-juridical aspect. On the other hand, they should aim above all at spreading measurable and assessable "good practices", as well as the use of innovative resources, models, different professional and non-professional roles and new skills.

The OASI 2018 Report also states that the health and social-health needs in Italy are increasing due to social fragmentation. In 2017, about 32% of families were made up of single individuals—about 8.1 million people—of which over half were over the age of 60. The process of social and family fragmentation makes the situation even more complicated. There is an urgency to take on the conditions of fragility, which is even greater if we consider that Italy has the highest ratio in Europe between the over-65 population and the active population (35%), and a persistent demographic crisis (1.34 children per woman) that undermines the basic conditions for the functioning of the current welfare system.

Despite that stated above, Italy's NHS shows solid results, placing Italy among the countries whose health levels are excellent. Life expectancy at birth is 82.8 years (higher than the UK, USA and Germany) and the rate of premature mortality in adult subjects (15–60) is the lowest among Western countries. Moreover, the system is cost-effective, where public expenditure per inhabitant is 50% less when compared to that of European countries with similar population records and statistics, such as Germany. In order to bring the Italian healthcare System closer to the European funding average, at least 10 billion euros should be allocated.

However, today's public debate on the NHS ignores the important results and the real criticalities of this sector, preferring instead to focus on very specific aspects (e.g. obligatory vaccination) or individual malpractice cases. A debate on the evolution of healthcare needs or the realistic policies to be adopted in order to avoid the progressive weakening of the system that might strengthen the collective awareness of the real situation of Italy's NHS is completely absent.

As stated in the 2014 OASI Report, the determinants of the sustainability of the National and Regional Health Service will also derive from possible future policies set in place, where a reduction in the input of economic measures must not result in a reduction in output, and therefore of the ability to satisfy the needs of the population in question.

The system's effectiveness can remain constant or be implemented only if there is a reduction in inappropriate performance, as well as a decrease in healthcare consumerism and a financial adjustment by the National Health Service, at the detriment of reducing the rate of public coverage of health needs in some areas of care.

The need to incorporate social innovation processes within welfare systems also arises from the increasing difficulty of countries with an advanced welfare state to secure resources to meet the growing demand for welfare services [9]. This also rings true in Italy, and the constant increase of the population that necessitates these measures. Moreover, the second half of the twentieth century was defined by the expansion of services offered by public bodies and by "the establishment of large public agencies that employ a large number of professionally trained workers and provide services to a large number of beneficiaries." (ALCOCK P., Editoriale, in Salute e Società, La social innovation nel cambiamento dei sistemi socio-sanitari, anno XIV, n. 1/2015).

The combination of the two aforementioned factors, growth in the demand for public welfare services and a simultaneous compression of resources have generated in politicians and policymakers the need to "Explore new avenues for a change in the system of services offered which reconciles these conflicting dynamics" (ALCOCK P., Editoriale, in Salute e Società, La social innovation nel cambiamento dei sistemi socio-sanitari, anno XIV, n. 1/2015). Therefore, the need to introduce innovation in the way public interventions and services are designed or implemented by paying greater attention to the local context in which they are designed, responding to the particular circumstances and needs of individual users. This occurs in a more specific manner involving the end users in design processes, in a local and participatory approach that contrasts with the standardized approach to the well-being of the population based on the "one-size-fits-all" concept [10].

Based on these viewpoints, we need to rethink the organization of services by calibrating these programs and actions to the emerging and submerged rights and needs of citizens, producing unexpected results. The result would be the development of a new type of welfare with noteworthy repercussions on the health of the individual and community, along with better use and management of social and healthcare resources.

1.2 The Specific Case of Trieste, Italy

The province of Trieste has 234,874 inhabitants, where 204,420 are residents in the municipality of Trieste (ISTAT data 2016), with a population density of 2402 inhabitants per km^2. The study "The Metropolitan City of Trieste—Territorial, Economic, Sociological and Legal Analysis" also highlights that Trieste has the characteristics of a metropolitan city, with a geographical position on an international border that makes the city even more unique [11].

The distribution by age of the population is also interesting, defined by a strong presence of elderly people over 65, who today make up 28% of the city's population (one of the highest percentages in Italy [12]), as shown in the graph in Fig. 2.

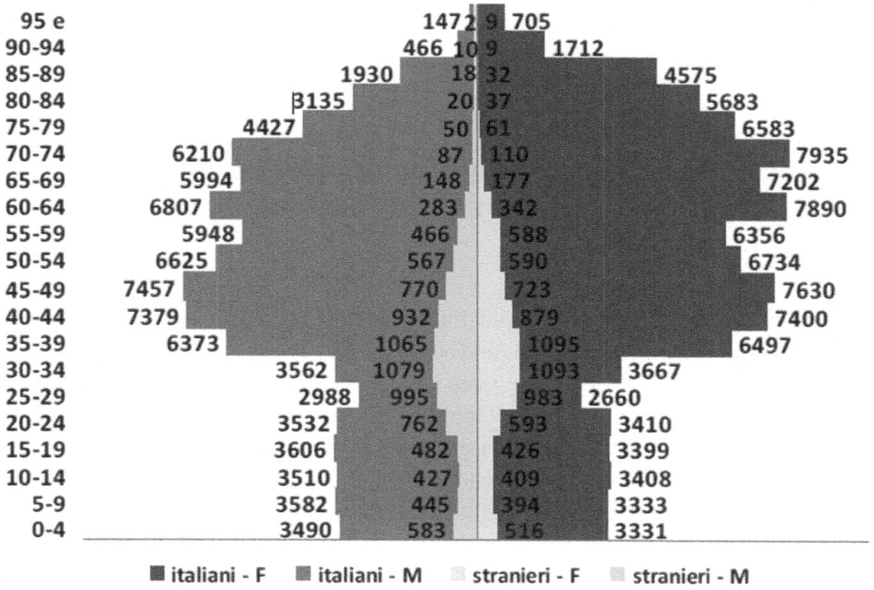

Fig. 2 Pyramid of age population resident in the district 1.2 Trieste, of which foreigners at the center at 31 December 2010 (from Trieste Province Social Policy Observatory elaboration on Istat Demo data). Italians (F/women), Italians (M/men), Foreign residents (F/women), Foreign residents (M/men)

The distinctive demographic distribution in Trieste makes the area a natural testing ground for what will likely be the Italian demographic situation in ten years' time. However, this is not the only unique trait of the city. More and more family units are made up of one or two people, and the noteworthy presence of lonely elderly people is an important characteristic. Out of the 57,414 people over the age of 65, 21,270 live alone (15,860 women and 5410 men). Furthermore, the clear majority of elderly people living alone are over 75 (over 13,000 people). The numbers on the elderly who live alone highlights one of the most important critical points of the Trieste population, which translates into assistance needs and support expressed by the elderly and their families [13].

Furthermore, the role of women has also changed. Both spouses often work, while education and the distribution of family roles have also changed. Separations and divorces are on the increase, conditions of juvenile delinquency and adulthood are also on the rise, there are more drop-outs, especially in peripheral areas of the city, and substance abuse in adolescents and young people is also a growing problem [13].

Within this complicated situation, it is important to intervene with projects that address critical issues pertaining to lifestyles, prevention, nutrition, substance consumption, socialization, education, continuity of care, psycho-physical well-being involving almost all those in a fragile state. In short, we need to act with targeted actions for the aforementioned social determinants of health, as outlined by Dahlgren and Whitehead in 1991 [14].

1.3 ASUITs, Local Welfare Laboratory and the Corporate Catalogue of Participatory Local Welfare Projects and Interventions

As a follow-up to this brief socio-epidemiological analysis, from an organizational point of view, the healthcare services and companies in Trieste context are defined by the rather unique presence of an Integrated University Healthcare Service established in May 2016 through the union of the University Hospital and the Health care service provider (Healthcare Company). This union was one the first of its kind in Italy, seeing the incorporation of a University Hospital within a Healthcare Company. Consequently, there was the need to implement the culture of welfare and the social and health vision in a context where professionals have always dealt with pathology and acute care rather than with transitional care. This also included the development of solidarity networks that enable people to take charge of their own contexts early on in life with an effective reduction in improper hospitalization in urban hospitals.

The newly created ASUITs [Integrated University Healthcare Companies of Trieste] employ around 4500 people who work in territorial and hospital organizations to carry out its activities. The various structures and facilities, in some cases individually and in others in a synergistic manner, carry out numerous projects.

Within such a complex system, which weaves through a dense network of relationships, the fragmentation of projects is a real risk that can undermine the synergy of the interventions and curb the positive effects on the population. Another problem is related to the tracking and monitoring of individual projects, due to the number of projects and their different aims.

In order to counter these weaknesses, in September 2015 the Social and Healthcare Coordination Service (now called the Department of Social and Health Services) began systematic interventions in order to maximize transparency towards stakeholders and ensure increasingly effective and efficient management. This strategy included the effective participation on all levels of the organization and was aimed at the pursuit of strategic objectives. Company representatives for welfare activities were identified by decree of the General Director and a working committee was set up, chaired by the Social and Health Coordinator (now Director of Social and Health Services). At least 2 referees participate in each of the 4 Districts and 3 Departments of ASUITs along with other members of the Directorate of Social and Health Services in order to provide technical support for the definition and optimization of project activities.

The Company Catalogue of Participatory Local Welfare projects and interventions (from here on the term "Company Catalogue" will be used), promoted by the Integrated University Health Service of Trieste (ASUITs), stems from the need to obtain evidence, while also monitoring and assessing all interventions of a social and health nature that ASUITs have promoted. Furthermore, the goal is to improve the quality of the design process of new projects and interventions using the tools of Project Cycle Management.

The idea was developed in 2015 by an initiative of the Social and Health Coordination, today called the Directorate of Social and Health Services, which involved all four Districts and the three Departments of ASUITs (Department of Addiction, Department of Prevention and Department of Mental health).

One of the tangible results that the Management has set itself is to publish the files of all ASUITs projects (therefore also involving hospitals) in the national database called Pro.sa. On a nationwide level, this is a tool for the collection, analysis and publication of projects, interventions and good practices in prevention and health. The goal is that of documenting, sharing and networking the projects of the participating Regions and their results to support activities of healthcare workers, policymakers and stakeholders in the field of health prevention and promotion.

To date, in addition to the three Departments and the four Districts already involved since the initial phases of the experimentation, the Cardiovascular Centre of the Ospedale Maggiore [General Hospital] in Trieste has joined the initiative, therefore beginning the process described above, which includes the involvement of hospital facilities with regard to new ways of approaching their work and services.

The main purpose of the Company Catalogue was to carry out a complete and defined mapping of all social and health interventions and actions carried out by the Districts and Departments of the ASUIT, enhancing the qualitative elements: design logic, objectives, monitoring, operational plan, communication and promotion, detection of innovative elements and best practices.

In turn, the mapping activity has had a dual meaning for the healthcare company. The first is training, given that it has strengthened the design skills for social and healthcare workers involved in the activity. The second aspect regards "certification", as it allowed the formulation of an overall final judgment on the projects and then their evaluation, opening the possibility to push and develop possible improvements.

These records and catalogues also have the strategic objective of maximizing the synergy of the project activities, creating new multi and interdimensional connections in the models of prevention, care, management, continuity of care and rehabilitation. Consequently, there is an increase in the efficiency and effectiveness of interventions to produce new positive effects on the territory, which will allow for the identification of best practices on which to focus and promote their use. Drafting and publication of guidelines with aim the of disseminating results also led to promotional and distribution projects in order to increase the number of beneficiaries reached, consolidating and expanding the networks of partnerships. This also saw a strengthening collaboration with other groups and workers in the third sector. Last but not least, the optimisation of public health spending was reached by strengthening the social fabric in order to prevent unnecessary requests for access to the healthcare system and reduce the demand for inappropriate services.

As a consequence, the Company Catalogue encourages attention to the effectiveness of services and performances, being itself a tool for evaluating the qualitative criteria of the project activities, as well as a useful tool for verifying the consistency between needs analysis, projects and interventions.

Starting in December 2016, the Company Catalogue is also accessible from ASUITs institutional website in order to promote the integrated community welfare experience and actions. In this way, all citizens and institutions can learn about the initiatives carried out by ASUITs, while also having access to all contacts and tools needed to participate.

In addition to mapping the interventions and promoting them, the Company Catalogue aims to become a complete company management tool in the social and healthcare sector, as we will see in the following paragraphs. Moreover, the Catalogue's functions and workings allow for the extrapolation and processing of qualitative and quantitative data, as well as the monitoring of the project costs of each single intervention.

In short, this system allows the user to divide the life span of an Intervention or action into four main stages: Design, Implementation, Monitoring and Evaluation. By design we mean the first "creative" stage in which an intervention or action is formulated so as to respond to certain needs or criticalities. Once the actions to be implemented are brought into focus, the second part is carried out, respecting the set times as much as possible. At the same time, monitoring is usually carried out, a crucial step that serves to identify and resolve any difficulties. Finally, evaluation (both in progress and ex post) is necessary to understand if the intervention is reaching or has achieved its objectives, generally in terms of efficiency, effectiveness, impact and sustainability.

The completion of a project form can be useful in all steps, acting as an easy-to-access information reference. Moreover, the form ensures that the designers of the intervention plan the actions based on the goal of achieving results, forecasting the means, division of tasks and monitoring. Therefore, the first need was to create a model of a user-friendly form that also provided all the necessary information.

The models of the summary form that are presented on the Pro.Sa database were analysed in order to create a form that would respond to the standards that would have been requested by the Regional Documentation Centre for the Promotion of Health—DORS of the Piedmont Region. Following that, there also needed to be the possibility to add the project forms to their "national catalogue". We chose to take inspiration from the working method of the DORS group, due to the fact that the professional skills of the Centre's operators not only refer to the biomedical and psychological culture, but also to document research models, training models, design and evaluation of prevention and health promotion actions, as well as social marketing and publication through information technologies and new media.

Secondly, the tools used in Project Cycle Management (PCM) were studied with the aim of adapting the forms to European and international design standards, in light of a possible expansion of local projects on a cross-border and international scale. The decision to use PCM, which involves the structuring in steps of project preparation and implementation and defines the role of the various people involved for each stage, was made in order to focus on the achievement of the set objectives and identify the true cornerstone of the design, the end users.

Once the first draft of the form was created, it was presented to the group of welfare representatives from healthcare groups and companies, in order to illustrate the contents and compiling methods. Moreover, these meetings were carried out in order to gather opinions and suggestions for the addition, or modification of some items on the form. The revision carried out with the company representatives, in different sessions, allowed us to optimize the usability of the form for the end users. As already mentioned, this form is designed to meet the criteria of the PCM, and contains spaces to transfer the contents of a Logframe, and the complete form, in its current version, can be viewed among the attachments.

At the same time, work was carried out to reproduce the form, previously created with a commonly-used text editor, in Epi Info, a software designed for the community of public health professionals and researchers. This software is used for epidemiological investigations in the field, the development of surveillance, clinical audits, visualization and reporting of data. Epi Info is distributed free of charge and allows you to work in multiple offices and professionals, centralizing data analysis and returning results. Epi Info also allows for the creation of IT modules for easy data recording, database building and data analysis with statistics, maps and graphs.

Upon opening the collection form/card created in Epi Info, the user is presented with 8 different forms to be filled out. They contain exactly the same entries present in the form which can be filled in with a text editor, which can also be analysed with this software in order to extract qualitative and quantitative data.

Using the tabs that can be filed in with a text editor, the project data is collected and then inserted into Epi Info. The compilation of the forms is carried out by the specifically trained professionals in each facility. Archiving in Epi Info is handled by the Directorate of Social and Health Services, with an objective of the 2016 incentive budget, intended for company contacts for welfare and to the District and Departmental directors, regarding the activities of census and insertion of the projects in the collection forms in order to support the participation and commitment of the professionals in this project.

After properly developing the collection form and records in Epi Info, company welfare representatives were asked to select a project from among those promoted by their district or department and to try to complete the text form with the help from an expert when needed. Consequently, the first 7 projects were collected (one for each district and department) and used to test the adequacy of the data sheet made in Epi Info with regard to the text-based form. The results were quite good, highlighting the need for some minor changes only.

After verifying and assessing the suitability of the collection and archiving tools, the Directorate of Social and Healthcare Services organized a corporate training course, ECM accredited. This course was open to all parties interested (including other government bodies such as the Municipality or the Region) in the planning of social and healthcare interventions. The goal was to promote the culture of structured planning aimed at achieving the objectives and to show the collection and record-keeping methods promoted by the Social and Healthcare Management. The corporate training course was attended by around 80 medical professionals and social workers, headed by a professional project-designer who works in Europe and internationally.

At the same time, company welfare representatives were asked to survey all the social and health projects promoted by their own district or department. The census resulted in a total of 47 projects, sometimes carried out across the various different facilities.

In view of the amount of planning brought to light after the census, additional hands-on training was scheduled by the Directorate of Social and Health Services dedicated to company representatives for welfare in order to assist them with an expert during the inclusion of projects in the collection forms. As the projects are inserted into the collection forms, the Social and Health Management will enter the data into the Epi Info software in order to compile and collect statistical data.

1.4 Conclusions

The processing of data in Epi Info has yielded interesting results, providing a fairly clear picture of the total number of interventions and actions that were surveyed and recorded. There are 47 projects recorded in Epi Info. Of these, 44 are completely inserted and 3 are under review, and the statistical calculations considered only the 44 projects that were 100% completed.

Initial data was provided by the number of projects presented by each structure involved in the experiment. The facility that presented the most projects was District n. 2 "Trieste Città Sud" [South Trieste], with as many as 14 projects with a social and health impact out of the total 44, followed by District n. 3 "Trieste est" [East Treiste], which included 8 projects in the catalogue, and 9 if we consider the project presented in partnership with the Municipality of Trieste. Another noteworthy figure is seen in the development phase, which included 44 projects, with 34 under in the design stage, 1 in the drafting phase, and 3 were renewed projects that had already started in previous years, and 6 are today completed.

Moreover, the software provides an interesting piece of data which can be obtained by the software if asked to return the 44 inserted projects classified by a General Objective; in this way it is possible to understand on which of the nine GOs the company is concentrating more at any given time.

Lastly, we can affirm that ASUITs concentrates the majority of its work on social and healthcare actions aimed at promoting good health and healthy lifestyles in Trieste's population. However, data also shows that inclusion and social support are also a priority for the Company, which is actually quite committed to also activating informal social networks in order to support people who suffer from loneliness and or show fragility in a multi-dimensional manner.

References

1. Verso un welfare generativo - da costo a investimento, Fondazione E. Zancan (2013)
2. Africa, Americas, Eastern Mediterranean, Europe, Southeast Asia and the Western Pacific

3. World Health Organization (2012) Addressing the social determinants of health: the urban dimension and the role of local government. World Health Organization, London
4. World Health Organization (2018) The European health report 2018. More than numbers—evidence for all. World Health Organization, Copenhagen
5. Le dimensioni della salute in Italia (2015) Determinanti sociali, politiche sanitarie e differenze territoriali. Istituto Nazionale di Statistica, Roma [The dimensions of health in Italy—Social determinants, health policies and territorial differences, National Institute of Statistics, Rome (2015)]
6. Fontaine P (2010) L'Europa in 12 lezioni. Bruxelles [Fontaine P.: Europe in 12 lessons, Bruxelles (2010)]
7. Le dimensioni della salute in Italia (2015) Determinanti sociali, politiche sanitarie e differenze territoriali, Istituto Nazionale di Statistica, Roma [Aspects of health in Italy—Social determinants, health policies and territorial differences, National Institute of Statistics, Rome (2015)]
8. Rotelli F (eds) (2004) Nodi, Trieste
9. Alcock P (2015) Editoriale, in Salute e Società, La social innovation nel cambiamento dei sistemi socio-sanitari, anno XIV, n. 1/2015 [Alcock P.: Editorial, in Health and Society, Social innovation in the change of social and health systems, year XIV, n. 1/2015]
10. Alcock P (2015) Editoriale, in Salute e Società, La social innovation nel cambiamento dei sistemi socio-sanitari, anno XIV, n. 1/2015 [Alcock P., Editorial, in Health and Society, Social innovation in the change of social and health systems, year XIV, n. 1/2015]
11. Carrosio G, Cesa M, Ciuffarin I, Cozzi A, Danielis R, Di Biagi P, Faraguna P, Gambini F, Giangaspero P, Marcon C, Marin A, Osti G, Rotaris L (2015) La città metropolitana di Trieste. Analisi territoriale, economica, sociologica, giuridica, Trieste, EUT Edizioni Università di Trieste, Trieste
12. ISTAT (2016) Rapporto Annuale 2016, Istituto Nazionale di Statistica, Roma [ISTAT, Annual Report 2016, National Statistics Institute, Rome (2016)]
13. Comune Di Trieste (2012) Piano di Zona 2013–2015—Ambito 1.2 Trieste, Comune di Trieste [Municipality Of Trieste, Zoning Plan 2013-2015—Area 1.2 Trieste, Municipality of Trieste, Trieste (2012)]
14. Dahlgren G, Whitehead M (1991) Policies and strategies to promote social equity in health. Institute for Futures Studies, Stockholm

Trieste's Microareas for Equity

Flavio Paoletti

Abstract "Micro-areas" arose from the project entitled "microwin-microareas", a project aimed at developing community welfare starting in 2005 by the Healthcare Services Company n. 1 "Triestina". The project includes the collaboration of the municipal area, of the territorial company for residential construction and housing (ATER) and of other social and healthcare facilities. The micro-area is a physically aggregated area (district, small municipality, cluster of houses) which includes between 500 and 2500 inhabitants, defined by ATER blocks of flats. From the point of view of the organizational analysis we can also define a "magnifying glass" focused on about 5% of the population of Trieste. Each micro-area is managed by a full-time nurse with the appropriate skills. The nurse's main role is to analyse the life context of the person, carrying out a general assessment of the person and their family. Moreover, this role works to identify the rights and needs not met, priorities for intervention, the institutional and innovative resources needed, as well as the different roles to be involved in the process of taking on social and health care.

Keywords Community welfare · Equity · Micro-area

1 Introduction

In order to respond to the new vision of healthcare, the ASS1 immediately built important partnerships aimed at developing participatory local welfare and high social and health integration.

Specifically, the project "microwin-microaree" [Microwin-Microareas], was conceived within the international laboratory win-welfare innovations to develop community welfare. The laboratory's first experiments were promoted in 2005 by the «Triestina» Health Services Company 1, through the identification of micro-areas. From the beginning, these projects have supported a collaboration among city government, the territorial company for residential construction and housing (ATER)

F. Paoletti (✉)
Azienda Sanitaria Universitaria Giuliano Isontina, Trieste, Italy
e-mail: flavio.paoletti@gmail.com

A. Battisti et al. (eds.), *Urban Health*, Green Energy and Technology,
https://doi.org/10.1007/978-3-030-49446-9_11

and other social and healthcare areas. Moreover, the laboratory also involves large companies and businesses, voluntary-work associations and active citizens from the territory.

This local action was initiated within nine quantitatively defined socio-demographic contexts, territorially delimited, which proactively intervene for the entire resident population and not only on that part of citizenship that presents specific health problems. The "micro-area" is a physically aggregated area (district, small municipality, cluster of houses) which includes between 500 and 2500 inhabitants, characterized by ATER blocks of flats. With regard to organizational analysis, we can also define it as a "magnifying glass" focused on about 5% of the population of Trieste.

The experiment's primary aim is the promotion of health and the increase in well-being within these delimited, often degraded areas. These were chosen on the basis of heterogeneous criteria, with a prevalence for areas with public housing and a minimum level of historical and "local" identity. Through this project, we try to combine the institutional mandate of a healthcare company with the person as an active protagonist in his or her own health project, capable of generating new resources and social benefits. The aim is that of real experimentation of integrated welfare and above all an effective participation of the different subjects in the identified territory: inhabitants, representatives of active citizenship, healthcare operators, as well as administrators and politicians.

The areas involved in the first experimentation are divided between the four health districts: Gretta (district 1), Città Vecchia, Ponziana and Vaticano (district 2), Giarizzole, Grego and Valmaura (district 3), Melara and San Giovanni (district 4).

This organizational and management methodology focuses on:

- Local action, as measured within a specific territorial context;
- Multiple action, since all the subjects active in that particular territory are involved and because the entire company participates and contributes to the experimentation;
- Global action, because through the rigorous inter-sectoriality of the interventions, the goal is to reach all the determinants of the health status of the population (social and health).

Micro-area work must strengthen and enhance the community by generating new health potentials while also reducing the institutional commitment of economic resources. A unique objective is certainly that of the direct knowledge of the inhabitants from a specific micro-area, especially those most at risk and not well-noted to the services. This highlights the proactive function of the institutions and in particular how healthcare that goes from being "waiting medicine" to one of initiative, generating a social resource. In order for the project to be implemented, the following actions were carried out:

- Appointment of micro-area representative, dedicated full-time to the project;
- Identification of the ATER apartments as physical locations of the micro-area also through spaces self-managed by the inhabitants for all those activities that fall within the construction of «active and participatory community»;
- Drafting of the maps, routes, premises and aggregation points of the individual micro-areas;
- Creation of the files and the documentation, shared by all the micro-area representatives and the various professionals of the Healthcare Company involved, as a useful tool for collecting information deriving from the direct knowledge of the inhabitants;
- Defined coordination meetings at a district and management level.

In order to measure the results, ten actions were identified as key aspects to be monitored during these three years of experimentation:

(1) Achieve maximum knowledge concerning the health problems of people residing in micro-areas;
(2) Optimize the interventions for home-living, in order to obtain all the necessary assistance (and counter institutionalization);
(3) Increase appropriate use of pharmaceutical drugs;
(4) Increase the appropriateness of diagnostic services;
(5) Increase the appropriateness for therapeutic services (curative and rehabilitative);
(6) Promote self-help and hetero-help initiatives by non-professionals (building communities);
(7) Promote the collaboration of organizations, associations and profit and non-profit organizations to improve the well-being of the reference population (mapping and development);
(8) Achieve an optimal coordination between different services that act on the same individual or the family;
(9) Promote equity in access to benefits (more quality for more vulnerable citizens);
(10) Raise the level of quality of daily life of people of higher fragility (for an active and independent life).

After this first experimental phase, the micro-areas increased in number. Once only experimental, they became stable services in the district offer and in 2010 they were connected to the simple departmental nursing service, directed by a nursing manager.

Each micro-area is managed by a nursing representative, (in one case also a physiotherapist and an administrative representative who graduated in sociology), who works full-time and has adequate skills.

The role of the representative is only rarely related to clinical-healthcare assistance. In few cases does the representative provide health services in the strict sense (blood samples, medications, etc.). Their main role is to analyse the living situation of the person, carrying out a general assessment of the person and his/her family. This work includes: identifying any rights and needs left unmet; priorities for intervention; the institutional and innovative resources needed; the different roles to be involved in the process of taking on social and health care; and, identifying the most appropriate indicators in order to then properly measure the results of the interventions made.

The representative plays a very different role from the nurses, who dedicate their work to home care and move within a Chronic Care Model calibrated more on the high sectors of the pyramid through models of disease management and case management.

Precisely due to the "unconventional" skills, attitudes and approaches that are required, expertise that not everyone may have developed, a specific job description was developed for the micro-area representative.

Job description of the micro-area representative;
Expected skills;
Community development and inclusion area, expertise in and the ability to:

- implement effective and adequate methods of communication and listening;
- establish adequate relationships with collaborators;
- establish adequate relations with the inhabitants of the community;
- motivate;
- delegate;
- foster autonomy;
- read the context and systemic vision;
- implement the problem-solving process;
- plan and plan;
- work in a team;
- mediate and negotiate;
- record-keeping;
- decision-making;
- use the integration;
- convene and manage work meetings;
- implement creative and innovative projects.

Key activity description.
Organization area:

- identification of organizational methods to meet the health needs of the community in a proactive and integrated manner;
- planning and planning activities;
- organizational coordination of activities;
- coordination and liaison with district and non-district services for the integration and approach of institutions to the needs of the population;
- management of assigned economic, structural and instrumental resources;
- management of the procurement and maintenance of goods;
- promotion of interventions aimed at developing and maintaining the decorum of the urban context of the reference context;

- organization of space and logistics;
- promotion of interventions to guarantee the safety of living, working and social environments;
- elaboration of monitoring reports and verification of results.

Management and development of collaborators and work groups:

- assessment of the skills and attitudes of Micro-area employees (volunteers from the national and civil service; volunteer associations; community volunteers; people in the stock exchange; public utility workers; third sector operators, type B and A co-ops);
- organizational coordination of the activities of Micro-area employees;
- assignment of objectives and activities related to the abilities and potential of the collaborator;
- monitoring and evaluation of the activities carried out;
- development of a good organizational climate;
- promotion of teamwork;
- administrative-bureaucratic management related to the economic area of the collaborator/volunteer/trainee;
- promotion of training and updating of employees.

Community development and inclusion area:

- planning of home interventions and in life contexts (home-living);
- activation of the network of services and convocation of multidisciplinary teams for disadvantaged situations;
- definition of personalized projects and home assessment in situations of fragility;
- periodic implementation of projects for the knowledge of community residents;
- development of the citizen's abilities in managing his health project by orienting care processes according to criteria of quality, efficiency and effectiveness;
- contrasting the institutionalization of elderly people with disabilities and minors;
- activation of integrated networks and communities to support the most fragile people;
- use of the Health Budget tool in favour of fragile residents;
- promotion of continuity of care;
- organization of health promotion and social inclusion initiatives and events.

Proficiency:

- use of computer and audio-visual technology;
- use of communication and relationship techniques;
- use of techniques and tools for the development of group work.

Specific knowledge:

- group management theories, team work, leadership, motivation;
- organizational models and innovative organizational tools in the field of community health;
- theories of design of the training process;
- economic reporting methods;
- communication theories and techniques;
- theories and techniques of management and development of human resources;
- elements of community epidemiology.

Titles and qualifications:

- all the professions present in the Company, after evaluation of the curriculum and post-basic training in community health planning and management

2 Activity

The activities that are organized and carried out within the micro-areas are aimed at orienting and supporting the exercise of health and citizenship rights by residents. These can be divided into four main areas of intervention/action:

1. Knowledge of all persons residing in the MA starting from those with the most relevant health problems;
2. Optimization of interventions for the permanence of people in their own homes to counter institutionalization and improper hospitalization;
3. Actions aimed at fostering collaboration between different institutions interact with the same individual and the same territory, through the active participation of the inhabitants;
4. Active and participatory community [1].

The activities carried out may be aimed at the entire resident population or at certain demographic groups, such as children, adults, the elderly, disabled or groups identified by specific factors, as well as individuals.

The aforesaid are mainly activities aimed at prevention and health promotion. As already illustrated, these actions are aimed at affecting social and health determinants through a set of synergistic and coherent actions whose impact focuses on health determinants such as: health, education, living environment, work, active participation in local democracy.

The goal of the program activities is to concretise the principles and declarations contained in national laws and international agreements. Therefore, these activities are based on the Essential Levels of Assistance (ELAs, or LEA in Italian) [2], through the National Health Service and public resources, that ensure the provision of social and health services aimed at collective prevention of public health, while also protecting the health of communities against environmental risks and correlated lifestyles [3] (Table 1).

Table 1 ELA (LEA in Italian) Section F, Surveillance and prevention of chronic diseases, including the promotion of healthy lifestyles and organized screening programs; nutritional surveillance and prevention (*Source* DPCM [2])

No.	Programs/activities	Program components	Assessment
	Cooperation of health systems with other institutions, with organizations and institutions of the community, for the implementation of inter-sectoral programs with the involvement of citizens, according to the principles of the National Gaining Health Program (DPCM 4.5.2007)	Community health profile Availability and use of information from current surveillance systems (infectious diseases, chronic diseases and road accidents, domestic and accident, lifestyle, health perception, use of health services), from surveys involving the community, in order to: – analyse the needs of the population – identify the risks of the population and the environment – assess the health impact of health, environmental and social interventions Promotion of awareness and participation Communication of data deriving from health profiles to institutional interlocutors, social organizations and associations, in order to promote health value in all regulation policies and instruments and to support the reorientation of the offer in compliance with the health needs of the community (advocacy) Communication of data deriving from health profiles to citizens in order to promote participation in health choices and to strengthen individuals in adopting healthy lifestyles (empowerment)	Development of health profile Report on the state of health of the community and on priority health problems Information and communication to institutions, citizens and healthcare professionals
		Promotion of synergies with other parties, building alliances and partnerships for health	

(continued)

Table 1 (continued)

No.	Programs/activities	Program components	Assessment
		Promotion of alliances between institutional, social, entrepreneurial and professional subjects to agree actions in support of health policies in order to promote well-being in all age groups	Activation of intersectoral healthcare/health processes in all policies
		Technical scientific contribution to health promotion Support for the identification of solutions to priority health problems, based on scientific evidence	Identification and provision of the most effective health promotion programs
F2	Surveillance of risk factors for chronic diseases and lifestyles in the population	Detection, analysis, communication and use for programmatic and evaluation purposes of information on risk factors for chronic diseases and lifestyles	Information and communication to institutions, citizens and health professionals also through structured reports
		Surveillance of temporal and spatial trends of the phenomenon to be prevented/contrasted and of related determinants	
F3	Prevention of the most epidemiologically relevant chronic diseases, promotion of healthy behaviour, according to priorities and indications agreed at national level	Programming, implementation and evaluation of interventions aimed at identifying individual risk conditions for MCNTs (also through analytical tests) and at the address towards an adequate take-over	Programming, activation and evaluation of public health interventions aimed at the prevention of MCNTs
F4	Prevention and fight against tobacco, alcohol consumption	Development by "setting" (school environment, work environment, community) of prevention programs for initiation and promotion of shared cessation between health and social-health services and educational institutions and between health and social-health services and "employers" Informative-educational campaigns aimed at the general population and/or specific targets Promotion of counselling by health professionals Monitoring compliance with the smoking ban Programs to promote alcohol-free driving also through mass media campaign	Activation of cross-sectoral programs for the prevention of risk factors Information on health risks Individual counselling offer

(continued)

Table 1 (continued)

No.	Programs/activities	Program components	Assessment
F5	Promotion of physical activity and health protection of physical activity	Clinical evaluation including examination and diagnostic and instrumental assessments, based on the protocols defined at national level, aimed at suitability for competitive sports for minors and people with disabilities and for non-competitive sports in schools Promotion and implementation of programs aimed at increasing the practice of physical activity in the general population and in groups at risk, promoting the development of opportunities and support from the local community Development by "setting" (school environment, work environment, community) of physical activity promotion programs shared between health and social-health services, educational institutions, "employers" Promotion of counselling on physical activity by health professionals Informative-educational campaigns aimed at the general population and/or specific targets Prevention and anti-doping programs Promotion of structured exercise programs for people at risk	Activation of intersectoral programs Information and communication to citizens and operators Individual counselling offer Issue of a certificate of suitability for non-competitive sports at the request of schools Issuing of a certificate of suitability for competitive sports for minors and people with disabilities
F6	Promotion of a healthy diet to promote healthy lifestyles	Promotion and implementation of programs aimed at encouraging the adoption of correct eating habits in the general population and in groups at risk and for " setting "(School environment, work environment, community, health facilities) shared between health and social care services, educational institutions," employers" Evaluation of the nutritional adequacy of the menus offered also in relation to specific dietary needs.	Activation of cross-sectoral programs for the prevention of risk factors Information and communication to citizens and operators Offer of individual counselling Support to institutions and institutions in the preparation of collective catering menus

(continued)

Table 1 (continued)

No.	Programs/activities	Program components	Assessment
		Interventions on tender specifications to improve nutritional quality	
		Informative-educational campaigns aimed at the general population and/or specific targets	
		Promotion of counselling on proper nutrition and by health professionals	
F7	Promotion, protection and support of breastfeeding and correct complementary nutrition	Training of health personnel on promotion, protection and support activities of breastfeeding, consistent with national guidelines	Offer of individual counselling Information and communication to citizens and operators
		Informative-educational campaigns aimed at specific population targets, such as pregnant/lactating women	
		Promotion of counselling by health professionals	
F8	Oncological screening defined by the State-Regions Agreement of March 23, 2005 and the National Prevention Plan for 2014–2018	Active call and carrying out of screening tests and in-depth study and therapy for the entire resident and domiciled target population	Information on health benefits deriving from adherence to the screening programs Active call and first and second level screening tests for target populations Send to another assistance setting for diagnostic-therapeutic management in relation to neoplastic pathology
		Periodicity and technical characteristics are defined nationally by the following acts:	
		– Screening for breast cancer: Recommendations of the Ministry of Health prepared in implementation of the art. 2 bis of Law 138/2004 and of the National Prevention Plan 2014–2018	
		– Screening for colorectal cancer: Recommendations of the Ministry of Health prepared for the implementation of art. 2 bis of Law 138/2004 and of the National Prevention Plan 2014–2018	

(continued)

Table 1 (continued)

No.	Programs/activities	Program components	Assessment
		– Screening for the cervical-carcinoma: guidelines drawn up in implementation of the National Prevention Plan 2014–2018 and the Ministerial Decree 5/8/11	
		Monitoring of the extension and acceptance of programs and assessments of the quality of the processes and the impact on the health of the population, also through the creation and management of information systems based on individual records	
		Involvement of risk groups and socially disadvantaged groups	
		Promotion of conscious participation and social reporting	
		Implementation and management of information systems based on individual medical records	
F9	Addiction prevention	Educational information campaigns aimed at the general population and/or specific targets, aimed at the knowledge of addiction risks	Activation of cross-sectoral programs for the prevention of addiction risk and to foster personal skills
		Development by setting (school environment, work environment, community) of health promotion programs aimed at prevention of addictions	

The development of these activities is founded on the knowledge of the resident population, a fundamental requirement in order to be able to plan and implement activities consistent with the context in which they are implemented. The knowledge and understanding of the population are not limited to a mere census. On the other hand, there is an in-depth study of the social, economic, health and life context of individual citizens, especially those with complex needs. The role of knowledge has the dual utility of acquiring fundamental information for the development and programming of micro-area activities and to make the target area known and recognized for the purpose of increasing the number of people who use the services offered by the micro-area and at the same time it contributes to the delivery of these services.

A possible classification of the activities carried out within the micro-areas is that which follows.

1. **Activities aimed primarily at health promotion, mainly focusing on health determinants**

   a. Orientation, support, help, individual or family support to facilitate access to social and health services and for the fulfilment of procedures related to housing, work and income support (facilitating relations with Offices and Agencies, help desk work, project in the city, work grants, public utility work or socially useful → aimed at encouraging the exercise of the right of citizenship.
   b. Accompanying and support at school, support for schooling also for children with special educational needs, specific learning disabilities (relationships with teachers and with educational institutions, after-school activities) → aimed at contributing to the respect of the right to education and training of minors.
   c. Organization of recreational, cultural, group, community and intergenerational activities (library, reading and poetry, theatre and cinema, singing and music, games of yesterday and today, trips, visits to exhibitions, parties and special events, language courses, computer and mobile use courses, courses for the creation of artistic objects) involving asylum seekers and refugees in the activities of the convention with ICS (Italian Solidarity Consortium) → aimed at developing community empowerment and promoting intergenerational and inter-ethnic knowledge and coexistence.
   d. Collection and distribution of unsold food (food bank), collection and distribution of toys, clothes, furniture, household appliances, household appliances and other materials, courses for the reuse of recycled material → aimed at optimizing the use of collective resources

2. **Activities mainly aimed at primary prevention to reduce the occurrence of diseases or injuries**

   a. Availability of Micro-area headquarters and/or other areas of the neighbourhood for group and community activities, home visits and individual meetings, self-help groups (anxiety, violence, …) → aimed at countering isolation and loneliness.

b. Organizations of meetings and lectures, to deal with topics related to lifestyles and health risk factors, also in collaboration with other corporate structures, such as the Departments of Prevention, Mental Health, Addictions and Voluntary Associations, offer of opportunities for recreational, physical and even intergenerational sports (games and sports for children and adolescents, gentle gymnastics, dancing, walks, group walking project, self-defence courses, …), cooking classes, care of the social garden, preparation and consumption of meals (socializing breakfasts and lunches) → aimed at encouraging the adoption of sustainable healthy lifestyles and, at the same time, socialization.
c. Awareness of individuals, families and the community also through the organization of dedicated meetings → aimed at supporting vaccination campaigns.

3. **Activities aimed primarily at secondary prevention to diagnose a disease early**

   a. Awareness of individuals, families and the community also through the organization of dedicated meetings → aimed at improving adherence to regional screening

4. **Activities aimed primarily at tertiary prevention to avoid the onset of complications or relapses resulting from a disease and/or quaternary prevention to avoid the effects of hyper-medicalisation**

   a. Organization of support and help for the performance of daily life activities at home and away from home, Promotion of assisted living and building of solidary condominiums, Information, guidance and support for Care Givers (Alzheimer Group, …) → aimed at encouraging fragile people to stay at home, avoiding institutionalization
   b. Health point, support, help and monitoring of adherence to dietary, therapeutic and rehabilitative prescriptions, facilitating relations with the General Practitioner, with district and health services in general (Wellness Program for people with heart disease, diabetes, COPD, management of the health notebook for people over 75 …) → aimed at contributing to the implementation of the care project and the integrated management [4]

In order to implement the Micro-area Habitat Program, in addition to the resources used by the Healthcare Company, the resources made available by the Municipality of Trieste, the Municipality of Muggia and the Territorial Residential Building Company (ATER) are also used to sanction the collaboration among these three bodies. The teamwork is important in order to maintain their active collaboration in the realization of projects and integrated interventions for community development, health promotion, improvement of the quality of life and housing conditions in some areas of the city, a protocol agreement was signed. The latest version is from 2018.

The protocol outlines the resources, aims and commitments of each Body and tracks the organizational and management aspects useful to guarantee the correct functioning of the Program which, for its implementation, envisages two bodies for management purposes:

1. **The Territorial Technical Group (GTT in Italian)**, one for each micro-area and made up of employees and contractors of the services of the three public bodies present in the territory. The GTT meets monthly with the aim of designing, organizing, documenting and verifying the interventions of competence of each institution and subject, favouring the connection between the various services that deal with residents in the area of competence. An open GTT is held on a quarterly basis and accepts the request for participation of representatives of the Circumscription, voluntary associations, neighbourhood committees and other public and/or private groups.
2. **The Coordinating Committee involved**, made up of a representative for each of the three bodies, has the function of identifying the general guidelines, the objectives to be pursued annually and the resources available. The committee meets every six months or as a result from pertinent request from one of the members.

A brief outline of the health status of the AAS1 micro-areas is given below by comparison with the resident population in the province of Trieste 10 years after the start of the trial. In particular, through the analysis of the demographic structure indices and the exemptions, we want to highlight with regard to the micro-areas and the weight in terms of both health, social and health, economic and social, as well as the complexity of the necessary and partly already put into action field, both in view of wanting to intervene on health non-health determinants, within and based on a logic of inclusion and equity of access and response to health needs.

From a demographic point of view, if it is true that the population of Trieste has decreased by 2.3% in 10 years, the micro-area population has decreased to an even greater extent: 12%. The main demographic indicators highlight a particularly bleak profile for micro-areas, starting from the disadvantage of AAS1 in comparison with regional and national reference values. The age index in micro-area, as a matter of fact, is more than double that of the FVG (Table 2).

If the exemptions of persons residing in the province of Trieste are then compared with the people residing in the 9 micro-areas from which the experimentation started in 2005, the resulting picture is quite clear. Firstly, the absolute values of the exemptions grouped by type were collected and, subsequently, the rate per 10,000 inhabitants was also calculated in order to highlight the comparison between AAS1 and

Table 2 Indices of micro-area demographic structure/AAS1/FVG

Demographic structure indices—2013	Micro-area	AAS1	Friuli-Venezia Giulia
index of youth addiction/dependency	14.24	18 (96%)	20.14
Ind. Dip. senile (%)	58.14	46.2	38.63
Addiction/dependency ratio	72.38	65.16	58.77
Age index	408.32	243.6	191.81

Table 3 Rate per 10,000 inhabitants calculated on the weighted population

Exemption type	AAS1	Total micro area
Pathology	3501	4670
Age	1900	2527
Disability	617	1.065
Income	356	857
Pregnancy	104	108
Disease, Rare	81	84
TOTAL	6560	9311

micro-areas. The rates are calculated using the population weighted according to the funding criteria, i.e. using the ministerial measurements, in order to make the comparison as correct as possible (Table 3).

For a more clear-cut comparison, the project built the ratio between the rate per 10,000 inhabitants of the micro-areas calculated with respect to the value of AAS1.

The types of exemptions taken into consideration were: pathology, age, invalidity, income, pregnancy and rare diseases. The main result is that the total number of micro-area exemptions is in a ratio of 1.42 compared to the total for 10,000 inhabitants of AAS1. This means that the total number of exemptions for the same population is 42% greater.The ratio of almost 2 and a half times of income exemptions is notable (2.40), as well as the exemptions for pathology and age are 1.33 times more frequent in the micro-area. Disability is also present in a much higher ratio, three-quarters higher (1.73).

Table 4 is a brief list of the exemptions that occur most frequently in micro-areas when compared with the general urban context.

Table 4 Report of the exemption rate of micro-areas compared to AAS1 of the most widespread exemptions

Code	Exemption	Frequency index compared to the urban context
014	Drug addiction and alcoholism	3.32
E03	Social pension holder	2.26
E02	Unemployed	2.13
S57	100% civilian disabled	2.03
L04	Occupational accident or illness	1.92
013	Diabetes	1.47
P 15	Hypertonia	1.39
031A	Arterial hypertension without organ damage	1.16
031	Arterial hypertension with organ damage	1.15
024	Chronic respiratory failure	2.39

3 The Current Situation

Upon completion of the experimental stage, the number of micro-areas rose. In 2019, there are as many as 17 active micro-areas, involving around 20,000 residents in their activities [5]. This work has turned from experimental into a stable service based on the provision and offer of district services.

Over the years, the services of the three partners involved have developed a working methodology based on operational and integrated planning. Their thinking is no longer in terms of intervention on the individual, but on the development of the entire community. Consequently, we have begun to analyse the capacity to change public services and on the strategies for facing the citizens' questions and demands.

A fundamental aspect of the work carried out within the micro-areas is the relationship that is created and strengthened between social-healthcare workers and citizens.

Several years after experimentation and implementation, there is a greater need to demonstrate the social and health-related effectiveness of the Habitat Micro-area program through objective and tangible results based on the health and development of social capital produced by the project.

References

1. The Trieste Microareas Habitat Program (2018) Planning and operational guidelines, document edited by the Directorate of Social and Health Services of ASUITs, Trieste [Il Programma Habitat Microaree Trieste (2018) Linee di indirizzo progettuali e operative, documento a cura della Direzione dei Servizi Sociosanitari di ASUITs]
2. Decree of the President of the Council of Ministers (2017, 12 January) Definition and updating of the essential levels of assistance, referred to in Article 1, paragraph 7, of the Legislative Decree of 30 December 1992, n. 502
3. Ibid.
4. The Trieste Microareas Habitat Program (2018) Planning and operational guidelines, document edited by the Directorate of Social and Health Services of ASUITs, Trieste
5. Fifteen (15) in the territory of the Municipality of Trieste and two (2) in the territory of the Municipality of Muggia

Micro-areas 10 Years Later. A Qualitative and Quantitative Assessment of Health Outcomes

Flavio Paoletti

Abstract In 2016, 10 years after the inclusion of the "Habitat Micro-areas" program in the Zone Plans (PDZ) Program agreements, the ASUITs began the process for the realisation of an initial quantitative research on health outcomes and results produced by the micro-area system, as well as a second qualitative research project. The latter is useful to report the development of the social capital and the health and wellness conditions reached in the joint action carried out by ASUITs, Municipal Social Services and the ATER Residential Housing Companies. Both research projects were entrusted to groups outside the Micro-area Habitat Protocol: for the research called "Evaluation of the Health Effectiveness of the MICROAREA Project (MA)" the Department of Medical and Biological Sciences of the University of Udine was chosen; for the second research project, entitled "Analysis of the effects on health of the social capital generated by the intervention in micro-areas", the Department of Political Culture and Society of the University of Turin were selected. Quantitative research highlighted the difference in the use of and access to the Regional Health System between Micro-area residents and non-residents in Micro-area, showing how the healthcare needs within the micro-areas are provided for more effectively. Importantly, qualitative research also highlighted how micro-area actions have increased the level and quality of social capital that is useful to the population's healthcare. The aspect concerns the aid received in order to address problems, including those who lack a family absence, as well as help offered to others.

Keywords Social capital · Health effectiveness · Qualitative and quantitative research

1 Introduction

In 2016, 10 years after the inclusion of the "Habitat Micro-areas" program in the Zone Plans Program (under the acronym in Italian *PDZ*) agreements, the ASUITs

---

F. Paoletti (✉)
Azienda Sanitaria Universitaria Giuliano Isontina, Trieste, Italy
e-mail: Flavio.paoletti@gmail.com

A. Battisti et al. (eds.), *Urban Health*, Green Energy and Technology,
https://doi.org/10.1007/978-3-030-49446-9_12

initiated the process necessary to implement what was agreed upon in 2016 Annual Implementation Plan referring to the 2016 PDZ. This referred to the development of a first quantitative research project focusing on the health results produced by the micro-area system, as well as start of a second qualitative research project for the development of the social capital and the health and wellness conditions reached in the actions carried out by ASUITs, Social Services of the municipal areas, and ATER (Residential Construction and Housing).

In order to avoid internal bias, this research work was entrusted to entities that are entirely external to those responsible for the Micro-Habitat Protocol. Consequently, for the research entitled "Evaluation of the Health Effectiveness of the MICROAREA Project (MA)" the Department of Medical and Biological Sciences of the University of Udine was selected. This decision was made in light of the epidemiological research group with national and international experience in etiological studies and in the quantitative evaluation of the effectiveness of health interventions that work in this department. Moreover, there are professional skills in the data management of the main regional databases as well as in-depth knowledge in carrying out multivariate and multilevel analysis, and for this reason Professor Fabio Barbone was chosen as the coordinator of the research group. For the second research project, entitled "Analysis of the effects on health of social capital generated by the intervention in micro-areas", the Department of Political Culture and Society of the University of Turin was selected. Scientific supervision of the research was entrusted to Professor Giuseppe Costa and scientific coordination to Professor Roberto Di Monaco, given their national and international experience in social policy studies and in assessing the social impact of public policies.

The majority of the research was financed by the ASUITs, with the contribution of the Municipality of Trieste, the ATER and the Municipality of Muggia.

2 Evaluation of the Health Effectiveness of the Micro-area Project (MA)

The main goal of the research work was to assess the efficacy of the Micro-area project through a historical epidemiological study of the groups.

Starting from the basic assumption that the Micro-area project proves effective if it intercepts the residents' healthcare needs by promoting adherence to prevention, diagnostic-therapeutic and structured care pathways, the proper management of a person's health determines, as an epiphenomenon, a more rational use of the Healthcare System. Access to the Healthcare System—a measurable parameter—was chosen as a useful tool for the evaluation and assessment of the efficacy and success of the Micro-area Project.

Therefore, two comparable groupings were formed by pairing residents in Micro-area (MA Group) with non-residents in the Micro-area (NMA Group) through the propensity score calculated by applying the following variables:

- Gender;
- Deprivation index 2001 according to Caranci;
- Age at the beginning (01/01/2006) of the follow-up;
- Charlson Index;
- Hypertension drugs;
- Diabetes drugs;
- Ulcer drugs.

The study began on 01/01/2006 and was completed on 31/12/2018 (start and end follow-up dates). In order to reduce misclassification, we excluded those people who transferred their residence from the Micro-area to a non-Micro-area area and vice versa, between the start and end dates of the project. Therefore, only permanent residents were taken into consideration.

3 First Results

A comparative study on the two samples created according to the parameters above—residents in micro-areas (made up of 7804 individuals) and non-resident in micro-areas (10,238 individuals)—showed that there is a difference in access to the Regional Healthcare System (under the acronym in Italian SSR) between the two samples.

As far as ordinary admissions for all causes are concerned, women were hospitalised at a lower rate (−8%). By stratifying the hospitalizations for a specific block of diagnosis, interesting results emerged: in women there is a clear reduction in the incidence rates of urgent first admissions for mental disorders (−61%), which goes hand in hand with an increase of 51% in the incidence rates of first admissions planned for the same cause. This data suggests that healthcare needs within the MAs are intercepted and more effectively taken into account.

A similar effect can also be observed in men. There was a decrease in the incidence rates of urgent hospitalizations (−9%), accompanied by an increase of 37% in the initial planned hospitalisations for the same cause.

As we further stratify the results of the analysis by specific diagnostic category, for women there was a substantial reduction (85%) in the rates of the first urgent admissions and hospitalisation for psychosis and 56% for acute respiratory infections. In men, on the other hand, there was a 28% reduction in the incidence rates of early urgent hospitalizations for endocarditis, myocarditis and pericarditis.

Regarding repeated hospitalizations, especially in women, results showed a 25% reduction in the incidence of repeated hospitalizations for fractures, while the analysis of visits to the ER highlighted a slight reduction in accesses with lower priority triage codes.

4 Analysis on the Health of the Social Capital Generated by the Intervention in Micro-areas (Trieste)

The purpose of this research was to explore the effects on health generated by the Habitat Micro-area program, specifically focusing on identifying the unpremeditated mechanism through which the program intends to improve residents' health and identify relevant empirical evidence on a theoretical and social level. Moreover, the aim was also to see if results were meaningful on a statistical level.

In order to achieve this goal, the research group worked closely and in full synergy with the group of operators involved in the research. from ASUITs and the epidemiological research group of the University of Udine, with whom the team worked in parallel on data regarding public health and healthcare.

The assumptions of the research begin with the understanding that the Habitat Micro-area program has introduced an element of innovation in the traditional functioning of the healthcare services and social services, changing above all the way services and recipients relate, focusing on those most exposed to socio-economic weaknesses and risks.

As previously illustrated, the program acted on three main axes:

- Personal relationships. Create and develop the relationship with the person at high risk for health problems, through dedicated operators, physical places and actions that approach the world in which the person at risk lives by observing, listening and creating a dialogue with the actual language of people in order to understand their point of view and the origin of their problems/risks;
- Relationship with the surrounding context. In order to increase the voluntary involvement of the primary recipient and of the people close to him/her in facing the problems, according to the logic of the research-action, proposing the cooperation of the operator himself and involving the other people near to him/her, in actions of reflection and organization support, mutual aid, gift, as well as instrumental and expressive activation of resources available in the context of life. Promote trust and recognition of results and people's satisfaction, in order to increase people's ability to control their own health (empowerment);
- Relationship with public institutions and professionals. Mobilize, based on the needs that emerged from people and possible actions, institutional and professional relationships (not only health), to help face the wide range of real problems (not only those foreseen by diagnostic and therapeutic pathways) that generate direct and indirect risks for health [1].

Acting through these three axes represents—based on theories of change—an approach that can be defined by individual and social capacity building, which has the effect of increasing the community and generative welfare processes. This approach is defined by two specific traits:

- The essential role attributed to the quality of the close social relationships (face to face, with the operator and with others) in raising the capacity of people—especially with scarce resources and individual skills—in controlling their own

health, through a process of cooperation and learning (growth of knowledge, skills and meaning);
- The role attributed to public services in the management of an articulated strategy, aimed at improving this quality, obtaining the active and voluntary involvement of people, assuming the burden of modifying the technical-bureaucratic nature of the traditional service, first of all by interfacing with the person and his/her environment and processes that directly involve him/her [2].

Consequently, the unique aspect of the Habitat Micro-area approach is that of attempting to overcome the scientific-technological and bureaucratic vision of public services through the construction of tighter relations between healthcare workers and the end user. These leads to a return, or the support, of technical, scientific and bureaucratic competences of the public body and its operators, a human dimension of understanding, individuality and proximity of the relationships that bring as close as possible to the demolition of the structural barriers that prevent the generation of individual and community welfare.

Starting from these assumptions, the research work was divided into three stages:

1. The first stage of assessment was carried out through an in-depth study with focus groups of professionals, analysing the work processes implemented in the intervention;
2. The second step of assessment consisted in the realization, by the operators and professionals themselves, of 600 interviews with three samples of subjects, designed in such a way as to create two control groups with respect to the target group of the intervention;
3. The third stage of the assessment involved discussions on the results obtained by the work group of the University of Udine, which carried out a longitudinal analysis on the same populations.

For the first step, the tool used was that of the focus group with the operators and professionals working in the context of the Micro-areas. These focus groups were aimed at analysing the work processes implemented in the intervention. Specifically, we studied the role of the operator/professional and the social mechanism through which the construction of social capital is realized, as well as its effect on health.

This first stage led to the mapping of the typical problems that people living in Micro-areas are facing. Among these issues, we identified problems relating to health as well as those issues afferent to the economic and social sphere. When combined with each other, they trigger a vicious cycle that is dangerous for the individual's well-being.

For the second stage of assessment and evaluation, a semi-structured questionnaire was used. It was specifically designed to investigate the relationship between health and the experience of facing critical health problems. In this questionnaire, the list of typical problems obtained in the first phase and for each problem was used. In the event that the person had to face it in the last two years, the relationship with the service process implemented by the public operators and with the network of neighbouring relationships was reconstructed, identified and measured based on different aspects. In particular, each problem was assessed and measured through the use of various indexes and techniques: the types of interlocutors involved, the chronology of action of the interlocutors, the speed of activation of the relationship, the continuity of the presence, the continuation of the network/connection to other networks, the adequacy of the relationship with regard to needs, as well as satisfaction with the help received and trust in the future relationship [2].

5 Results

The second stage of this research provided statistically significant results, which are reported in the following paragraphs. The overall sample population (600) showed, as expected, the capacity to control their health directly that was proportional to their individual resources and abilities. Mental health is more influenced by short-term conditions and the lack of resources at a specific point in time. Physical health is more exposed to the effect of long-term deficiencies, specifically education, which defines the course of life.

Challenges regarding control show negative effects on mental health when the person is faced with one or more problems that he/she cannot manage. These problems include eviction, followed by financial hardships, deprivation, and humiliation, which amplifies stress and generates further negative effects on other aspects of daily life.

With the same resources and individual abilities, people who have close relationships that are activate, meaning those who have more social capital (someone is on their side and helps them), are able to better control the problems that arise and mitigate risks to mental health.

Actions in the micro-areas have increased the level and quality of social capital that is useful to health, which the people treated can count on (albeit they generally have less resources and individual capacity than the average member of the population). This concerns the aid received to address the problems, even in cases of absence of the family, as well as helping others, assuming an active role as aid providers. The social capital created by the interventions and actions, measured by the evaluation process, is explicitly recognized by the people. They consider the help received adequate and satisfactory and feel less alone when facing their problems. This aid does not appear "in excess" when compared to the need for help that people experience.

Moreover, the people for whom these actions and interventions took place, in addition to the greater aid received and given, also experienced the growth of social capital in other parts of their lives. This included trust in the people who work to improve their community and the perception that their close relationships are a point of reference to address future problems. This growth occurs despite the fact that these people have more personal problems and that their neighbourhood shows a greater degradation with regard to their social life and the physical environment.

As expected, regarding those who received aid, mental health is on average worse when compared to their counterparts in other areas. Clearly, these interventions and actions focus on people with greater discomfort. However, if we assess health using econometric tools—in the event that they had the same resources and capacity as their peers (and therefore better) but without the intervention of those working in the Micro-area—we can see that their health would have been worse off. This is consistent with the fact that in order to produce positive effects on the health of socially disadvantaged people, improving available resources is not enough. However, a direct intervention on the problems paired with the strengthening of the social capital is effective, allowing the individual to better face health-related problems [2].

6 Conclusions

On June 14th and 15th, 2018, the conference entitled "The Community that Creates Health. The micro-areas of Trieste for equity" was held in Trieste. This conference saw the participation of about three hundred and fifty healthcare professionals, including Professor Michael Marmot, from the social and housing sectors, in order to discuss the Habitat Micro-area program. These talks focused on the project's history, the culture of reference, and the organizational structure of the territorial services involved, with particular attention placed on the social and health sector and the district. Following the conference, some of the guidelines for the future of Micro-areas and the "Trieste Declaration on the Community that Creates Health" was signed by the council members for services and social policies of Trieste and Muggia, as well as the General Managers of the ATER and ASUITs.

With these guidelines, given the results obtained by the two research projects, the ASUITs committed to consolidating and improving the joint planning of the new levels of integrated assistance, provided through community interventions guaranteed to the citizens through the Micro-Habitat Program [3]. Furthermore, they defined a list of six priority needs in order to achieve this purpose, namely:

1. Obtain updated population data in order to identify priority health problems and consequently focus the proactive work of the Mas in a proper manner;
2. Consolidate methods and tools for monitoring and evaluating activities (e.g. auditing, etc.), with particular attention placed on the outcomes and results;
3. Continue constant work focused on the verification and methodological innovation of the main operating mechanisms, also for the purposes of their dissemination, publication and the possible adoption of the HM program in other territories;
4. Strategically orient activities and resources, periodically verifying system criticalities and coherently identifying the priority areas of interventions and actions;
5. Support the MA Referrals through specific training programs that favour the consolidation of skills and the spread of good practices;
6. Reach the definition of a specific annual Budget dedicated to the implementation of the Micro-area Habitat Program [4].

Moreover, the declaration also states that:

> More social capital allows for a greater ability to take charge of the problems and therefore fewer undesirable effects such as inappropriate and avoidable admissions and hospitalisations.

This is one of the few occasions in Italy when a demanding program is evaluated with semi-experimental methods in order to verify and assess if the interventions and actions truly work and can therefore be recommended and transferred to other areas. This would clearly involve taking into due consideration the particularities of territories, inhabitants and communities. The stringent constraints of public accounts and funding with regard to sustainability, including those of the social and healthcare systems, require every programmer and assistance provider to consider the effectiveness and convenience of how public resources are spent. They must also ask themselves whether or not significant health results are achieved. ASUITS, Municipalities of Trieste and Muggia and ATER have shown that their joint planning provides new levels of integrated assistance that promote health and help avoid unwanted events.

Public and private financing are increasingly trying to find social investment instruments and tools (such as social impact bonds) that are appropriate for financing and funding effective innovative actions. However, this requires a detailed and clearly-defined set of actions and interventions (such as those mechanisms that generate social capital in the Micro-area Project) as well as adequate data to support the expected benefits (such as those resulting from the assessment).

International organizations support the need to reinforce local communities so that they can promote and protect health not only thanks to welfare programs, but also thanks to the activation of the community's own resources, as shown by the Habitat Micro-area Program. The same community interventions and actions are those of greatest impact for the reduction of health inequalities.

Furthermore, the conference allowed the participants to discuss, in an open and critical manner, the project's results. They concluded that the interventions and actions used to strengthen the communities are generally still too rare, episodic and poorly valued. Therefore, the conference members invited all the main stakeholders and policymakers to consider the positive results obtained in the Trieste Micro-areas in order to assess their transferability into the agenda of future social and healthcare planning.

The conclusions also raised awareness regarding the evaluation and assessment tools used in the project as indicators to measure the ability to generate resources for health in local communities, to be used in all investment and social innovation interventions and actions that are funded and promoted by national and local planning and donors. Lastly, they proposed using the results of the project to transfer the logistics of action, skills and tools in all circumstances and situations that intend to pursue the same objectives [5].

References

1. Di Monaco R, Pilutti S (2018) Analysis of the effects on health of the social capital generated by the intervention in the Micro-areas. Trieste), Turin
2. Ibid.
3. The Trieste Microareas Habitat Program (2018) Planning and operational guidelines, document edited by the Directorate of Social and Health Services of ASUITs, Trieste
4. Ibid.
5. The Trieste Declaration on the Community of Health, Trieste (2018)

Recovery-Net: A Multilevel and Collaborative Approach to Mental Healthcare Transformation

Daniela Sangiorgi, Fabio Lucchi, and Marta Carrera

Abstract A recent orientation of therapeutic practices in mental healthcare is moving from focusing on the treatment of the disease (clinical recovery) to the promotion of wellbeing (personal recovery) that implies a growing engagement of users toward co-production. This transformation requires the innovation of individual services and organisations, but also the collaboration with a wider set of local actors, able to guarantee the continuity of care, and enhance the potential for rehabilitation and social inclusion. This chapter will illustrate the first step of an action research project—Recovery-Net—toward the establishment of 3 Recovery Co-Labs in the Lombardy region in Italy, intended as the operational mechanism to activate and operationalise this transformation. The text will focus on the specific Co-Lab to be established in the city of Brescia, in the urban periphery of San Polo District.

Keywords Recovery · Co-production · Co-design · Mental health

1 Mental Healthcare Toward Recovery

A recent orientation of therapeutic practices in mental healthcare is moving from focusing on the treatment of the disease (clinical recovery) to the promotion of wellbeing (personal recovery) that implies a growing engagement of users toward co-production [1]. This transformation requires the innovation of individual services and organisations, but also the collaboration with a wider set of local actors, able to guarantee the continuity of care, and enhance the potential for rehabilitation and social inclusion.

A recovery orientation is embedded in national mental health policy in many countries across the Anglophone world and it is spreading globally since it has been embraced by professional groups and associations worldwide. We are living a period

D. Sangiorgi (✉) · M. Carrera
Dipartimento di Design, Politecnico di Milano, Milan, Italy
e-mail: daniela.sangiorgi@polimi.it

F. Lucchi
UOP23, Diparimento di Salute Mentale, AST Spedali Civili di Brescia, Brescia, Italy

A. Battisti et al. (eds.), *Urban Health*, Green Energy and Technology,
https://doi.org/10.1007/978-3-030-49446-9_13

in which traditional cornerstones in psychiatry are challenged by new and conflicting evidences that lead to reconsider diagnostic systems, efficacy of pharmacological treatments, delivery of services, what is meant to be mental health and how to promote it: in such a complex time, ideas and practices stemming out from the recovery movement gained strengths to become a more definite paradigm for the mental health system.

Traditional definitions of health have been challenged for their scarce contribution to support concrete actions for "a good life" in which the experience of wellbeing could be made by each person with or without an active mental disorder. If wellbeing research has been conducted on a variety of groups (general population across the life-span and persons with specific health-related problems) [2] there have been calls for a stronger focus on wellbeing in mental health systems [3] especially in relation to supporting recovery.

Considering the context of mental illness, the notion of recovery has a long history in mental health services and it has been traditionally understood as a "return to normal" or symptom remission. However, in the past three decades a new concept of recovery emerged from personal accounts of people affected by mental illness who described in public and in different ways what helps and what hinders in their journey toward a life worth of living even with the limitations caused by illness.

This new understanding of recovery—more based on a process dimension than on an outcome—places emphasis on subjective experiences, and personal meanings aiming to a new identity beyond the role of patient. Priscilla Ridgway stated in this direction: "the field of psychiatric disabilities requires an enrichment knowledge base and literature to guide innovation in policy and practice under a recovery paradigm. We must reach beyond our storehouse of writings that describe psychiatric disorder as a catastrophic life event" [4].

The spread of this approach is debated and sometimes criticized by user associations that see in this the risk of a sort of institutionalisation of a movement holding a radical message that is not easily squared by frameworks running in statutory health and social services with traditional mandates. This consideration leads directly to the issue of power also in mental health services where power, responsibility, and risk are strictly interconnected within a balance not easy to find and to preserve. The co-production approach—that protects the patients' rights to be properly informed about their condition and to participate to treatment decisions and care planning and delivery—gives a valuable contribution in order to start a conversation among different voices and positions on contemptuous topics also for the general public [5].

Wellbeing and recovery have some overlaps supported by scientific evidence about the contribution to the wider community that can come from recovery and its implications. A conceptual framework for personal recovery has been defined to inform strategies and practice of mental health services and to take in appropriate consideration elements from persons with lived experience.

Slade et al. [6] identified thirteen characteristics of the recovery journey among which recovery intended as an active, individual, unique, non-linear, life-changing process. This can be reported in a thirteen-stage models of recovery all of which can be mapped to the Transtheoretical Model of Change [7] and five overarching recovery processes comprising connectedness, hope, optimism about the future, identity, meaning in life and empowerment. This framework, called CHIME, can be considered as a focus for understanding the complexity of the recovery process and in identifying how mental health workers can facilitate recovery [8].

Although guidance on recovery-oriented practice exists, there remains a lack of clarity regarding best practice [9]. In the countries that adopted in some way the recovery approach a wide range of experiences have been synthetized in four levels of recovery oriented practices: supporting personally defined recovery, working relationship, organizational commitment and promoting citizenship [10]. The first two domains involve the content and process of care and are addressed in person-centred approaches [11]. The third domain has been addressed through national programmes such as ImROC in England, Partners in Recovery in Australia or Recovery in Practice in the USA, while the fourth recorded much more limited progress.

Ten evidence-based recovery supporting interventions have been identified [12]: peer support workers, advance directives, Wellness Recovery and Action Planning, Individual Placement and Support, Recovery Colleges, Trialogues, manualised interventions such as Refocus, Illness Management and Recovery.

All of them contribute to the development of an empirical evidence-based for supporting recovery indicating also an overlapping with wellbeing research. Points of linkage include the emphasis on connection, the importance of developing a resilient identity, the focus on strengths rather than on deficit amelioration and the need to contribute as well as receive. Similarly, emergent findings about the importance of lived experience as a source of knowledge in the context of recovery can inform approaches to increasing wider societal wellbeing.

Meaning, in particular, has emerged as a key component of models of psychological recovery [13] contributing on helping people explore their spiritual and religious lives, develop personal goals in their lives or better understand the nature and the best use of their strengths [14]. Meaning in life predicts better response to psychological treatments and it is linked to better psychological wellbeing, to the recovery of psychological functioning following both traumatic events and psychological disorders.

Positive emotions and future orientation are common across recovery and wellbeing, particularly through hope and goal setting, in the CHIME framework and Psychological Wellbeing Framework [15] and Wellbeing Theory [16].

Identity features strongly in all mental health recovery processes [17]. Responsibility and empowerment suggest a common agency or autonomy theme among recovery and wellbeing theory [18].

From this knowledge base, how service provision can be delivered to support recovery? How can organisations be changed so that they can offer recovery consistent services? Researchers summarized a large body of data and experiences in two guiding principles and four components of a general model of service delivery [19].

The first principle is the assumption that recovery is an individual process and it encourages individuals to take responsibility for their own well-being [20]. It implies that while symptom management is important, it is only one part of the overall recovery process that can be considered as moving from an avoidance/escape dimension in the present to an approach goal setting for the future [21].

The second principle is based on collaboration and autonomy support and it emphasizes aspects of the working alliance in assisting human growth. As outlined in self-determination theory, autonomy support refers to environments that support autonomy in turn impacting upon wellbeing. This seems to be important in mental health contexts generally conditioned by a history of paternalism and control.

Change enhancement is the first component to be considered: are mental health services interested in promoting change? Many people with severe mental illness tend to believe positive change is not possible so this ingredient directly challenges fixed mindsets [22] that can be shared by users, staff-members and the organization itself. It aims to encourage people to learn about the change and personal development process [23].

The second component is focused on strengths and values and their use to reach personal goals [24]. This might be very different from what happens in clinical contexts where deficits and impairments are scrutinized within the avoidance and escape dimension.

The third component is a collaborative life visioning and goal setting that, despite adversity, considers each person capable of developing an own vision for life, consistent with his or her personal values and strengths. The general aim of this ingredient is to support people in setting goals more to achieve positive attributes than to remove negative attributes [25].

The fourth component is a collaborative action planning and monitoring informed by research on health behavior change, self-regulation, self-efficacy and monitoring [26].

The combination of all these aspects in a broad systematic framework can guide a range of interventions with service users, caregivers, staff and organizational systems towards recovery-oriented services [27]. Positive institutions enable people to use their positive traits and in mental health service organizations require change to enable staff and consumers to utilize strengths and to enable the possibility of the benefits of positive emotions [28]. Without such a comprehensive change, recovery oriented services are unlikely to succeed.

Aside and synergistically with the adoption of a recovery approach, the contribution that coproduction can give to the health sector and mental health services in particular is considered a pillar of a general strategy towards a person-centred community-based mental health system [29].

2 Transforming a Mental Healthcare Ecosystem in Italy: A Multilevel Approach

Given these premises, transforming mental healthcare toward recovery principles require deep cultural change across a complex ecosystem. Changes within single service encounters and organisations are not enough, as individual recovery journeys move in between institutional care and more informal and community-based solutions that need to collaborate. To achieve a full Recovery, it is fundamental a transformation also at the societal level to overcome other barriers that relate to stigma and social inclusion, and a supporting policy frame.

With this perspective in mind, this chapter will illustrate the first steps of an action research project titled Recovery.Net funded by Cariplo Foundation,[1] that is working toward this kind of transformation meaning a Recovery oriented and community-based psychiatry in the East of Lombardy region in Italy. Starting from the recognition of the limitations of the current mental healthcare system and at the same time of a wide range of available resources and assets, partners with different roles and mission in mental health and public services joined together to design a project that could bring on the same ground recovery and ways of collaborative working among users and services aiming to test a pathway toward the transformation of the current practices. The project brings together a wide array of partners: two mental health departments of the cities of Brescia and Mantova, three universities representing the fields of design, sociology and psychology, two cooperatives, three family associations and a theatre company. The main objectives of the project are: (1) to activate and create synergies amongst the territorial resources of Lombardy and develop the necessary competences and tools to experiment and evaluate a model of psychiatry oriented toward recovery and co-production, active on the territory and based on the community; (2) to support the creation of regional and local forms of network governance able to manage care paths centred on people, co-produced and integrated in the territory.

Given the complexity of transforming and re-orienting the service ecosystem toward a recovery oriented and community-based psychiatry, the project has been conceived from its start as a multilevel process, simultaneously operating at the micro (co-production of the individual treatment plan), meso (service and organisational change toward recovery and co-creation), and macro (cultural change in society and informing policy making) levels (see Fig. 1).

At the **micro level**, the coproduction of individual treatment plans can be considered the "native code" of a mental health service that chooses to orient its activities to facilitate a recovery process. The condition for this is a complex mixture of elements coming from different agents. First of all the whole service has to imagine itself as an open environment able to hold complexities, conflicts, different visions and to manage all these aspects in a shared picture in which users, staff members and also the local community can play a role. Recovery.net proposes a pathway towards this, starting from a space called "recovery co-lab" to be implemented outside formal service facilities, with holding features in which all these ingredients could interact and grow.

The project planned training programmes aimed to transfer new competences to staff members of mental health services enabling them to adopt evidence-based and recovery oriented interventions such as Individual Placement and Support (IPS), Cognitive Remediation techniques, or co-design methodologies in order to define

[1] http://welfareinazione.fondazionecariplo.it/it/project/recoverynet/33/.

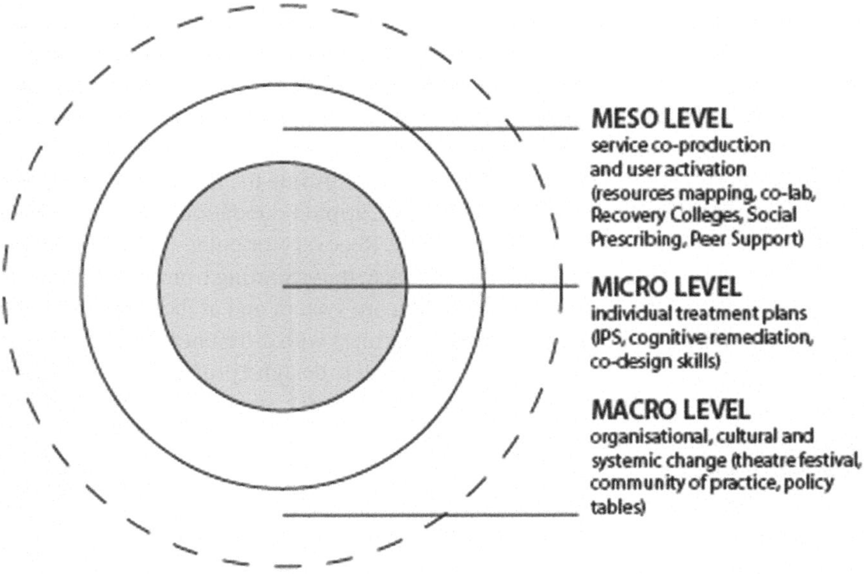

Fig. 1 Multilevel project organisations

together with users and their family coproduced treatment plans following the Mental Health Recovery Star approach.

IPS is a manualized method that has been evaluated through many randomised controlled trials that demonstrated its efficacy in promoting employment of people with severe mental illness. The method is based on a "zero exclusion" criteria and on the recognition of a genuine willingness to work as the only real driver to achieve a job on the free-market. IPS is considered the most efficacious method to promote employment in persons with severe mental disabilities.

Cognitive remediation is a set of techniques based on neuroscience, learning and behavioural therapy aiming at overcome cognitive deficits in persons with different psychiatric diagnosis. The impact on real life of persons with mental illness of these deficits are impressive in terms of the ability to cope for community integration, to socially relate, to find and maintain a job, to fulfil educational attainments. Within this framework, social cognition seems to play a central role in supporting recovery and reduce self-stigma that has a central role in hinders the agency of a person with complex mental health needs.

Also co-design techniques can be conceptualized as a metacognition exercise where users, relatives and staff can become familiar with a creative and collaborative process and approach to service improvement, learning to move from personal experiences and field work exercises to re-imagine the services they use and work for. Participating in the co-design of mental health services is also a fundamental prerequisite for co-production.

The Mental Health Recovery Star is instead a tool designed by Triangle Consulting, a social enterprise based in the London area, that has been translated and piloted in the Italian context by Associazione il Chiaro del Bosco.

Among the strengths of this tool, intended as a method for the coproduction of individual treatment plan with a clear orientation towards recovery, there is the journey toward transformation based on the trans theoretical model of change proposed by DiClemente and Prochascka and confirmed by different research on the recovery process [30] and its visual feature that helps users and key-workers in working together easily.

The project will support the coproduction of a definite number of individual treatment plans to achieve recovery goals as the result of agreed and shared actions among users and their key-workers with the support of their natural networks and the resources that the project will be able to activate in the local community.

At the **meso level** two complementary and fundamental mechanisms have been initiated (action 1): a dynamic mapping of territorial resources led by the Department of Sociology of Bicocca, and the set-up of three innovation labs in the three main territories (cities of Brescia, Mantova and Castiglione delle Stiviere) of the project.

The dynamic and collaborative mapping activity is an ongoing process, where micro-equips of users, relatives and service providers explore and identify potentially useful local resources for rehabilitation journeys, that are then mapped, archived, and activated; this database will become then a fundamental resource for personal treatment plans as well as materials to inform the co-design and implementation of new initiatives leading to the establishment of the so called "local community for mental health".

The innovation lab has been instead originally intended as the activation—within the participants' organisations—of competences, spaces and permanent practices leading toward co-design, co-production and co-evaluation of care paths, services and initiatives oriented toward the principles and ideals of Recovery.

Also at the meso level Recovery.Net has foreseen the design and activation of innovative service models, recognised as best practices in mental health related literature: three recovery colleges (one of them in a forensic mental health facility), a social prescribing programme, and two peer-support training programmes.

Recovery colleges have reached in the last ten years a large diffusion in UK, USA, New Zealand and Australia and more recently they have been implemented in Asian and European countries. The first experiences of "educational centers" in which training programmes have been proposed to support recovery competences took place in the USA and then the model has been largely adopted in England where in 2018 there were 85 recovery colleges running. Recovery colleges give an opportunity to mental health services to put in practice an educational approach to recovery through the coproduction of a set of courses co-delivered with the contribution of peer-workers.

Social Prescribing is a way of addressing social determinants of health in primary care, connecting general practices and secondary care to wider community resources. Social Prescribing has been adopted to reduce the medicalization of social problems and to promote social inclusion as a mean to cure diseases influenced by social and relational factors and in the same time it helps in strengthening community ties between formal and informal networks.

Peer support is considered as an important contribution to a working system in which the lived experiences can help in orienting people with similar conditions, especially in the so-called "life-changing diseases" that imply a profound process of coping and restructuring of affect, cognition and behaviours.

Finally, at the **macro level**, the project is supposed to inform, as the result of its bottom-up approach, strategies to promote mental health in local communities and at the policy level. One fundamental strategy is the use of theatre as a mean and as a vehicle for society transformation, engaging users in co-producing a theatre festival (e.g. Metamorfosi Festival) that becomes also an opportunity to share and promote a new understanding of mental health across the city. Also, promising and best practices which are running within the project or are adopted by its partners, will be mapped and exchanged through the establishment of a "Community of Practice", engaging eventually also stakeholders not directly involved in Recovery.Net. One of the output of the project will be an instrument to evaluate and monitor the orientation toward coproduction and recovery of organizations, and the facilitation of policy tables to orient regional government decision making for better mental healthcare frameworks.

3 Co-designing for Mental Healthcare Transformation

Designing for this complex transformation is inevitably an interdisciplinary effort, where different approaches are operating and converging toward the aimed for change. In line with a Recovery vision, together with a multi-level approach, Recovery.Net has adopted the ideal of working in a collaborative manner as a way to challenge current power dynamics and modes of service design and delivery, and to give voice to the different actors involved, patients and relatives included. Service Design intended as a creative, person centred, collaborative and experimental approach to service innovation [31], has been specifically introduced to strengthen the collaborative nature of the project.

Service Design is a specific area of application of Design, that has emerged in the '90 s thanks to the intuition of few scholars in Europe who have proposed the need to redirect the contributions and skills of design professionals from tangible products to more intangible and complex objects such as services. The advent of the so called service or experience economy, together with the call for more radical societal transformations, have justified the urgency to bring design approaches to the service sector.

In the healthcare arena in particular, Service Design applied design ethnography approaches [32], bringing the study of human experiences to the fore, while complementing the original focus of healthcare improvement studies on processes, pathways and systems [33]. By applying an experience-based design approach, Service Design pays attention to the role emotions play in healthcare recovery, and helps healthcare staff and organizations to increase the ability to empathize with and to design the service around patients and their experiences, as a fundamental basis to imagine and implement people-centered care [34].

At another level, the human-centered approach of Service Design is revealed through the capacity to actively engage people in the design and innovation process [31]. Service Design aims to develop more inclusive, efficient and integrated care [35], applying co-design approaches with people with different forms of disabilities and vulnerabilities, such as elderly people [36], people with cognitive impairments [37], mental health concerns [38], or chronic conditions [34]. In general, patient engagement– intended as patients taking an active role and being engaged in their own care—is highly valued in healthcare as it contributes to better health outcomes, to enhance patient's care experience, to improve illness self-management and adherence to therapies, and to reduce care costs [39]. At the same time, as it is implicit in the recent views on patient centred care, patients bring their own and personal sense of value, that might transcend adherence with medical decisions and include a wider set of actors and factors [40]. In this view, patient's participation, can go beyond the simple engagement with their own care, when they become involved in both the design and delivery of the services they use [41]; service co-production challenges the traditional bio-medical view of care, while it mobilizes the hidden resources of users to innovate service solutions and enhance healthcare outcomes [42]. This increased participation and collaboration are though limited by cultural difference and information asymmetry between providers and users, making it hard to establish an effective co-creating partnership [42]. Service Design provides the tools and approaches to inform more levelled interactions based on a deeper understanding of users' voices and experiences and informed by notions of "equality, equal contribution, and mutual respect" that are "proving difficult to establish in health care contexts where traditional roles of provider and recipient of care are clearly demarcated" [43].

This experience-based and collaborative approach of service design has proved valuable for improving patients' healthcare experience and the delivery processes in very diverse settings and levels of care [44]. The centrality of people in Service Design, does not stop though with patients, but include healthcare staff, relatives and other potential actors that are directly or indirectly affected by or contributing to healthcare value co-creation [45], leading toward a more systemic perspective.

This human centred and collaborative approach well fit with the necessary transformations mental healthcare is undergoing, and the challenges Recovery.Net is addressing in its multilevel intervention. In the last few years, there has been a growing number of action research projects studying how to apply Service Design for mental healthcare with a special attention to the contradictions and complexity of this sector.

Service design has been applied within mental health to help draw out the lived experiences of stakeholders and inform the design of solutions that most effectively meet their needs [46], orient existing services toward recovery [47], or build design capacity in organizations to enable ongoing systems transformation [48]. Operating within the mental healthcare sector, presents though issues that are peculiar if compared with work with other kinds of vulnerable populations. In a recent review of action research projects [38], five key areas of contention were identified: organizational constraints; the challenges of ensuring a meaningful participation; culture clashes; power dynamics and the need for systems approaches. Amongst these contention areas the "effective and genuine participation of all stakeholders involved" was perceived as being "key to creating the most effective outcomes for all parties" (p. 13).

Combining a multi-level and interdisciplinary approach with collaborative and creative methods, Recovery.Net has been set up to challenge current limitations within the mental healthcare sector, with a special focus on urban areas. The relation between mental health and cities has been subject of studies and speculations. The next chapter will reflect on the special connections existing between urbanization and mental health, focusing on the case of Brescia, and in particular of peripheral areas, such as the San Polo district where one of the Recovery co-lab is now in the process of being implemented.

References

1. Slay J, Stephens L (2013) Coproduction in mental health. New Economics Foundation, London
2. Hatch S (2010) A developmental-contextual approach to understanding mental health and well-being in early adulthood. Soc Sci Med 70:261–268
3. Hanlon P, Carlisle S (2008) What can the science of well-being tell the discipline of psychiatry and why might psychiatry listen? Adv Psychiatr Treat 14:312–319
4. Ridgway P (2001) Restoring psychiatric disability: learning from first person narratives. Psychiatr Rehabil J 24(4):335–343
5. Clark M (2015) Co-production in mental health care. Mental Health Rev 20(4):213–219
6. Slade M, Adams N, O'Hagan M (2012) Recovery: past progress and future challenges. Int Rev Psychiat 24:1–4
7. Prochaska JO, DiClemente CC (1982) Transtheoretical therapy: toward a more integrative model of change. Psychother Theor Res Pract 19:276–288
8. Eriksen K, Arman M, Davidson L, Sudfor B, Karlson B (2014) Challenges in relating to mental health professionals: perspectives of persons with severe mental illness. Int J Mental Health Nursing 23:110–117
9. Lakeman R (2010) Mental health recovery competencies for mental health workers: a Delphi study. J Mental Health 19:62–74
10. Le Boutillier C, Leamy M, Bird V, Davidson L, Williams J, Slade M (2011) What does recovery mean in practice? A qualitative analysis of international recovery-oriented practice guidance. Psychiatr Serv 62:1470–1476
11. Tondora J, Miller R, Slade M, Melton J, Le Boutillier C (2014) Social factors and recovery from mental health difficulties: a review of the evidence. B J Soc Work 42:443–460
12. Slade M, Amering M, Farkas M, Hamilton B, O'Hagan M, Panther G (2014) Uses and abuses of recovery: implementing recovery-oriented practices in mental health systems. World Psychiatr 13:12–20
13. Andresen R, Oades L, Caputi P (2003) The experience of recovery in schizophrenia: towards an empirically validated stage model. Aust N Z J Psychiatr 37:586–594
14. Slade M, Wallace G (2017) Recovery and mental health. In Slade M, Oades L, Jarden A (eds) Wellbeing, recovery and mental health. Cambridge University Press, Cambridge, pp 24–34
15. Ryff CD (2003) Psycological wellbeing revisited: advances in the science and practice of Eudaimonia. Psychother Psychosom 83:10–28

16. Seligeman MEP (2011) Fluorish: a new understanding of happiness and wellbeing. Free Press, New York, NY
17. Buckley-Walker K, Crowe TP, Caputi P (2010) Exploring identity within the recovery process of people with serious mental illness. Psychiatr Rehabil J 33:219–227
18. Deci EL, Ryan RM (2013) The importance of autonomy for development of wellbeing. In: Sokol BW, Grouzet FME, Muller Y (eds), Self-regulation and autonomy: social and developmental dimensions of human conduct. Cambridge University Press, Cambridge, pp 19–46
19. Oades L, Deane FP, Crowe TP, The collaborative recovery model: positive organisations enabling the use of strengths and values to serve recovery in enduring mental illness. In: Boniwell I, David S (eds) Oxford Handbook of Happiness, Oxford, pp 1050–1066
20. Andresen R, Caputi P, Oades L (2003) The experience of recovery from schizophrenia: towards an empirically validated stage model. Aust N Z J Psychiatry 37:586–594
21. Elliot A (2006) The hierarchical model of approach-avoidance motivation. Motiv Emot 30:11–116
22. Dweck CS (2006) Mindset: the new psychology of success. Random House, New York
23. Bridges W (2004) Transitions: making sense of life's changes. Da Capo Press, Cambridge
24. Veage S, Ciarrochi J, Deane FP, Andresen R, Oades L, Crowe TP (2014) Value important success and congruence in the workplace: links with well-being and burnout amongst mental health practitioners. J Contextual Behav Sci 3:258–264
25. Clarke S, Oades LG, Crowe TP (2012) Recovery in mental health: a movement towards wellbeing and meaning in contrast with an avoidance symptom. Psychiatr Rehabil J 35:297–304
26. Kelly PJ, Deane FP, Kazantins N (2006) Use of homework by mental health case managers in the rehabilitation of persistent and recurring psychiatric disorders. J Mental Health 15:95–102
27. Davidson L, Rakfeldt J, Strauss J (2010) The roots of recovery movement in psychiatry: lesson learned. Wiley-Blackwell, Oxford
28. Park N, Peterson C, Seligman PEM (2004) Strengths of character and well-being. J Soc Clin Psychol 23:603–619
29. Lewis A, King T, Herbert L, Repper J (2017) Coproduction-Sharing our experiences. Reflecting on our learning. ImRoc. Centre for Mental Health, Pune
30. Leamy M, Bird V, Le Boutillier C, Williams J, Slade M (2011) Conceptual framework for personal recovery in mental health: systematic review and narrative synthesis. B J Psychiatr J Mental Sci 199:445–452
31. Meroni A, Sangiorgi D (2011) Design for services. Gower, Aldershot
32. Blomberg J, Giacomi J, Mosher A, Swenton-Wall P (1993) Ethnographic field methods and their relation to design. In Schuler D, Namioka A (1993) Participatory design: principles and practices. Lawrence Erlbaum Associates, Hillsdale, pp 123–155
33. Bate P, Robert G (2007) Bringing user experience to healthcare improvement: The concepts, methods and practices of experience-based design. Radcliffe. Stacey & Thether, Abingdon
34. Tsianakas V, Robert G, Maben J, Richardson A, Dale C, Wiseman T (2012) Implementing patient-centred cancer care: using experience-based co-design to improve patient experience in breast and lung cancer services. Support Care Cancer 20(11):2639–2647
35. Fisk RP, Dean AM, Alkire L, Joubert A, Previte J, Robertson N, Scott Rosenbaum M (2018) Design for service inclusion: creating inclusive service systems by 2050. J Serv Manage 29(5):834–858
36. Kälviäinen M, Morelli N (2013) Developing services to support elderly everyday interaction Vælg. In: Miettinen S (ed) Service design with theory: discussions on change, value and methods. Lapland University Press, Rovaniemi, pp 38–49
37. Carr V (2018) Adapting the design process for different learning styles and abilities. ServDes2018—Service Design Proof of Concept. Linköping University Electronic Press, Linköping
38. Sangiorgi D, Farr M, McAllister S, Mulvale G, Sneyd M, Vink J, Warwick L (2019) Designing in highly contentious areas: perspectives on a way forward for mental healthcare transformation. Des J 22:309–330

39. Barello S, Graffigna G, Vegni E (2012) Patient engagement as an emerging challenge for healthcare services: mapping the literature. Nursing Res Pract 2012:1–7
40. Joiner KA, Lusch RF (2016) Evolving to a new service-dominant logic for health care. Innov Entrep Health 3:25–33
41. Boyle D, Harris M (2009) The challenge of co-production. How equal partnerships between professionals and the public are crucial to improving public services. NESTA, London
42. Palumbo R (2016) Contextualizing co-production of health care: a systematic literature review. Int J Public Sector Manag 29(1):72–90
43. Donetto S, Pierri P, Tsianakas V, Robert G (2015) Experience based co-design and healthcare improvement: realizing participatory design in the public sector. Des J 18(2):227–248
44. SDN. Service design impact report: health sector, service design network. gGmbH, Köln
45. Freire K, Sangiorgi D (2010) Service design and healthcare innovation: from consumption to co-production to co-creation. Nordic Service Design Conference. Linköping University Press, Linköping
46. Nakarada-Kordic I, Hayes N, Reay SD, Corbet C, Chan A (2017) Co-designing for mental health: creative methods to engage young people experiencing psychosis. Des Health 1(2):229–244
47. Carrera M, Sangiorgi D, Foglieni F, Segato F, Lucchi F (2018) Developing recovery oriented services and co-production in mental healthcare: building-up on existing promising organisational practices. ServDes2018—Service Design Proof of Concept. Linköping University Electronic Press, Milano, pp 414–426
48. Pierri P, Warwick L, Garber J (2016) Embedding design in a mental health network. In: Morelli N, de Götzen A, Grani F (eds) Proceedings of ServDes.2016. Service Design Geographies. Linköping University Electronic Press, Linköping, pp 580–585

Mental Health and Recovery in the Urban Setting: Brescia and the San Polo District

Daniela Sangiorgi, Fabio Lucchi, and Marta Carrera

Abstract Urban settings have been historically associated with an increase of mental illness, in contrast with more rural environments. Also the de-institutionalisation of mental healthcare has seen the coming-back to town of former psychiatric hospital inpatients, initiating other forms of seclusion associated with stigma and self-stigma and stimulating the activation of several community-based initiatives. This chapter reviews the city-mental health relationship, introducing the specific case of Brescia in Italy, and the work of a operative unity for psychiatry—UOP23—leading a transformational project in the San Polo district.

Keywords Recovery · Co-production · Co-design · Mental health

1 Mental Healthcare and the Urban Setting

Today more than a half of the world population lives in cities and the ongoing urbanization is paralleled by an increase in prevalence of mental disorders, and, more in general, of manifestations of urban suffering [1]. Urbanization historically has been determined by global trends in economies that lead to an increase of wealth but at the same time we are assisting to the downsides of this impressive worldwide process. The challenge of urbanization is global and include health inequalities, insecurity, housing problems, access to basic services, healthcare included, especially for people living in informal or disadvantaged settings [2].

For as long as psychiatry has existed as a medical specialty, researchers have speculated that city environment could be toxic for mental health and that more people with mental illness live in towns in comparison to countryside. The common notion is that the urban environments are harmful because they are noisy, burdened with pollution, traffic, narcotics, homelessness, etc. while the countryside can provide

D. Sangiorgi (✉) · M. Carrera
Dipartimento di Design, Politecnico di Milano, Milan, Italy
e-mail: daniela.sangiorgi@polimi.it

F. Lucchi
UOP23, Diparimento di Salute Mentale, AST Spedali Civili di Brescia, Brescia, Italy

A. Battisti et al. (eds.), *Urban Health*, Green Energy and Technology,
https://doi.org/10.1007/978-3-030-49446-9_14

more access to nature, rest, more quality food, etc. Following this logic, strategies for urban improvement tried to make cities "more rural" through the provision of green spaces, care-free zone, etc. but this turned out to be too simple: the link between cities and mental health seems to have a higher degree of complexity [3].

Many studies suggest to consider which mental illnesses are eventually more prevalent in urban contexts considering the balance between protective and risk factors for each of them and taking into account the manifest and hidden resources cities provide.

Recent evidences demonstrate that city living is associated with higher risk of psychosis [4] and "urbanicity" became one of the strongest predictor of schizophrenia even if there is not a complete agreement on what does it mean: is it a composite measure for social deprivation, low-income, insecurity, mistrust and exclusion, high level of stress or the consequence of a social drift that brings disadvantaged people to live in socially deprived suburbs? or is it the consequence of the presence in urban settings of services with the consequent risk to be more easily diagnosed in comparison of area with less accessible services? Similar observations and doubts have been proposed for other mental health conditions such as depression, anxiety, substance use disorders.

Organizing mental health services in urban contexts is consequently difficult and even if there are not clear guidelines to assist in their setting up in such particular environments, many good practices and projects can give an orientation about what it works under the circumstances of overcrowded, multi-determined, multi-layered urban settings [5].

But asides epidemiological considerations, the relationship between mental health and cities has roots in the history of mental health services. If the asylums were generally built outside the cities for the cure and the seclusion of citizens with psychiatric problems, deinstitutionalization can be seen as the coming-back to town of former psychiatric hospital inpatients and from then on the issue has been finding a home or, more in general, having citizenship rights for those who have been so long separated by the cities. The new condition of "being in the community" put at risk of new forms of segregation through subtler mechanisms than bricks and mortars such as stigma, self-stigma and the request of control that the cities make in order to be safe.

The urban landscape of mental health has therefore different intertwining dimensions and it can find a metaphor in "Marco Cavallo", the blue horse that has been produced inside the Psichiatric Hospital in Trieste, that in the years of the 180 Law, was brought in the city with a parade that became the symbol of the madness willing to go out of the old institution and give back mental wellbeing to the town through inclusion and affirmation of civil rights.

The organization of community mental health services from the seventies to nowadays is an ever ending process aiming to find a balance among continuity of care, access to services, prevention, social inclusion and citizenship rights, risk management, prevention and early detection of incident cases, health and social care integration through multisector and multidisciplinary contributions [6].

Without a wide participation of community stakeholders supporting the notion that mental health should be transversal to all the policies to be correctly addressed, any effort to establish efficient and efficacious mental health systems seems difficult to accomplish [7].

In recent years many national plans have been proposed to improve the critical aspects of mental health care that in large cities are generally more evident with a top-down approach and, in the same time, many good or promising practices have been run giving significant contributions in terms of innovation with a bottom-up approach.

What is still lacking is a vision that brings together all the pieces of this complex puzzle in a general framework and this task should be more clearly put on the agenda of the institutional bodies and among them an important part can be played by who hold responsibilities for the wellbeing of our cities.

2 The Mental Health Scene and Experience of Brescia

In the province of Brescia and in its main urban context, Recovery.Net (see Chap. 13) operates in the catchment area of the psychiatric unit involved in the project, the Operational Psychiatric Unit n. 23 (UOP23). UOP23 is part of the Mental Health and Substance Abuse Department of Azienda Socio-Sanitaria Territoriale Spedali Civili, a health organisation that operates under a regional framework assuring continuity of care from acute settings to ambulatory care for persons with psychiatric disorders through clinical, psychological, social and rehabilitative interventions. UOP23 is composed by: an acute inpatient unit, two community mental healthcare centres covering about 220,000 inhabitants in the area of Brescia, a day-centre and two rehabilitative residential units with different levels of care. The multidisciplinary team of UOP23 is staffed with psychiatrists, psychologists, nurses and social workers. Public services work in collaboration with private services (generally social cooperatives or no-profit organizations) which provide interventions according to a common accreditation system.

In the set-up of the project, mental health services data of the Lombardy Region and of Brescia area, had been collected to inform the action research plan. This data suggested how mental health systems tended to rely on interventions and instruments that are bringing to different forms of institutionalisation more frequently and for longer period of time than in the past.

During the period from 2010 to 2015 adult mental health services had an increase of 15% of their interventions while infant and adolescent mental health services raised of 108% with psychopharmacological prescriptions growing of 11%. At the end of 2017, 257 adults were in psychiatric residential facilities: 78 of them were users of Brescia UOP23 catchment area and 9 were above the threshold of the maximum length of stay allowed by regional regulations.

Regional data of the catchment areas of the psychiatric units involved in the project in Brescia and Mantova, describes a picture at community level in which 8142 people are in contact with mental health services and among them 742 have an individualised treatment plan (ITP), signalling the presence of complex needs that require coordinated interventions by a case-manager and a mulidisciplinary team. The 50% of these people with a ITP were in psychiatric residential facilities. The difficulties of the system to engage on a regular basis service users are described by the high numbers of "drop-out", meaning people that don't keep contact with the services: in 2017 they were about 698, a slightly higher number comparing to the previous years.

In the catchment area of UOP23, considering the average number of 500 people admitted to the acute impatient unit during a year, the number of people that are then readmitted before 30 days from the discharge, had grown from 6% in 2015 to 8.35% in 2017.

Two other proxy indicators contribute to a framework in which access and being in charge are elements of weakness: in 2018, 101 persons living in Lombardia were in forensic residential facilities with Mental Health Departments unable to provide a reintegration plan to their communities; moreover, in 2017 there had been 1030 persons with psychiatric problems in jails in Lombardia of which 235 were in jails in the Brescia and Mantova areas.

This tendency to new forms of institutionalisation, that is confirmed for the whole Region but also for many other European countries, is the "dark side" of the provision of care in the community: notwithstanding policies that give emphasis on community-based care as an appropriate approach to promote person-centred interventions and to reduce costs linked to hospitalisation and residential care, community services and mental health services have been neglected in terms of funding, staff, training and innovation. The consequences of this have been an impoverishment of the service culture and capabilities to work "on the ground" with users; this has led to the adoption of "defensive" and disengaging practices with a significant expansion of the provision of residential psychiatric facilities, representing in 2018, the 70% of the total regional budget for mental health care.

Because of this scenario, the UOP23 in 2012 started a process of revision of its current user involvement practices as part of their clinical and social inclusion activities. The first step had been the introduction of the Mental Health Recovery Star, an organisational methodology to facilitate conversations towards the co-production of care pathways, recovery and social inclusion. Besides the specificities of the instrument, the Mental Health Recovery Star became a powerful opportunity for staff members to work more efficaciously in the context of mental health services and for users themselves to be more prepared to cope with life-changing diseases.

This initial experience was then followed by the implementation of a Recovery College, following the inspiration and support from the ImROC project coordinated at that time by Geoff Shepherd and Julie Repper. The Recovery college can be defined as a formative space for the acquisition of competences to spend in supporting recovery processes open to users, staff members, citizens interested in mental health promotion. The first experiences have been established about ten years ago and in 2018, 85 recovery colleges are running in England while many others have been set up in Australia, New Zealand, USA, Asian and different European countries as well.

In the same time a new conversation started with the wider community considering the generative power of connecting and valuing resources embedded in the real life of the city. Aiming to explore the potential that expressive arts and social theatre could bring to mental health promotion in real life context, a theatre festival called "Metamorfosi: mental scene in transformation" was launched and organized through recent years.

3 San Polo District

The special relation of Brescia with the theme of mental health has a long history with a peripheral area, called San Polo, that is the most populous area of the Eastern district of the city with over 20,000 inhabitants. San Polo is a very controversial and multifaceted neighbourhood, known for hosting problematic cases of fragility—individuals and families, with a high percentage of foreigners and migrants—in high council houses (called "towers"), with the consequent concentration of very active social cooperatives and associations dealing with the criticalities of the area such as children education, social inclusion, or poverty.

Beyond the "towers" San Polo is characterized by terraced villas owned by middle class families, inserted in a green context. The neighbourhood is also well known for being very polluted because of a large steel factory and the proximity with highways. Towers are seen as a reality apart from the neighbourhood, both from a demographic point of view and from residents' perceptions.

Recovery.Net identified one of these towers (called Torre Cimabue)—and specifically some spaces in its first floor—as the possible location for the new co-lab. The Cimabue tower is owned by the Brescia municipality and managed by ALER, the regional residential building company. There are 188 apartments of which 150 are inhabited and about thirty vacant for legal recoveries. The population of the tower is varied: elderly people living here for decades; foreign families with many children; housing for social service; a set of apartments for mental health patients managed by a social cooperative.

The Towers have been firstly inhabited by families moved away from the historic center of the town that underwent renovation projects and consequently by immigrants and other disadvantaged groups. In this way, the Towers have gathered people with many features that the scientific literature considers as significant risk-factors for developing mental health disorders: immigration, poverty, social exclusion and loneliness, unemployment, difficulties in accessing basic services and health care. This situation has been consolidated through the years and also the surrounding part of the suburb developed discriminatory attitudes towards people living in the towers even if they share much of the same problems in community living and quality of life.

In this way, San Polo district clearly represents the downside of urban areas for mental health, while manifesting alternative forms of isolation and segregation of fragility in the city. Studying closely this context became part of the collaborative design effort to establish a recovery co-lab in the area.

During a 2-month collaborative contextual field research in San Polo, a local co-lab research team, supported by the Politecnico di Milano design team, explored the neighbourhood identifying key actors to interview while conducting some visual documentation. The interviews were intended to collect experiences of those who live in the spaces of San Polo district and the Cimabue tower and specifically: key stakeholders working in the Cimabue tower, key actors operating in the San Polo district and residents of the neighbourhood and Cimabue tower.

Among these, there were representatives of local associations working with fragilities, members of informal groups of interest (walking Group, sewing group), a holistic centre, institutional groups of citizens (neighbourhood council, community centre), a professor working on projects regarding the green area of the district, a tower inhabitant, an ecclesial organisation, a nurse of the Mental Health Department working in the neighbourhood. From the interviews and the visual documentation, 8 key opportunities and challenges, described below, were identified and used as starting material for the co-design process:

- *Integration and cohabitation*: The neighbourhood is characterized by several cultural identities and prejudices against the foreigners. However, there are some cases in which the opening up to foreign knowledge has enabled the establishment of mutual relationships. Complaints are frequent in the tower neighbourhood for the noise and the rubbish, while inside the tower, there is an ongoing conflict for the use of common spaces;
- *Spaces of aggregation*: San Polo as a district lacks a real meeting and aggregation place like a square. Before its decline, the old shopping center was the main meeting point. The ecclesiastic centre is still a strong reference point, but it does not exist a lay equivalent. As for the tower, logistics, aesthetics and spaces do not favour the socializing among tenants;
- *Value of the common good*: Especially because of the high turnover of tenants, a difficulty in recognizing the value of common spaces has been reported, in particular for families with difficulties to actively engage in the local initiatives. On the contrary, citizens living in the private houses, manifested a rediscovered care for the common good, often as a consequence of the participation to some awareness raising events for the maintenance of public spaces;
- *Tower isolation*: Among the citizens of Brescia the tower is seen as a wrong political choice, concentrating tenants with fragilities in few high buildings. For this reason, the tower is perceived as detached from the neighbourhood;
- *Wealth of initiatives but lack of dialogue*: The neighbourhood, closely monitored by the municipality, hosts several and very active informal groups, associations and individual citizens that operate in the area, in a mostly fragmented manner;
- *Green district*: The neighbourhood has been, since its original project, conceived as contemplating many green areas with bicycle lanes. Green—and its preservation—is a theme which unites citizens; the neighbourhood council demonstrates a particular interest towards environmental sustainability and has organized over the years, cleaning up or planting groups involving also the local schools;

- *Youth and the neighbourhood*: young people has limited venues and offer in the neighbourhood. There isn't a proper street education and it is difficult to intercept youth needs. For the little ones, up to elementary schools, there is the toy library. Here the integration between foreign children and Italian ones—who prefer other after-school offers—does not exist. In the school the exchange between cultures is inevitable and its frequentation makes it a meeting and interaction place between parents on issues related to children and the neighbourhood.
- *Elderly and the neighbourhood*: The neighbourhood is getting old: there is no generational turnover. There are good services for the elderly, who still have though difficulty in moving, to reach the various dislocated services in the neighbourhood area (e.g. shopping, cemetery, etc.). All these insights have been the basis to inform the co-design of an experimental space in the Cimabue Tower, that could address both the objectives of Recovery.Net project and the concerns of San Polo district.

References

1. Saraceno B (2014) Discorso globale, sofferenze locali. Analisi critica del movimento di salute mentale globale. Il Saggiatore
2. Heinz A, Deserno L, Reininghaus U (2013) Urbanicity, social adversity and psychosis. World Psychiatry 12:187–197
3. Gruebner O, Rapp MA, Adli M, Kluge U, Galea S, Heinz A (2017) Cities and mental health. Dtsch Arztebl Int 114:121–127
4. Van Os J, Kenis G, Rutten BPF (2010) The environment and schizo-phrenia. Nature 468:203–212
5. ICSU (International Council for Science Regional Office for Asia and the Pacific) (2011) Science Plan on Health and Wellbeing in the Changing Urban Environment
6. WHO (World Health Organization) (2014) Mental Health Atlas. WHO, Ginevra
7. Vandecasteele I et al (2019) The future of cities—opportunities, challenges and the way forward, EUR 29752 EN. Publications Office, Luxembourg

Co-designing Innovation Labs as Engines for Mental Healthcare Ecosystem Transformation

Daniela Sangiorgi, Fabio Lucchi, and Marta Carrera

Abstract Transforming mental healthcare ecosystem is an ambitious aim, that requires different and convergent interventions. Recovery.Net project, with its multi-level, multidisciplinary and collaborative approach is an example of the complexity of this level change. This chapter presents one of the actions of this experience, aiming to co-design a Lab in the city of Brescia, resulting in a hybrid integration of the qualities of the so called Innovation Labs, Living Labs and Community Hubs. This collaborative design process is described as a mean in itself as it worked as a prototype of a collaborative and generative approach to service design and provision, that is fundamental to a more recovery orientation to mental healthcare. The illustration of this process discusses both the potentials and challenges of this long term endeavour.

Keywords Recovery · Co-production · Co-design · Mental health

1 Co-designing Innovation Labs as Engines for Mental Healthcare Ecosystem Transformation

San Polo district has been the context of a co-design process for the establishment of one of the three recovery co-labs of the Recovery.Net project. As anticipated in chapter 13, Recovery.Net project decided to activate 3 local laboratories outside the institutional services, intended as both physical and social spaces with the three-fold aim to help innovating services, supporting social inclusion and co-creating with the territory. The Politecnico di Milano design research team is facilitating this ongoing development, following a three-stages co-design process, alternating action and reflection (see Fig. 1): (1) the transversal search for a hybrid model of innovation

D. Sangiorgi (✉) · M. Carrera
Dipartimento di Design, Politecnico di Milano, Milan, Italy
e-mail: daniela.sangiorgi@polimi.it

F. Lucchi
UOP23, Diparimento di Salute Mentale, AST Spedali Civili di Brescia, Brescia, Italy

A. Battisti et al. (eds.), *Urban Health*, Green Energy and Technology,
https://doi.org/10.1007/978-3-030-49446-9_15

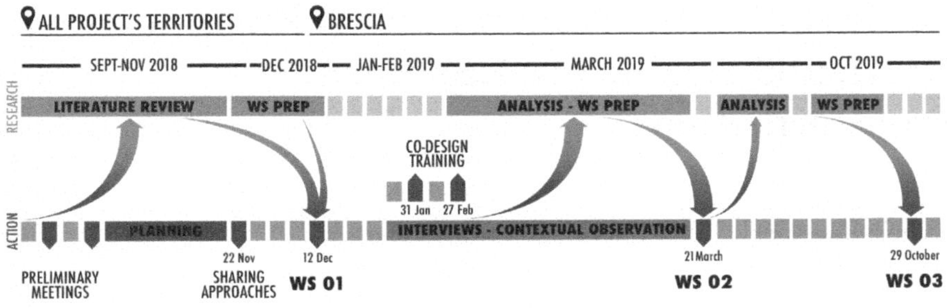

Fig. 1 Co-design process for the set-up of the co-lab in Brescia

lab, via desk research and a common co-design workshop (WS01); (2) collaborative field work to contextualise each co-lab; (3) a collaborative design process to move from general scenarios to local plans, facilitating two co-design workshops in each location (WS02 & WS03). The co-design process involved users, relatives, caregivers, doctors, and local actors over a year of research and collaborative and creative sessions (see Table 1). This section will review the activities that were carried out for the specific context of Brescia, where all the anticipated complexity and contradictions of San Polo illustrated in the previous chapter, have become material for discussion and imagination.

2 The Search for a Hybrid Lab

The first step for the establishment of the innovation labs, consisted in preliminary conversations with the key actors of the project to reflect on how to support the process of co-designing each individual lab. Specific sessions to gather preliminary visions for the lab and to understand the current activities were conducted as a starting point to map the existing resources and to activate relations. This also helped to identify who was able to actively contribute in the design research activities, establishing a smaller group responsible for the development of each lab.

Moreover, in preparation of the co-design sessions, a specific meeting was organised to share operational and design approaches: participants reflected on how decisions and processes were currently managed, who was involved and the roles and capabilities needed. This phase helped to align knowledge both on the participants and design team sides.

A preliminary literature review on Innovation Labs was then conducted to identify lab categories, that could be in line with the multiple aims of Recovery.Net, meaning to enable: (1) policy and systemic change; (2) organisational and cultural change; (3) service innovation; and (4) societal change and co-creation. This desk research led to the identification of three main kinds of labs: (1) Innovation Labs, intended as safe experimental spaces working mostly on service innovation and cultural change within public sector organizations or Government [1]; (2) Living Labs, intended

Table 1 Summary of participants to the co-design process of the Brescia co-lab

Phase	People involved		No.
Workshop 01		3 Patients 3 Patients' relatives 1 Mental health doctor 8 Caregivers (supervisors, nurses, social workers) 11 Local actors (social workers of social cooperatives and associations, volunteers of family member associations, a theatre company member)	26
Fieldwork	Co-lab team members	2 Mental Health Department patients 1 Mental Health Department patients' relatives 3 Mental Health Department caregivers	6
	Interviewed	A staff member of a local open centre for elderly people A staff member of the local associations' centre The founder of a local cultural association with focus on holistic wellness A staff member of a social cooperative with focus on social housing A staff member of a social cooperative with focus on children and youth inclusion A member of the sewing group for foreign women A staff member of a charity association A member of the local walk group for elderly people The president of the local neighborhood council An inhabitant of the tower A sociologist, professor at the local university A music teacher A volunteer at the local Italian Associations for Christian Workers A staff member of the local community hub A nurse at the local Mental Health Department	15
Workshop 02		6 Patients 2 Patients' relatives 1 Mental health doctor 11 Caregivers (supervisors, nurses, social workers) 8 Local actors (social workers of social cooperatives and associations, volunteers of family member associations, a university professor)	28
Workshop 03		4 Patients 1 Mental health doctor 9 Caregivers (supervisors, nurses, social workers) 7 Local actors (social workers of social cooperatives and associations)	21

as physical or digital venues managed by private-public-people (PPP) partnerships aiming to co-create and test in real-life contexts new solutions or technologies [2]; and (3) Community Hubs, intended as hybrid and multifunctional urban spaces managed with and by local communities promoting social inclusion, new welfare services and cultural activities [3]. Starting from this classification, the design research team identified key qualities for each category (see Table 2) to then relate them with several representative examples to inform the co-design process that were represented in the form of design cards (see Fig. 2). The intention was to provide a starting point for project participants to imagine the future co-labs, positioning the scenarios in-between these three ideal models and selecting which qualities could be implemented, as described in the following section.

Furthermore, semi-structured interviews with key members of three representative labs were conducted: La 27e Région[1] (innovation lab) in France, Malmö Living Labs[2] in Sweden; and Punti di Comunità[3] (community hub) in the North-East of Italy. The aim of these interviews were to deepen the processes that led to their establishment and their current working model, to gain inspiration.

La 27e Région was selected for a particular program they run called La Transfo that resembled the Co-Lab one, as it facilitated the set-up of innovation labs in public authorities; this was enabled by a multidisciplinary team of "residents" (designers and sociologists) during a period of 14–18 months that collaborated with teams of 20 very diverse local "ambassadors" via monthly sessions, to work on practical changes, testing and therefore prototyping how the future lab could work in the future. Only after testing the design methodology in concrete projects, they started to imagine the future lab, developing as a final outcome a poster—"future lab map"—with key information on the lab roles, activities, rules, space qualities, etc.

Malmö Living Labs, instead, was an example of a university unit moving from applying participatory design approaches within working environments, to explore how to increase democracy in other processes outside organisations in cross-sector collaborations between public sector and other social actors. This led to ad hoc social innovation projects that, in order to implement innovative solutions in complex contexts (e.g. immigration services), aimed to facilitate a process of learning, appropriation and change in public sector organisations at different levels. By participating in change projects, they aimed to introduce different ways of working and collaborating in the public sector informed by living lab approaches, identifying "pockets and spaces" of opportunities; being humble and adapting processes to fit the organisational contexts they collaborated with and creating also physical environments conducive of change were specific insights from this case.

[1]La 27e Région is an innovation lab in France conducting action-research programs with public and private stakeholders to experiment with new innovation methods and design for innovative public policies (http://www.la27eregion.fr/en/).

[2]Malmö Living Labs is a university research unit that works with participatory design approaches for social innovation in the city of Malmö (http://medea.mah.se/malmo-living-labs/).

[3]Punti di Comunità are physical spaces aiming for supporting information, reflection and peer support in the city of Brescia, as part of a project funded by Fondazione Cariplo, called Gener_azioni: http://www.welfaregenerazioni.it/punti-di-comunita/.

Finally, a project called Gener_Azioni funded by Cariplo Foundation, developed the so called "Punti di Comunità" intended as very diverse physical places in the province of Brescia aiming to promote peer support, information and the activation of new relationships based on a new understanding of community and welfare. These

Table 2 Synthesis of key definitions and qualities of three types of labs

Definition	Key qualities
Innovation lab	
Innovation labs are generally separated units operating as change agents within public sector organisations and government to introduce new innovative approaches and capabilities[1, 2, 4–7].	– Dedicated and safe space for experimentation – Multidisciplinary teams and approaches – Foster collaboration inside and outside the public sector – Embrace human centred design concepts and methods – Systematise and codify innovation processes and methods – Support organisational learning – Aim to change the mindset of organisation – Co-creation (engagement) with citizens – Focus on exploration/ideation stages of innovation – Conduct quick and dirty experimentation – Small, separated and autonomous unit in government – Work for both policy making and policy implementation – Produce most of their work for or with the ministerial departments and other government agencies – Has the capacity for self-renewal
Living labs	
Living labs are physical regions, virtual realities or interaction spaces where private-public-people (PPP) partnerships collaborate to co-create and test in real-life contexts new solutions or technologies[1, 8–12].	– Active user involvement (people as resources) – A real-life setting – Multi-stakeholder participation (4Ps) – A multi-method approach – Co-creation – Medium and long term experimentation – Allow for technical testing – Connect bottom up grassroots initiatives with more established top down actors – Balance between emergence and strategic design (not over design) – Continuous process of building relations – Friendly hacking the system
Community hubs	

(continued)

Table 2 (continued)

Definition	Key qualities
Community hubs are hybrid spaces led by and for the community that offer alternative welfare services, support social inclusion and cultural initiatives and, often focused on health and wellbeing[13–15].	– Hybrid and multipurpose spaces – Informal and Open spaces to participation – Aggregating physical space – Favour socialisation – Promote social cohesion and inclusion – Provide social and integrated services for and by the community – Support community led urban regeneration – Improve individual skills and knowledge – Invite for participation in civic activities – Adopt a widened and inclusive governance models – Action research places – Use a diverse range of income sources – Places to create social value and work opportunities

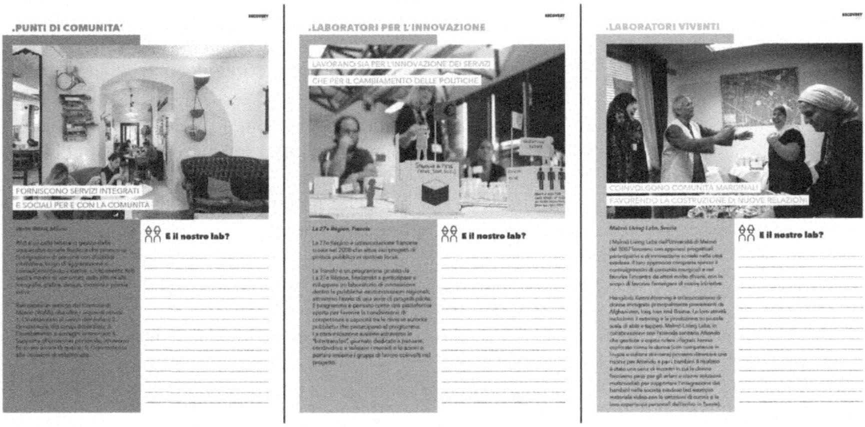

Fig. 2 Examples of case study cards with key lab qualities

places are led by trained profiles called "community facilitators" working 15 h a week in synergy with the social worker of the City Council. The Punti di Comunità favours the encounter between distant people and organisations and supports, also economically, local initiatives of proximity or experiential laboratories, proposed and led by single or group of citizens, addressing an identified need of the community while being potentially engaging and generative in the long term.

All this information was elaborated to inform a fist co-design workshop held in December 2018 involving 26 participants including doctors, caregivers, patients and expert patients from mental health services and social actors from local associations of the 3 territories involved in the project. The aim of this event was to envision possible ideal and transversal scenarios for the future co-labs starting from what emerged during the desk research. The session was articulated in the following steps:

1. An icebreaking activity in which each participant was asked to place a sticker with its own name on its territory of reference and tracing lines of connection with the people with whom they already cooperated, creating a map of relationships;
2. A presentation of the 3 types of labs (innovation lab, living lab and community hub) with the three illustrative case studies and exemplifying user stories;
3. A scenario development activity in four groups, where participants had to position selected representative case studies cards in a map with three polarities (i.e. innovation labs, living labs or community hubs) to help position and define the key qualities of their ideal co-lab;
4. A storyboarding activity where participants had to imagine practical activities the lab could do;
5. Groups presentations of their ideal lab as developed in the workshop (Fig. 3).

The polarity map in particular was asking participants in groups to first choose exemplar cases summarised in coloured cards (one colour for each typology), representing the identified key qualities of the 3 types of labs (see Fig. 2); once selected the cards, these were positioned in the polarity map, close to their belonging typology, representing visually which kinds of hybrid lab was emerging. Based on this exercise, each group was then asked to write on the same poster, the key values of the

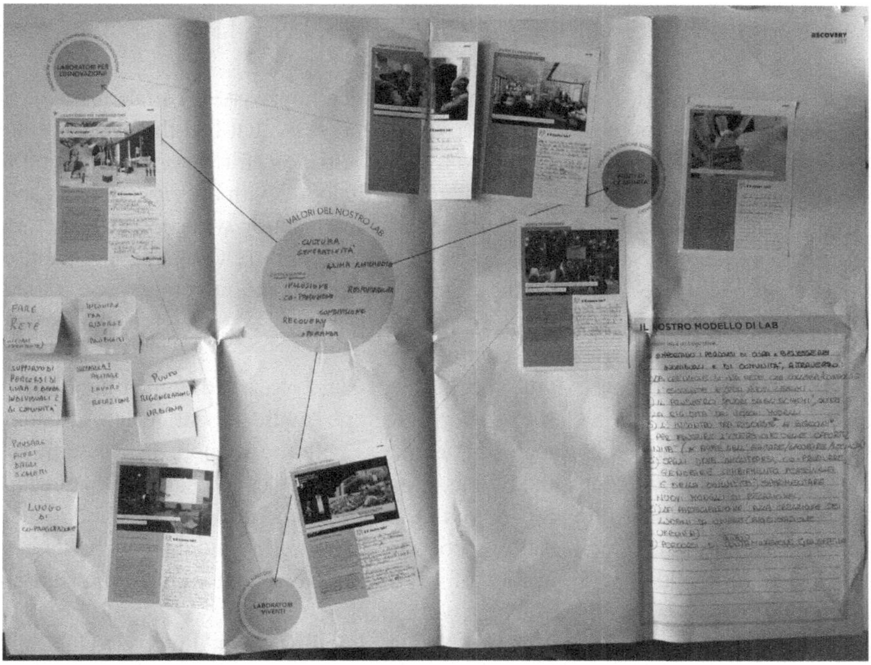

Fig. 3 Example of a polarity map for scenario development

future co-lab and to describe what would happen in this kind of environment. The storyboarding activity was then helping to bring this hybrid lab to life, telling possible stories and activities that could happen in these spaces.

The four scenarios of hybrid labs that emerged from these activities were:

- *The co-lab as a place of discovery and experimentation of wellness*: Alongside physical and mental health, the co-lab promotes the value of social health intended as the ability to form satisfactory interpersonal relationships with others through the development of transversal skills such as relational and communication skills, or the use of an accessible language;
- *The co-lab as a co-living space*: sharing a space, and doing together help to better know each other, and overcome stereotypes and fears. This lab is a non-partisan place with the aim of stimulating a renovated debate with the territory and institutions on mental health;
- *The co-lab as a co-design space*: learning about people's needs helps to generate new ideas and initiatives, imagined by the community for the community. The co-lab becomes the space where these new ideas take shape, are shared and tested with different actors in the territory;
- *The co-lab as a place of generative paths and positive contamination*: the encounter between diverse resources and needs favours the emergence of new opportunities in a generative way through innovative methods and tools.

3 A Collaborative Design Process in Brescia

The transversal scenarios emerged in the first workshop were then taken by each territory as a starting point for a local co-design process, that had the aim to bring these ideas to the reality of their contexts. In particular, each territory had to find a possible location for the future co-lab, starting a dialogue with the city councils and local associations. In Brescia, as mentioned earlier, a location was soon identified in the peripheral area of San Polo, in the first floor of the Torre Cimabue, in a centre previously used as a day centre for the elderly. The identification of this space started a process of negotiation with both the city council and the several associations that live and use the spaces close to the centre.

At the same time, because of the specificity of San Polo, a 2-month collaborative contextual field research in San Polo was developed with a local co-lab research team of 8 people. Trained by the design team and with the support of ad hoc interview guides and district maps, the co-lab research team was in charge of exploring the neighbourhood identifying key actors to interview and conducting some visual documentation. As an outcome of this process, opportunities and design challenges were identified together with profiles of key local actors, that were formalised as design materials for a second co-design workshop.

The second co-design workshop, was held in March 2019, and involved 34 participants from the Brescia area—including doctors, caregivers, patients, expert patients from mental health services and social actors from local organisations. The aim of this event was to revisit the original common scenarios of hybrid labs emerged in the first workshop, to address both the Recovery.Net project aims and ambitions, and the specific needs and resources of the location of San Polo.

As a starting activity, the groups were introduced to the context by the research team that presented the highlights of the research including the challenges and opportunities of San Polo, supported by photographic material. Then, the four groups had to choose the most relevant hybrid scenarios for the local area and were asked to adjust those visions to address both the needs of Recovery.Net project and the qualities of the local area. Using co-design tools such as "challenges and opportunities cards" or "actor cards" representing the collected field work data to inform their imagination, groups had to describe the future lab in terms of values, activities, and main participants (Fig. 4).

The developed scenarios were strongly affected by the contextual information of San Polo leading to the proposal of a wide understanding of mental health that would concern and engage the surrounding neighbourhood with its complexity and contradictions:

- *The co-lab as a caring place:* here the interests and individual capabilities of local actors and users are integrated to reactivate and take care of people and the spaces of the Cimabue tower and of the surrounding neighbourhood;
- *The co-lab as a place for encounters and bottom-up generative contaminations*: here mental health patients, inhabitants of the tower and the neighbourhood can

Fig. 4 Scenario building using challenges and opportunities cards

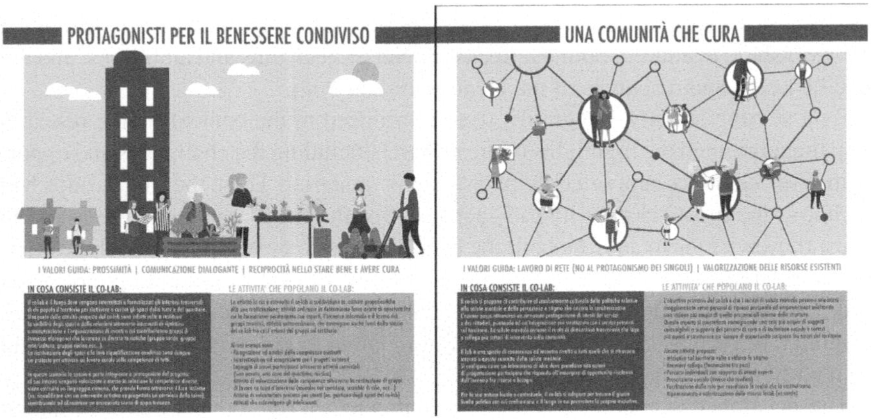

Fig. 5 Example of visualisation of the four scenarios for the co-lab

learn and exchange knowledge acting as an informal living room, where everyone feels welcomed;

- *The co-lab as a place for policy and cultural change in the city of Brescia*: here service users and citizens are protagonists and mental health is a transversal value that connects multiple sectors of intervention in the community;
- *The co-lab as a place that promotes social health*: here active citizens, and mental health patients are trained to become facilitators to promote social health, engaging San Polo neighbourhoods and the existing local organisations.

The co-lab scenarios were then visualised (Fig. 5) and shared across the project community to gain feedback through an offline and online survey, to be then presented at the opening of a theatre festival, partly hosted in the future lab location and organised by the theatre company partner of the project. These actions and a constant dialogue with institutions and local organisations led to a round table with the local associations: this brought to the drawing up of a common letter with proposals addressed to the city council to ask access and future management of the lab's space in the Cimabue Tower. The request induced the city councillor for social services to concede the use of the identified spaces and municipality took on the burden to bring it up to the code. This led to opening up a public call to address security issues of the Cimabue Towers and if this on one side could be seen as a first good outcome of the project, on the other side this process is delaying the access to the co-lab's space; as a temporary solution then, the municipality offered alternative spaces to host some activities of the project, namely the forthcoming recovery college.

Once the agreement was settled, the next step was a meeting with a smaller co-lab team of Brescia, to discuss the four emerged scenarios to converge them toward a unified vision. During this session it was underlined the need to distinguish the developing co-lab from the community centres already existing in San Polo, by reinforcing its mental health connotation and link with the Recovery.Net project. In fact, the co-lab, as it is located in a place that is already strongly active in the social sector, needs to be distinguished to avoid ending up in the background of a controversial context: the co-lab, therefore, is an experiment on mental health. It emerged also as fundamental to keep the lab open to the neighbourhood: the integration with existing projects that already insist on the neighbourhood is an aspect to be pursued and strengthened.

The unified scenario used the metaphor of an "invisible city"—adapting the title of the book from Italo Calvino, operating for the needs of mental health, but whose spaces are crossed and influenced by the different actors of the territory, resulting in hybrid functions and initiatives.

Four macro-themes qualified the metaphor of the Invisible City:

1. *The Crossed City*, in which the co-lab spaces open up to temporary thematic re-interpretations, being contaminated by guests and co-workers. Some of these open activities are recreational and convivial ones using internal and external resources, while an itinerant version of the co-lab can bring its mental health vision in other contexts;
2. *The Informing City*, a space where to train and inform about mental health issues. It is also a promoter of a new vision of mental health open to the territory and to political representatives. The proposed activities involve training, neighbourhood board and political tables aiming for awareness raising towards mental health issues;
3. *The Welcoming City*, with spaces where patients feel comfortable and at their ease while meeting with co-lab participants to co-organise and plan initiatives. Examples of activities in this area are an active welcoming desk which offer mental health orientation with the support of available resources, thematic open days for new users and intimate and convivial spaces for users.
4. *The Generative City*, that hosts an updated and accessible archive of territorial resources, intended as a starting point to imagine new initiatives for rehabilitation and social inclusion. Here dedicated equips work on the dynamic mapping of local resources, the co-design of initiatives and events, the requalification of spaces for social inclusion purposes.

The final third co-design workshop, held in October 2019, involved 21 participants including doctors, caregivers, patients, expert patients from mental health services and key actors, partners of the project and representatives of local organisations. The event aimed to articulate the activities proposed for the Invisible City, imagining in four separate groups, the required roles and competences, the governing rules, and the equipment and features of the physical spaces. The second part of the workshop focused on the space layouts, working on a scale plan of the co-lab positioning furniture cards in each room to imagine possible space configurations, to then compose a mood-board, choosing from given style furnishings examples (Fig. 6).

Fig. 6 Co-design of the space layouts and configurations

4 Reflection on the Process

The co-design process that we presented in this chapter, as one of the main actions of Recovery.Net, suggests how urban health should be the result of a collaborative endeavour that transcends the boundaries of institutional care. The co-labs have been imagined with the double intent to change and open up traditional service providers while connecting and collaborating with actors from the local community, informed by a wider understanding of mental health. This collaborative journey is not though a linear process as it does face several resistances and setbacks when trying to engage and orientate professionals, users, relatives and organisations toward the principles and practices of recovery, when entering the complexities and contradictions of urban peripheral areas such as San Polo, and when in particular aiming for a systemic and sustainable transformation.

We started in chapter 13, introducing the concept of personal, as opposed to clinical recovery and the key changes service providers need to address in order to become recovery-oriented services. Valuing autonomy, experiences and participation, building a positive emotions and future orientation environment, means asking patients, relatives and staff members of different organisations to significantly change the approach and expectations toward mental healthcare. Together with the introduction of innovative service models or approaches, the co-design process, as described in the previous sections, was intended both as a mean and as a goal in itself.

As a mean it worked as a "multistakeholder forum" to orchestrate dialogue and deliberation across multiple agencies and actors, favouring more distributed forms of leadership and governance [16]. Also, establishing a collaborative environment and a sense of participation, became the fundamental ingredient to gradually establish different operating models and relationships. The size and formats of the co-design sessions presented inevitably limitations in the possible level of engagement, as well as in the depth of organisational involvement for all participant stakeholders. In this sense co-design worked more as a prototype of a collaborative and generative approach to service design and provision, that has then led and informed the ideation and set-up of the co-labs; the envisioned co-lab has become the materialisation of a co-production culture and the result of a concrete intention to de-instutionalise mental healthcare where patients play a central role. Still strong organisational resistances persist, with limited engagement of staff members and doctors in the mental healthcare services, that interpret the project as an experimentation with limited evidence and political support. Resistances come also on the patient sides, where motivation, assistance and ability to participate can change significantly. This is where individual organisations need to keep working in their own authorising environment to leverage legitimacy and support, while building the needed operational capacity to co-create public value. In public value theory, it is here where the project needs to move to more "institutionalized arenas—legislative, executive, and administrative settings—for making and implementing policy decisions" [16].

The internal change struggles have met also external challenges when interacting with the urban setting and arena. The slowness of bureaucratic processes to access the co-lab, together with the need to open a public competition to repair the fire system of part of the Tower in San Polo is putting at risk the project, as we are losing the momento and enthusiasm the vision for the co-lab has generated. Also, the complexity of the location in itself with its issues of isolation, security, garbage and stigma bring into the project a further layer of challenge, with the risk of other forms of segregation and stigma. Counteracting this trend with attention to aesthetics, quality and care toward the physical and social environments, are dimensions that need to be carefully safeguarded in the implementation journey and beyond.

Furthermore, as the project is aiming for a systemic change, the different actions of the project that have been gradually advancing in an individual manner, need to start now synchronising to create synergy and amplify their impact. The co-design of the co-labs are meaningless without the ongoing territorial dynamic mapping activity that help individuals to value local resources in a different manner and work toward their activation; these resources are starting to be used as discussion materials for the co-production of the individual treatments plans and rehabilitation initiatives, and should become design resources to imagine new care models, support information for Social Prescribing, or courses within the Recovery College. At the moment the coming theatre festival will use the newly activated territorial resources as potential locations for their distributed shows, to continue in the promotion of a different understanding and participation to mental health in the city of Brescia. All this synergy requires effective coordination, and the co-lab should function in the long term as its operational centre supporting its main activities, while using and adapting at best to emergent opportunities or barriers. The change process is perceived as fragile; it is very important to demonstrate impact soon, but in a systemic change process this is difficult and there is the risk of losing political support, enthusiasm, or local champions. Sustainability of change is also a fundamental part of this process. Recovery.Net is funded for other 2 years, and questions on its continuation are already asked. This is bringing the attention to the need to define a sustainable governance and management models that do not depend on the single mental healthcare provider, but that relies on a collaborative effort. Discussions are starting on how to define an evaluation tool able to measure the ability to orient and create a sustainable ecosystem in the city that activates a wider local community for mental health. Fundraising mechanisms are also starting to be elaborated and implemented to bring public attention to the initiative, while testing its economic viability in the long term.

5 Conclusions

Transforming mental healthcare ecosystem is an ambitious aim, that requires different and convergent interventions. The vision of community psychiatry rooted in the deinstitutionalisation movement of the seventies is under the pressure of economic cuts, of a general request for more security and control, that is leading to coming-back of explicit and implicit forms of institutionalisation that make working in the community a less perceived sustainable way to promote mental health.

This general attitude is causing a shift of the budget for mental health in many Italian regions toward residential care: community care is not only impoverished in terms of material resources but also in terms of culture and competences and the consequences are disempowering processes for mental health services and users themselves. Policy-makers are considering to use financial leverages to orient mental health provision of care toward health and personal budget following the assumption that this could reduce costs also through the mobilisation of community resources according to welfare community framework.

The risk is that these potentially efficacious tools could be managed without appropriate competences by mental health services and without real engagement of users and communities.

Mental health systems need to find forms of governance that bring a wide arrays of local resources at decisional levels and forms of real engagement of users in defining individual treatment plans measured on meaningful individual, recovery-oriented outcomes. This transformational approach needs not just people, plans and pathways but also places that bring all the community assets together aiming to demonstrate the sustainability also in difficult times of community mental health. The Recovery.Net project in its complexity and the vision of the Recovery Co-Labs are endeavours in this direction.

References

1. Carstensen HV, Bason C (2012) Powering collaborative policy innovation: can innovation labs help? Innov J: Public Sect Innov J 17(1):2–25
2. Schuurman D, Tõnurist P (2016) Innovation in the public sector: exploring the characteristics and potential of living labs and innovation labs. Technol Innov Manage Rev 7(1):7–13
3. Bagnall A-M, South J, Di Martino S, Southby K, Pilkington G, Mitchell B, et al (2018) Places, spaces, people and wellbeing: full review. What Works Centre
4. Thenint, H (2009) "Labs for a more innovative Europe" Report. INNO-GRIPS Global Review of Innovation Intelligence and Policy Studies
5. Tõnurist P, Kattel R, Lember V (2017) Innovation labs in the public sector: what they are and what they do? Public Manage Rev 19(10):1455–1479
6. Junginger S (2014) Public innovation labs–a byway to public sector innovation? In: Christensen PR, Junginger S (eds) The highways and byways to radical innovation-design perspectives, Kolding, Design School Kolding & University of Southern Denmark, pp 117–129
7. Fuller M, Lochard A (2016) Public policy labs in European Union Member States; EUR 28044 EN. http://dx.doi.org/10.2788/799175
8. Westerlund M, Leminen S (2011) Managing the challenges of becoming an open innovation company: experiences from living labs. Technol Innov Manage Rev 1(1):19–25
9. Almirall E, Lee M, Wareham J (2012) Mapping Living Labs in the Landscape of Innovation Methodologies. Technol Innov Manage Rev 12–18
10. Ballon P, Schuurman D (2015) Living labs: concepts, tools and cases. Info 17(4). http://dx.doi.org/10.1108/info-04-2015-0024
11. Følstad A (2008) Living labs for innovation and development of information and communication technology: a literature review. eJOV: Electron J Virtual Organ Networks 10
12. Hillgren, PA (2013) Participatory design for social and public innovation: living labs as spaces for agonistic experiments and friendly hacking. In: Manzini E, Staszowski E (eds) Public and collaborative: exploring the intersection of design, social innovation and public policy, pp 75–88. DESIS Network
13. Bagnall A-M, South J, Di Martino S, Southby K, Pilkington G, Mitchell B, . . . Corcoran R (2018) Places, spaces, people and wellbeing: full review. What works centre
14. Nava E (2016) Community Hub. I luoghi puri impazziscono. Accessed at http://www.communityhub.it/wp-content/uploads/2016/10/Community-Hub.compressed.pdf
15. Locality (2020) The community hub handbook. How to run a successful hub and make your neighbourhood thrive. Accessed at https://www.powertochange.org.uk/wp-content/uploads/2020/02/Community-Hubs-Handbook-Final.pdf
16. Crosby BC, 't Hart P, Torfing J (2016) Public value creation through collaborative innovation. Public Manage Rev 19:655–669

Methodological Comparison of Different Projects

Livia Maria Salvatori, Maurizio Marceca, Lorenzo Paglione, Aurora Angelozzi, Susanna Caminada, Miriam Errigo, Marco Tofani, Alessandra Battisti, Asia Barnocchi, Chiara Bodini, Martina Riccio, Rita Maralla, Valeria Gentilini, Francesca Cacciatore, Elio Trusiani, Rosalba D'Onofrio, Roberta Cocci Grifoni, Mariano Pierantozzi, Enrica Petrucci, Ilaria Odoguardi, Graziano Enzo Marchesani, Corrado Sgrò, Chiara Camaioni, Daniela Sangiorgi, Fabio Lucchi, Marta Carrera, Flavio Paoletti, Alessandro Dario Greco, and Silvia Iorio

Abstract In order to compare the methodological aspects of the different projects, while also placing them within a common framework, a form was specially drafted. This form was filled out in May 2019 by one or more members of each work group

L. M. Salvatori · M. Marceca · L. Paglione · A. Angelozzi · S. Caminada · M. Errigo · M. Tofani
Department of Public Health and Infectious Diseases, Sapienza University of Rome, Rome, Italy

L. Paglione
Department of Civil, Building and Environmental Engineering DICEA, Sapienza University of Rome, Rome, Italy

A. Battisti · A. Barnocchi
Department of Planning, Design, and Technology of Architecture, Sapienza University of Rome, Rome, Italy

C. Bodini · R. Maralla
Centre for International and Intercultural Health, University of Bologna, Bologna, Italy

M. Riccio · V. Gentilini · F. Cacciatore
Centre for International and Intercultural Health, Bologna, Italy

E. Trusiani · R. D'Onofrio · R. C. Grifoni · M. Pierantozzi · E. Petrucci · I. Odoguardi · G. E. Marchesani · C. Sgrò · C. Camaioni
School of Architecture and Design, University of Camerino, Ascoli Piceno, Italy

D. Sangiorgi · F. Lucchi · M. Carrera
School of Design Polytechnic, University of Milano, Milan, Italy

F. Paoletti
Healthcare Services and Planning of Social and Medical Activities, Trieste University, Trieste, Italy

A. D. Greco
Integrated Healthcare Office, Planning of Social and Medical Activities, Trieste University, Trieste, Italy

S. Iorio (✉)
Department of Molecular Medicine, Unit of History of Medicine and Bioethics, Sapienza

A. Battisti et al. (eds.), *Urban Health*, Green Energy and Technology,
https://doi.org/10.1007/978-3-030-49446-9_16

(Ascoli Piceno, Bologna, Milano, Roma, Trieste). The form was divided into three different sections ("Context characterisation methods"; "Community involvement methods"; "Networking methods"). Each section was created in order to highlight multidisciplinary aspects, the collaboration among different roles, and the problems and limitations the could have been faced. The sections differ in their design, although a common scheme was used in nearly all parts: narrative description, players, actions, instruments and sources. Consequently, all projects were therefore analysed according to the following matrix. Considering the specificity of the Recovery-Net project, this project was analysed solely for context characterisation methods.

Keywords Networking methods · Action research · Health equity

1 Context Characterisation Methods

This section was designed to investigate how the research/working group characterised the context under study, not only from a socio-demographic point of view, but also regarding the health characteristics of the population, as well as the architecture and urbanism of the area, with special regard to any critical points caused by social inequalities or lack of stable housing. Furthermore, this section was divided into two sub-sections, one of which focused on socio-demographic and healthcare methods and another on urban-architectural methods. The first sub-section was further divided into two parts in order to collect the description of qualitative and quantitative methodologies separately. Under "quantitative methodologies", all the methodologies that implied the use of epidemiologic, social, economic population data sources were considered. On the other hand, the "qualitative" methodologies were those used to obtain information on the context without any statistical support, directly involving the subjects under observation. Both the quantitative and the qualitative parts are similarly structured—after an initial narrative description, a schematic collection of players, actions, instruments and sources follows. The description of any remarks closes both of the parts related to quantitative and qualitative socio-demographic and healthcare area methods. The sub-sections related to urban-architectural methods is structured in the same way as the parts on qualitative and quantitative methods (narrative description, players, actions, instruments, sources, as well as any remarks).

2 Community Involvement Methods

This part of the form was designed to investigate the research/working group approach to the community. It focused on how the project was able to involve the

University of Rome, Rome, Italy
e-mail: silvia.iorio@uniroma1.it

community and provide tools and knowledge that would be useful in order to improve living and health conditions, as well as the control on the urban context with regard to empowerment. After an initial schematic part (narrative description, players, actions, instruments, sources, any remarks), a wider space was dedicated to the narrative reporting of the main results, limitations and problems encountered, as well as any possible remarks.

3 Networking Methods

This section is aimed at investigating the research/working group-building methods in terms of institutional involvement (e.g. Universities, local health authorities, municipalities) as well as social networking. Starting from associations, this section also includes information on "informal" aspects (parishes, organised groups, associations of residents, neighbourhood committees) present in the context in question. Firstly, the tools used to involve institutional as well as non-institutional stakeholders were explained. Secondly, the players/stakeholders that were involved in formal and non-formal networks were described.

4 The Form: Working Methods

4.1 Context Characterisation Methods

This section investigated how the research/working group has characterised the context under study, not only from a socio-demographic point of view, but also in the field of the health characteristics of the population and of the architecture and urbanism of the area, with special regard to any critical points due to informality and social inequalities.

Socio-demographic and healthcare area methods
Briefly describe the socio-demographic/healthcare context characterisation methods used.

Qualitative methods
Which of the methods used for the socio-demographic/healthcare context characterisation were qualitative?

- Which **players** were involved?
- Which **actions** were implemented?
- Which **instruments** were used?
- Which **sources** were considered?

Quantitative methods
Which of the methods used for the socio-demographic/healthcare context characterisation were quantitative?

- Which **players** were involved?
- Which **actions** were implemented?
- Which **instruments** were used?
- Which **sources** were considered?

Remarks

4.2 Urban-Architectural Area Methods

Briefly describe the methodologies used for the characterisation of the urban-architectural area:

- Which **players** were involved?
- Which **actions** were implemented?
- Which **instruments** were used?
- Which **sources** were considered?

Remarks

4.3 Community Involvement Methods

Briefly describe the initiatives and the practices adopted for the engagement of the target communities:

- Which **players** were involved?
- Which **actions** were implemented?
- Which **instruments** were used?
- Which **sources** were considered?

Main results

Limitations and problems encountered

Remarks

4.4 Networking Methods

Involvement tools: Briefly describe the main networking instruments used.
Which instruments were used to involve:

- **Institutional stakeholders**
- **Associations/third sector**
- **Informal community networks**

Institutions involved: Briefly describe the institutions involved

Remarks

Glossary

Players: both institutional (universities, government organisations) and non-institutional (associations, NGOs, etc.) as active participants in the described action.
Actions: the properly speaking activity carried out by the players.
Instruments: eventual physical and non-physical tools (e.g. datasets, maps, workshops, etc.) used by the players to carry out the actions.
Sources: information sources, that are both data sources and bibliography/references used.

5 Ascoli Piceno

5.1 Context Characterisation Methods

(a) **Socio-demographic and healthcare area methods**

CCUHRE wants to start a system of scientific knowledge shared between public administration, research community and local community in order to evaluate climate change plans adapting projects and choose the most beneficial in terms of health effects. Object of study is the neighbourhood of Monticelli (Ascoli Piceno). Qualitative and quantitative methodologies have been used, through: interviews, historical and demographic recognition of the neighbourhood, questionnaires on the health and social aspects of the population, in order to create a profile of the neighbourhood community and identify climate and health indicators.

Qualitative methods

- Bibliographic research

- Participation in world Café activities of the project “R3 Monticelli-resilience, re-use and reactivation of urban capital” sponsored by the municipality of Ascoli Piceno
- Interviews with the stakeholders of the District and the City.

Which players were involved?

- Municipality of Ascoli Piceno
- ASUR (Regional Health Authority)
- Parish
- Senior club
- Private citizens
- ERAP (Regional Public Housing Organisation).

Which actions were implemented?

- Meetings and interviews (with private citizens, neighbourhood assemblies, educational institution, senior club, sport association)
- Meetings with the municipality of Ascoli Piceno and ASUR.

Which instruments were used?

- “Furia Map”—Open Source Urban planning: questionnaires and quality control of the places (with the technological use of GIS and BIM) by the students of the faculty of architecture and design
- Newspaper articles to promote the project.

Which sources were considered?

- Interviews with private citizens and with stakeholders
- Demographic surveys: PRG (Ascoli Piceno General Regulatory Plan), Regional Register
- ASUR (Regional Health Authority) web site
- European projects: LIFE SEC ADAPT PROJECT
- Upgrading Sustainable Energy Communities in Mayor Adapt initiative by planning Climate Change Adaptation strategies.

Quantitative methods

- Demographic surveys in the neighbourhood area (by census data)questionnaire administration about the Daily life of families
- PASSI (Progress of Local Health Authorities in Italy) questionnaire administration
- Data collection regarding climate and urban environment quality.

Which players were involved?

- Municipality of the city of Ascoli Piceno
- ASUR (Regional Health Authority)
- Educational institution; Parish; cultural and sports associations
- ISTAO (Adriano Olivetti Institute, managerial school).

Which actions were implemented?

- Administration of questionnaires and interpretation of data: characterisation of the different areas of the neighbourhood
- Social, demographic and urban planning reports
- Implementation of the Monticelli Community's Health Profile
- Identification of themes of the project concerning climate change effects on health.

Which instruments were used?

- Questionnaires
- Climate and health indicators
- GIS (Geographic Information System) Technologies
- Communication activities between UNICAM (University of Camerino) and ISTAO
- Open-Source Urban planning.

Which sources were considered?

- Census data of Ascoli Piceno
- National and international research/studies about climate and health indicators
- Suburban plan, PRG (Ascoli Piceno General Regulatory Plan).

Remarks

CCHURE research is ongoing: only some activities have been carried out.

(b) **Urban-architectural area methods**

The activities carried out concern the urban characterisation of the district through the reading and interpretation of the settlement system, the environmental system, open spaces and urban instrumentation and planning.

This reading will be in-depth with the citizens within the focus groups that will be activated following the construction of the Community Profile (CHP). The Focus Groups of experts and citizens will have the task of selecting a list of indicators to assess the effects of the climate change that will have the greatest impact on the health of citizens with reference to the Community Profile and which involve the fundamental themes of the urban planning: land use, mobility, building, open spaces and meeting spaces, natural environment—and some topics of technological design—contemporaneity and flexibility, etc.

The next step will be to propose a methodology for the public administration to select adaptation/mitigation scenarios of the effects of climate change, through the use of real-time analysis, data feedback mechanisms and non-instrumental interaction with local communities, through:

- Climate Health Lab (CHL): construction of a platform of sensors and automation technologies (Urban Internet of Things, IoT), which will provide measurements in real time of the environmental conditions of the neighbourhood. This platform will be implemented with the contribution of citizens through the use of mobile crowd-sensing techniques, which allow users to interact with IoT devices. With CHL, it will be possible to;

- analyze and evaluate the difference between subjective and objective measurements of quality of life indicators to understand how the perception of different environmental conditions varies in the neighbourhood;
- verify and compare the performance in terms of health and well-being of the identified scenarios and their evolution over time.

Which players were involved?

- Municipality of Ascoli Piceno
- Inhabitants of the Monticelli district
- Cultural and Sports Associations of the District
- Seniors Club
- Public administrators
- ASUR (Regional Health Authority)
- Researchers from different disciplines
- ISTAO (Adriano Olivetti Institute, managerial school).

Which actions were implemented?

- Selection of climate-health indicators
- Survey and systematization of the state of the art for the selection of actions and combinations of actions for adaptation and mitigation, with reference to the "fundamental themes" of urban design: land use, mobility, construction, open spaces, and spaces of encounter, natural environment—and some topics of technological design—contemporaneity and flexibility, etc.
- Research on methodologies adopted by the public administration to select adaptation/mitigation scenarios of the effects of climate change, through the use of real-time analysis and data feedback mechanisms and interaction with local communities.

Which instruments were used?

- Participatory processes
- Focus Group
- Open Source Urban Planning
- GIS (Geographic Information System) and BIM (Building Information Modeling) technologies.

Which sources were considered?

- International and EU researches for the indicator selection
- Best Practices projects and plans.

5.2 *Community Involvement Methods*

In CCUHRE Citizens become providers and evaluators of data concerning health and well-being becoming simulators and assessors of climate change adaptation strategies, becoming actively involved in the design of their own living environments affected by climate change. This will promote: a dialogue between public administration, citizens and researchers; citizen participation and knowledge about the decision-making of the city; greater understanding of the need/opportunity to adopt an integrated and interdisciplinary approach, which is the only one able to respond to the complexity of the effects of climate change on health and urban areas.

It is therefore necessary to communicate and establish cooperation between citizens and public administration by sharing information and ensuring:

(a) quality control of the data collected;
(b) the assessments of climate change adaptation strategies through direct interaction between experts, public administration technicians and citizens. This collaborative process will mean that citizens will give more credit to the project and will earn a more effective knowledge of the "smart city approach"

Which players were involved?

- Target Groups of citizens
- Municipal administration
- ASUR (Regional Health Authority)
- Experts (facilitating decision-making processes, communicators).

Which actions were implemented?

- Meetings with the population to illustrate the aims of the research;
- Distribution of a questionnaire to the families about the quality of life in the neighbourhood
- Distribution of PASSI (Progress of Local Health Authorities in Italy) questionnaire
- Quality control of collected data
- The assessments of climate change adaptation strategies should take place through direct interaction between experts, public administration technicians and citizens
- Involvement of the population (target groups) through the developing of apps that will allow smartphone users to interact with the CHL platform to give information for the adaptation and mitigation scenarios assessment.
- Implementation of a protocol aimed at selecting citizens' focus groups: specification of the sample of participants.

Which instruments were used?

- Focus Group
- Public meetings
- Smartphone APPs.

Which sources were considered?

- European and international research about citizens involvement with the support of new technologies.

Main results
The first partial results are currently being analysed.
Remarks

This activity has not been realized yet.

5.3 Networking Methods

Involvement tools

- The main goal of CCHURE is to effectively convey the progresses and results of the project to the scientific community, the decision-makers, the private citizens and other stakeholders, in order to:
- strengthen partnerships with other universities and research institutions, national and international public bodies and enterprises on Urban Health, climate change, ICT technology and IOT;
- raise awareness of local communities, in particular of young people, about climate change and its effects on health;
- increase awareness of the importance of the project for the city and the surrounding territories, for its possible replicability;
- influence decision-makers' decisions on climate change/urban health.

In order to achieve these aims, the following will be executed:

- The development of a project identity (logo, power point, poster)
- Social media strategy: LinkedIn, Twitter, Facebook updates about conferences, events and other activities to promote the project
- Electronic newsletter to be published every 4 months online
- Events to present, discuss and disseminate the project to a wide audience of stakeholders. The final meeting will be open to international experts, to the territory and to other cities, with which the research group will collaborate in the project of "healthy city"
- Participation in national events: Forum PA, Ecomondo, etc.
- Scientific publications on international paper and an initial web-based report, an interim report and a final report
- Participation to conferences and international conferences (Salus -Conference Healthy city Design, ISUH, UrbanPromo)
- Educational activities and creative workshops for young people.

Institutional stakeholders

- KOM (Kick-Off Meeting); interim and final meeting to present, discuss and disseminate the project to a wide audience of stakeholders. The documents will be published on the website.

Associations/third sector

- Website; Facebook; Twitter
- Electronic newsletter to be published every 4 months online.

Informal community networks

- Website; Facebook; Twitter; LInkedin.

Institutions involved

- University of Camerino
- District of Ascoli Piceno, ASUR-Area Vasta 5
- Researchers from other foreign and Italian universities
- Other territorial and urban entities through shared conventions (municipality of Avezzano General Regulatory Plan).

Remarks

- CCHURE research is still ongoing: only some activities have been carried out.

6 Bologna

6.1 Context Characterisation Methods

(a) **Socio-demographic and healthcare area methods**

- Interviews with General Practitioners/Paediatricians/SerT (Addiction Treatment Service) providers
- Contact with a social worker from Navile working in the protections of minors
- Processing data on local social services access
- Observational epidemiological retrospective study on Bologna Census sections.

Qualitative methods

Which players were involved?

- General Practitioners and Paediatricians
- CSM (Mental Health Facility) and SerT
- One local social worker.

Which actions were implemented?

- Gathering a list of all General Practitioners and Paediatricians in the area subsequent personalised phone-calls
- Meeting with a social worker from the neighbourhood.

Which instruments were used?

- Semi-structured interviews.

Quantitative methods

- Data collection and processing from Iperbole (Civic Net of Emilia-Romagna) and data flows from local health authorities
- Observational epidemiological retrospective study on 18 socio-economic and demographic indicators drawn up by the statistical area of the Municipality of Bologna and 14 indicators drawn up by the Epidemiology operative unit of the Public Health Department.

Which players were involved?

- Medical Doctor under fellowship from Emilia Romagna local health authority
- Social workers
- Bologna Health District director
- Public Health Department director
- Epidemiology operative unit of the Public Health Department
- Statistical office of Bologna Municipality.

Which actions were implemented?

- Contact with a social worker
- Reports of qualitative and quantitative initial data were shown to the Health District director and to the Public Health Department director.

Which instruments were used?

- Demographic data collection and subsequent "concentric" comparison between Bologna Municipality, Navile neighbourhood, as well as the area called Lame and Pescarola statistical area
- Collection of data regarding social services performances in Pescarola area
- Acquisition by the Epidemiology—Health Promotion—Risk Communication operative unit of personal and medical information flows regarding the resident population of the City of Bologna. Aforesaid data were processed, after record linkage, through statistical analysis that enabled the researchers to calculate indicators of diseases, use of services and outcomes, disaggregated by statistical area. At a later time, after signing an agreement with Bologna Municipality on data transmission, an analysis was carried out with the aim of correlating the social and economic disadvantaged areas found during the Municipality study to the territorial distribution of worse health outcomes and access to services. The goal was to integrate social and health indicators in a single map of the urban state of

health. These data allowed the team to gain more in-depth understanding of the various levels of vulnerability in the area of Pescarola.

Which sources were considered?

- Iperbole—Programming, Control, Statistical area of Bologna
- Garsia—Social-health informative system
- Demographic and socioeconomic data were provided by Bologna Municipality, Programming, Control, Statistical area, which carried out a study entitled "Suburbs of Bologna: vulnerabilities and opportunities. A proposal of measurement for other Italian cities". This study provides demographic data (percentage changes of the population, natural decrease, population age, etc.), social data (social isolation, foreign population replacement, education, minors and single parents, unoccupied conventional living, etc.), economic data (percentage of illegally occupied housing for rent, individual and household incomes, etc.)
- The observational retrospective study concerned the resident population of the City of Bologna from 2012 to 2016, provided by the Registry Office of the Municipality of Bologna, including the census and statistical area
- For the resident population of each statistical area, data was provided on the following: standardised mortality and BMR rates, incidence and prevalence of diseases (diabetes, stroke, etc.), standardised rates of hospitalisation and emergency department access, indicators of access to specialist medical services, participation in oncological screening programmes, and drug consumption in order to assess whether there was a difference between the areas in comparison to the entire territory covered by the Bologna Municipality
- Databases from the Local health authorities: SDO (Hospital Discharge Forms), AFT (Local Pharmaceutical Assistance) and directly provided drugs register, exemptions of medical dispensations, CEDAP (Birth Assistance Certificate), outpatient services, emergency department accesses database, oncological screening database, records of mortality.

(b) **Urban-architectural area methods**

- Participatory mapping with local residents and the research-action group.

Which players were involved?

- Children from the socio-educational centre
- Foreign women attending Italian courses.

Which actions were implemented?

- Participatory mapping
- Mapping by CSI (International Health Centre) and the Sociology Department.

Which instruments were used?

- Investigations, through mapping, of subjective perceptions on resources and criticalities present in the territory from the point of view of different groups of people

- Mapping of the resources present in the territory.

6.2 *Community Involvement Methods*

- Participant observation
- Contacts with groups already operating in the area: neighbourhood volunteers (Voluntary associations coordination of Lame—CVL), participation in their activities (food and clothing distribution)
- Contact with the Residents' Committee (*Acer Agucchi—Zanardi*).

Which players were involved?

- Voluntary associations coordination group of the Lame area (CVL)
- Residents' Committee Acer Agucchi-Zanardi
- Inhabitants of the section of the council housing.

Which actions were implemented?

- Participant observation during CVL activities
- Writing and sharing of a journal
- Attending CVL meetings; Focus groups with CVL
- Attending Residents' Committee meetings
- Planning of different events (Christmas party, "castagnata"—chestnut party, Carnival) in network with the other organisations
- Weekly opening of a common space ("Spazio Comune", inside the block, managed by CVL) open to anyone, aimed at collecting and facilitating the expression of social needs and questions about health issues relevant to the local population
- Facilitating meetings with ACER (Public Housing Organisation)
- Facilitating internal meetings between the residents.

Which instruments were used?

- Direct contacts with the inhabitants and the neighbourhood
- Narrative meetings and workshops with the inhabitants regarding their experiences of health and disease and their relationship with social health services
- Community care
- Self-production workshops
- Theatre workshops
- Shared investigation on the theme of housing, quality of life
- Distribution of flyers for meetings.

Main results

The issues raised during the gatherings and meetings were: depression, lack of bonds of solidarity, sense of loneliness, nutrition, racism and discrimination within the area. However, the was also satisfaction of finding a place in which they can talk and listen in a way that is different from their daily lives. This opportunity decreased their sense of loneliness and isolation, triggering a process of sharing of community resources in order to tackle problematic situations. We also noticed an increase in the social relationships and in the mutual understanding among the inhabitants.

Limitations and problems encountered

- The weekly presence on the territory does not allow a constant presence and it does not enable groups to structure activities that can engage the inhabitants at a higher level
- Often, there was a strong feeling of the boundary between the inhabitants and research group
- Difficulties in expanding participation
- Sometimes, tensions among the participants with the "Spazio Comune" [common spacde].

6.3 Networking Methods

Involvement tools

- Meetings with institutional players
- Presentations at conferences on inequalities/community participation
- Participation in calls with other groups operating in the block/area
- Events (parties, meetings, workshops, etc.) in partnership with other groups.

Institutional stakeholders

- Monthly coordination meetings with other groups operating in the block/area: meetings promoted by the Urban Centre of the Municipality of Bologna as part of the "Bilancio Partecipativo 2017" [2017 Participatory Report] and "Piani di Zona 2017 e 2018" [2017 and 2018 Zone Plans]
- Meetings with the president of the neighbourhood watch (during organisational meetings of the members of the local network)
- Meetings with the contact person of the neighbourhood social service
- Facilitating meetings with ACER for the residents' committee and other block inhabitants
- Working group about the "Casa della Salute" (Medical centre) in Navile.

Associations/third sector

- Participation in calls, organisational meetings, planning of events.

Informal community networks

- The research-action group's primary goal was the strengthening of the Committee of residents while supporting networking with the other partners.

Institutions involved

- Neighbourhood watch president
- ACER (Public Housing Organisation)
- Bologna Health District Director
- Social services of the neighbourhood.

7 Milan

7.1 Context Characterisation Methods

(a) **Socio-demographic and healthcare area methods**

The geographical areas involved in the project—Brescia Sud (San Polo), Mantova and Castiglione delle Stiviere (with a focus on REMS, a facility created after the takeover of the penal psychiatric hospital)—have been characterized through interviews with privileged stakeholders. Due to their institutional mandate, personal history, or activities concretely carried out, these stakeholders were able to provide qualitative and quantitative data. This process allowed the team to draw up a profile of each territory, defining their strengths, weaknesses, opportunities, and threats with regard to potential "mental health scenarios", and therefore able to support processes of social inclusion, co-production, engagement and recovery.

Data regarding the users directly involved in the project actions were collected from "Psiche" electronic register as well as a set of validated instruments specifically created for the project, obtaining personal and clinical features and the users' engagement towards Recovery.net themes, along with individualized results of each project.

At the same time, we collected data regarding the operators and the territorial service groups involved with regard to their approach to recovery and co-production.

Qualitative methods

- Interviews were conducted, also with the participation of users as interviewers
- Standardised instruments or specifically created questionnaires were used.

Which players were involved?

- Stakeholders belonging to public and private/social services
- Mental Health services workers, users and their families
- Representatives of different projects and initiatives of the territory
- Project partners (university, associations, social cooperatives)
- Local authorities (municipalities, community).

Which actions were implemented?

- Mapping of the resources of the territories involved in the project

- Training of users and operators through workshops concerning the project's themes
- Co-production of individualised therapeutic pathways according to the project's methodology.

Which instruments were used?

- Co-design instruments and techniques
- Questionnaires and other standardised tools
- Semi-structured interviews specifically designed for the project.

Which sources were considered?

- Scientific literature, regional guidance documents
- Stakeholders from the territory involved in the project
- Case studies.

Quantitative methods

- We organised workshops open to users and operators concerning the project's themes, as well as training seminars, focus groups, semi-structured interviews.

Which players were involved?

- Stakeholders belonging to public and private/social services
- Mental Health services workers, users and their families
- Representatives of different projects and initiatives of the territory
- Project partners (university, associations, social cooperatives)
- Local authorities (municipalities, community).

Which actions were implemented?

- Mapping of the resources of the territories involved in the project
- Training of users and operators through workshops
- Co-production of individualised therapeutic pathways according to the project's methodology.

Which instruments were used?

- Co-design instruments and techniques
- Questionnaires and other standardised tools
- Semi-structured interviews specifically designed for the project.

Which sources were considered?

- Scientific literature, regional guidance documents
- Stakeholders from the territory involved in the project
- Case studies.

(b) **Urban-architectural area methods**

Recovery.Net, in order to contextualise the planning and launch the Recovery Co-Lab, has started a collaborative research project and an analysis of the context/neighbourhoods in which these facilities will be implemented. For each of the three territories, we established a mixed team of users, relatives and workers in order to carry out a photographic investigation and a series of semi-structured interviews with residents and key players. This research has led us to define the needs and potentials of the territory.

Which players were involved?

- Users and workers from the three CPS (Mental Health Centres) involved in the project
- Inhabitants of the contexts-neighbourhoods under study (Brescia)
- Players with a key role in the context and who share the goals of the project, with whom the mental health services had already worked or who seemed interested in a future collaboration, with special regard to groups near the co-lab. Among these, we involved social cooperatives who deal with fragility or different associations active in the context under study. Institutional bodies operating in the territory were also involved, including the community council. Furthermore, particpants also included stakeholder representatives from some groups (sewing or walking groups), representatives of meeting places, holistic healing centres, sports clubs (UISP) of the neighbourhood, and representatives of associations or cultural initiatives (Circolo ARCI o Mantova Festivaletteratura), as well as meetings with district doctors.

Which actions were implemented?

- Training sessions on research for design
- Meetings to plan interviews in the field
- Meeting for the collaborative analysis of data.

Which instruments were used?

- Photographic investigation of the neighbourhoods
- Semi-structured interviews
- Analysis of challenges and opportunities.

7.2 Community Involvement Methods

We planned an activity of dynamic mapping in the project's three territories, aimed at the activation of available local resources that could create a relationship with the partners and plan different projects in the field of mental health. The data, collected through a semi-structured interview proposed by working groups made up of workers, users and relatives, were inserted in a database that will be used to create an interactive app aimed at facilitating a wider fruition of the mapped resources. Furthermore, we facilitated co-design processes aimed at the definition of the three co-labs, starting from the analysis of existing types of laboratories for innovation (Innovation Lab, Living Lab, Community Hub) for the definition of local scenarios that qualify the activities and spaces of the laboratories in the three territories.

Which players were involved?

- Small teams of users, relatives and workers from three Mental Health Centres
- Group of Co-Lab, users, relatives, workers from the CPS and a selection of key players from the territories took part in the interviews aimed at studying the context
- Universities.

Which actions were implemented?

- Training sessions about dynamic mapping and co-design
- Meetings for the guidance of the dynamic mapping of the three territories
- Case studies research and literature research
- Co-design workshop transversal to the three territories/for each territory
- Co-design workshop for the web-app project.

Which instruments were used?

- Dynamic mapping
- Design games and scenarios; storyboards
- Online database.

Main results

The primary result of the dynamic mapping was the gradual activation of users, relatives and workers in the three territories. These people are currently meeting weekly in order to develop the database and activation of contacts and collaborations with players of the territory. This mapping, which is still in progress, is turning into a resource for the individual rehabilitation interviews of the users. In the future it will become a key resource for generative sessions of initiatives and activities co-created in the territory.

The main result of the co-design process is the definition of development scenarios for the local co-labs in terms of types of activities and implementations for the start of the processes of preparation and redevelopment of the identified premises/areas.

Lastly, a joint result has been the creation and development of skills and knowledge of users, relatives and workers regarding mapping and the co-design processes.

Limitations and problems encountered

Each territory showed a natural resistance to the active involvement in the mapping activities, due also to the limited availability of time and resources of the three territories. Some territories started late, a delay caused by the logistic aspects of the projects and the specific challenges of some areas, such as the REMS of Castiglione delle Stiviere. Given the goal of putting workers, users and relatives at the same level in the definition of the resources and in their involvement, particular attention has been paid to the bottom-up change that requires more time. In the case of the co-labs, the choice and the activation of the spaces saw numerous delays due to bureaucratic obstacles linked to authorisations and concessions from government offices and associations. These processes significantly slowed down the co-design process and the requalification of the facilities.

7.3 Networking Methods

Involvement tools

Since the very beginning in the planning phase, also those subjects and institutions not directly involved as partners showed interest in the themes of the project. Moreover, they expressed their willingness to participate in the periodic meetings aimed at sharing the experiences and creating a discussion regarding good or emerging practices in terms of the keywords of the project: co-production, engagement and recovery. For the purpose of facilitating good practices in recovery and co-production through concrete and reproducible experiences, we are currently developing a tool aimed at assessing how organisations took on the principles of recovery and co-production, in a logic of continuous improvement of the quality. This tool will also be useful to highlight good practices in mental health services (public and private), therefore defining services and information available all the partners and members of the network. It will be made accessible through the communication channels of the project, such as the website and integrated social networks.

Institutional stakeholders

- A seminar for partners and network members was organised at the headquarters of Lombardy Region; other seminars and workshops are being planned.

Associations/third sector

- Public initiatives, workshops, seminars open to associations and third sector
- The mapping activity is allowing the building of relationships among different realities of the third sector and associations.

Informal community networks

- Since the beginning, the project focused on territorial community networks already active in mental health.

Institutions involved

- Regional government, municipalities, departments of social services and culture, social cooperatives, community points, local health units, universities, etc.

8 Rome

8.1 Context Characterisation Methods

(a) **Socio-demographic and healthcare area methods**

The action research project in the Ex-Bastogi [or simply "Bastogi"] area aims to characterize the context from both a qualitative and quantitative point of view—through the involvement and empowerment of the community—in order to plan, program and implement urbanistic, architectonical, social and health-related interventions. The actions were carried out by a working group made up of the Local Health Authority Rome 1 (ASL Roma1), the XIII Municipality of Rome, the National Institute for Health, Migration and Poverty (INMP) and Sapienza University of Rome. Each institution includes various professional roles from different areas of study and skill-sets, in order to guarantee a multidimensional assessment of the physical and social characteristics of the context.

Qualitative

- Community consultations, used for each research activity as a tool for detecting data and qualitative information about the local population
- Focus Groups involving both citizens and third sector associations operating in the context, led by professionals within the work group
- Semi-structured interviews with the local population
- Institutional reunions, used as a tool for analysis and observation of the several Institutions involved.

Which players were involved?

- Local Health Authority Rome 1 (ASL Roma1)
- Sapienza University of Rome.

Which actions were implemented?

- Periodic meetings with the local population
- Periodic coordination meetings between institutional players.

Which instruments were used?

- Focus Group
- Community consultations
- Interviews
- Institutional reunions.

Which sources were considered?

- Direct experience and knowledge of the residents' context
- Volunteer associations working in the area.

Quantitative

- Evaluation of the use of hospital services by the Ex-Bastogi population
- Comparative assessment of the primary social determinants of health between Ex-Bastogi and neighbouring areas
- Evaluation and assessment of Bastogi population's perception of the area's social-health workers
- Assessment of the self-perceived health status through the administration of the PASSI questionnaire (Progress of Local Health Authorities in Italy)
- Questionnaire addressed to social and health personnel regarding the perception about the population residing in Bastogi.

Which players were involved?

- Department of Epidemiology, Local Health Authority Roma1
- Sapienza University di Roma
- INMP (National Institute for Health, Migration and Poverty).

Which actions were implemented?

- Data extraction from Regional health information systems (SIS) databases
- Data from ISTAT (National Institute of Statistic) census databases
- Administration of questionnaires.

Which instruments were used?

- Descriptive and analytical statistical elaborations
- PASSI questionnaire (Progress of Local Health Authorities in Italy)
- Validated questionnaire on health literacy
- Questionnaire on critical issues of the housing and urban context
- Questionnaire for social/health personnel of the Local Health Authority.

Which sources were considered?

- Hospital Information System (SIO)
- Sanitary Emergencies Information System (SIES)
- ISTAT (National Institute of Statistic) Census 2011 datasets
- Questionnaires results.

Remarks

The qualitative and quantitative methods were simultaneously developed and constantly adapted on the basis of the progressive results from both. Specifically, the quantitative analysis of the use of hospital services was carried out. Moreover, issues in the relationship between citizens and services emerged from the focus groups. The results of the quantitative analysis were then explained to the residents in subsequent meetings.

(b) **Urban-architectural area methods**

- Urban Analysis: urban framing of the case study at a municipal scale, obtained through the collection and elaboration of statistical data and the analysis of mobility, green areas, services and facilities → first identification of the case study in a reference-framework, followed by an in-depth analysis.
- Local analysis: moving to a local scale limited to the Bastogi residential complex. Study of the evolution of the complex; analysis of the architectural approved project; map and comparison of past and present intended uses; map of the property distribution; statistical and demographic analysis; surveys on the outdoors area, on the ground floors and in 7 residential buildings; thermal and energy simulations; administration of questionnaire, interviews to the inhabitants. → in-depth investigation. Identification of the quantitative and qualitative characteristics of the residential complex and its inhabitants.
- SWOT (Strengths, Weaknesses, Opportunities, Threats) analysis: identification of Strengths, Weaknesses, Opportunities, Threats. → development of proposals and strategies to achieve an urban and social regeneration.
- Development of a Protocol as a guideline for regeneration. → delineation and definition of urban regeneration steps; generation of cooperation among stakeholders; implementation of concrete actions; suggestions and ideas regarding actions/policies.
- Participation: involvement of players through meetings, seminars and workshops → Promotion of the inhabitants' participation in local policies or actions, in order to have common decisions and obtain support of stakeholders in local action plans.

Which players were involved?

- Sapienza University of Rome, Department of Planning Design and Technology of Architecture (PDTA)
- XIII Municipality of Rome
- Inhabitants of the building complex
- Religious and sports associations of the building complex
- Prosolidar foundation.

Which actions were implemented?

- Data collection and processing
- Completion of three master thesis on architecture
- Participation processes
- Regeneration through zero ground consumption: realization of a soccer field and a playground with recycled materials; design of urban gardens, market and fab labs.

Which instruments were used?

- Inspections
- Photographic and architectural surveys
- Ecotect and Envimet Software (Thermal and energetical simulations)
- GIS (Geographic Information System)
- Meeting with the inhabitants
- 'Social-Living' questionnaire
- SWOT (Strengths, Weaknesses, Opportunities, Threats) analysis
- Development of a Protocol.

Which sources were considered?

- General Regulatory Plan (PRG) of Rome of 1965, New General Regulatory Plan (NPRG) of Rome of 2008, Regional Territorial Plan (PTPR) of Lazio of 2007
- Open Data of Rome Municipality
- Google Maps
- Open Street Map
- National Institute of Statistic (ISTAT)
- Approved project of the building complex filed in the Municipality of Rome, at the Department of 'Public Work and Urban Maintenance'
- European researches and studies on similar study-cases
- Inhabitants of the building complex.

8.2 Community Involvement Methods

All research and activities were planned and programmed involving the local population—at times privileged players or individuals, who could represent large groups of the population, were identified and included.

The actions were aimed at understanding the self-perception of the inhabitants (and of the community as a whole) regarding the living and health conditions in relation to the physical and social environment as well as local institutions.

The aim of the study was to make it possible for external parties to understand how the local community perceives health in a context characterized by socio-economic vulnerability, housing instability and institutional abandonment. Moreover, the research and actions were carried out in order to allow local institutions to gain a greater understanding of the context and consequently contribute to the creation of social, health and urban planning programs and policies targeted to tackle heath inequities. Community participation in local policies or actions was also promoted and addressed.

Which players were involved?

- Sapienza University of Rome
- Local Health Authority Roma1
- INMP (National Institute for Health, Migration and Poverty)

- XIII Municipality.

Which actions were implemented?

- Participated activities to design and analyse the physical and social environment of Bastogi
- Community therapy interventions
- Proximity health assistance
- Physical education activities
- Community sharing initiatives
- Events aimed at sharing results and dedicated to health promotion.

Which instruments were used?

- Community consultations
- Focus groups
- Community nurses
- Specialist visits
- Screening targeted hard-to-reach groups.

Which sources were considered?

- Local population.

Main results
Renovation of outdoor areas, planning on common areas use.

Limitations and problems encountered
Low participation of an institutionally and structurally marginalized social group

8.3 *Networking Methods*

Involvement tools
All work was carried out through a cooperation among the players, groups and individuals involved. ASL Roma1 and INMP were the promoters. With the passing of time, the project has seen an increasing involvement of departments and personnel of the three institutions, and finally that of the XIII Municipality, the local territorial institution. The growing complexity in the structure of the involved institution led to the decision to stipulate an Inter-institutional Operational Protocol that established timing and roles of each player. In any case, each operating unit has maintained its autonomy to carry out its own mandate, even if the coordination framework was the same.

Informal relationships were established with the Associations working in the area. This action allowed for the establishment of a trust-based relationship between institutional and non-institutional subjects, in order to guarantee the involvement of the community.

Institutional stakeholders

- Inter-institutional Operational Protocol.

Associations/third sector

- Direct involvement in the activities.

Informal community networks

- The periodic coordination meetings laid the foundations for a collaboration with the associations working in the area. At the beginning, the meetings were held in rooms used as a gathering centre by religious personnel. In following, other abandoned common areas owned by the Municipality of Rome were restructured and then used as a point of contact with social and health services. Citizenship was also involved thanks to public events, such as the inauguration of the refurbished football field or a health promotion day organised by the ASL Roma1. The constant presence of the staff of the operating units allowed for fruitful interaction with certain segments of the community.

Institutions involved

- Local Health Authority Roma1: Prevention Department—Hygiene and Public Health Service—Unit of Screening; Department of Epidemiology (DEP) of the Health Service of the Lazio Region; XIII District; Department of Mental Health—Unit of Mental Health XIII District; Inter-district Unit of migrant health; ASL Social Service; Unit of Nursing Assistance
- XIII Municipality of Rome; Social Service
- INMP (National Institute for Health, Migration and Poverty)
- National Network for social and health care
- Sapienza University of Roma:
  - Department of Public Health and Infectious Diseases
  - Department of Molecular Medicine
  - Department of Planning, Design, and Technology of Architecture
  - Department of Social Sciences and Economics
  - Department of Medical and Surgical Sciences and Biotechnologies.

Remarks

The work was carried out in a context that is defined by a great deal of distrust for public institutions, Consequently, players in the community had to find a way to maintain a constant balance between the necessary formality in the relationships among the institution involved and the informality needed in this type of community. The associations operating in the area were included, as well as the existing religious and non-religious networks, which allowed for a solid level of awareness and capillarity of the actions carried-out. This multi-level organisation has proven to be quite effective, albeit with the necessity of a constant effort of institutional coordination in order to avoid the possibility of sending conflicting messages to the community.

9 Trieste

9.1 Context Characterisation Methods

(a) **Socio-demographic and healthcare area methods**

The program is based in Trieste, within 17 micro-areas of the city. These Micro-areas are the most disadvantaged parts of the city, due to social, housing and health problems. The program serves around 19,000 inhabitants: an average of just over one thousand inhabitants for each micro-area, ranging from 500 to 2500.

Qualitative

- Community consultations, with the primary objective of becoming acquainted with the resident population, uncovering and detecting any complexities and pertinent issues
- Focus group for specific targets (e.g. the elderly, minors, etc.)
- Social activities to get to know the inhabitants (lunches, parties, cinema).

Which players were involved?

- Trieste Integrated University Health Service (ASUITs)
- ATER (Public Housing Organisation)
- Municipality of Trieste and Municipality of Muggia
- Volunteer Associations
- Social Cooperatives
- Non-profit Organisations
- Merchants.

Which actions were implemented?

- Monthly meetings between Local Technical Groups (GTT)
- Quarterly meetings between the coordination groups
- Specific meetings with Volunteer Associations and Social Cooperatives.

Which instruments were used?

- Focus Group
- Interviews
- Role play.

Which sources were considered?

- Stories of life of inhabitants
- Contributions of Volunteer Associations
- Feedback from the social and health services involved in the project.

Quantitative

- Analysis of socio-demographic structure indices

- Analysis of diseases registries
- Analysis of health indicators in the regional health authority database
- Analysis of support requests of services from the municipal authority.

Which players were involved?

- Trieste Integrated University Health Service (ASUITs)
- ATER (Public Housing Organisation)
- Municipality of Trieste
- Municipality of Muggia.

Which actions were implemented?

- Continuous census of people with health, housing and social problems
- Analysis of demographic structure and exemptions.

Which instruments were used?

- Indicators: people resident per micro-area, index of demographic structure (elderly index), exemptions rate per 10,000 inhabitants based on weighted population, ratio per type of exemption
- Longitudinal health research. University of Udine.

Which sources were considered?

- Regional and Council information system
- Micro-areas Database.

Limitations

- Privacy restriction and difficulty to have health and social individual profiles
- Difficulty to create a pathology' register
- Difficulty to have information about drugs consumers and health services
- Need to create a comprehensive network of health data with social, salary and work information
- Need to have an electronic integrated health record.

(b) **Urban-architectural area methods**

Since the start of the project, the Sociology and Architecture Degree Courses have been involved. The goal was that of mapping the different territories in question and verifying the meeting points for the individual targets, as well as extra-institutional resources present and green areas to be restored with the help of the citizens themselves.

The actions taken can be summarized in:

1. Analysis of the territory on site
2. Involvement of citizens in identifying the aggregation points of the territory
3. SWOT (Strengths, Weaknesses, Opportunities, Threats) analysis
4. Elaboration of an integral protocol

5. Organisation of Focus Groups, local seminars and workshops.

Which players were involved?

- University of Trieste
- Volunteer Associations and Social Cooperatives
- Districts and Municipalities
- Merchants
- Schools
- ATER (Public Housing Organisation)
- ASUIT (Integrated University Health Service of Trieste) departments.

Which actions have been implemented?

- Community participation
- Involvement of students in the drafting of specific degree theses based on socio-health and architectural research
- Data collection and processing
- Regeneration of green spaces (e.g. social gardens).

Which instruments were used?

- Inspections; Surveys
- Meetings with citizenship.

Which sources were considered?

- General Regulatory Plan of Trieste
- Topography of the ATER (Public Housing Organisation) flats in the city
- Google Maps
- ISTAT (National Institute of Statistic).

9.2 Community Involvement Methods

"Habitat-microaree" is specifically aimed at promoting well-being and social cohesion. It proposes to create action in five sectors: health, education, habitat, work and local democracy. Community involvement is therefore a pivotal activity. The project is implemented by three main players (ASUITS, ATER and Municipality of Trieste); since 2006, operators have a specific-project facility for each micro-area and they interact with inhabitants on specific problems. Consequently, micro-area headquarters become a point of reference to develop mutual aids in order to increase confidence and become stimulus for a proactive community.

Which players were involved?

- Within each micro-area, in a specific facility, different organisations are regularly present:
- Trieste Integrated University Health Service

- Social cooperatives for ATER (Public Housing Organisation) and for Trieste Municipality
- Volunteer organisations.

Which actions were implemented?

- Referent: full-time worker of the Local Health Authority
- Social Reception Desk: social cooperatives on behalf of the Municipality of Trieste and ATER
- Socio-educational activities: social cooperatives
- Low-threshold health programs
- Follow-up for people with non-communicable chronic diseases
- Different stakeholders organise in each micro-area different actions, such as social, leisure and educational activities. The aim is to promote community integration of marginalized people, prevent stigma and reduce conflict situations.

Which instruments were used?

- Micro-area facility with electronic apparatus
- Minibus to promote transfer of people with motor impairment
- Walking-group and Adapted Physical Activity
- Self-help and self-help groups
- Culinary events for socialization
- Specific micro-projects for each Micro-area
- Research activity with University of Turin to measure social capital generated within Micro-areas.

Which resources were considered?

- Lisbon European Council, March 2000
- "Agenda for Social Policy". European Commission, 2005
- Regional and National Law for social and health integration
- European Strategy Health 2020
- Local Health Implementation Plan
- ASUITs catalogue of projects and local participatory welfare interventions.

Main results

In 2016, a quantitative longitudinal research project was assigned to the University of Udine in order to explore different health indicators: number and type of hospitalisations, emergency room access, and deaths. At the same time, another research project was assigned to the University of Turin in order to measure Social Capital generated within the Micro-areas. Samples were obtained with matching techniques in order to guarantee proper balance within different variables, such as health, demographic and social information. Results of both research projects were presented during an international conference in June 2018. Activities and services of the Micro-areas improved healthcare of the people, with a reduction of inappropriate hospitalisations for the elderly as well as individuals with mental illness. Research also revealed an increase in social capital, allowing for improved social and health care.

Limitations
The first challenge was in identifying and matching samples, due to the fact that some information was restricted due to privacy policies.

Any difficulty was the involvement of people who did not live in the Micro-areas. About one out of three people agreed to participate in the research. This led to a lengthening of the research project's timetable.

9.3 Networking Methods

Involvement tools
The program is clearly focused on networking and the collaboration of different institutions with heterogeneous characteristics: the Municipality of Trieste, the Municipality of Muggia, ATER and ASUITs. Furthermore, different actions are associated with a local network of organisations.

Institutional stakeholders

- Joint programming initiative
- Regular meetings and protocol between institutional stakeholders
- June 2018 conference "The Health-Giving Community: the Trieste Micro-areas for Equity". Health, social and housing professionals discussed together about Habitat-Microarea program
- The conference ended with joint signing of the "Trieste Declaration on Health Giving Community" between Municipality of Trieste, Municipality of Muggia, ATER and ASUITs.

Associations/third sector

- Non-profit organisations were activated
- Creation of autonomous and spontaneous groups of citizens.
- Creation of formal organisation of people who live in a Micro-area
- Promotion of inter-associative network.

Institutions Involved

- Municipality of Trieste
- Municipality of Muggia
- ATER
- ASUITS.

10 Comments

10.1 Context Characterisation

For each area, socio-demographic characteristics and health aspects were described by the combination of different qualitative and quantitative methodologies. The qualitative methodologies most used by the research groups were community consultations, focus groups and semi-structured interviews. Review and research on literature of historical, social, demographic and health characteristics in the neighbourhood under study was only carried out in one case. In an attempt to involve the local community, events already present in the neighbourhood were used and social activities were also promoted.

In almost all projects, the qualitative survey involved municipalities and local health authorities (called ASLs in Italy). Moreover, the Bologna group specifically involved general practitioners, paediatricians, mental health and addiction treatment service providers and a social worker. The Rome project also had the university as one of the promoters of research. In several cases the third sector was involved in its various components: voluntary associations, cooperatives, groups for the elderly and church parishes. The projects in Ascoli Piceno and Trieste also involved local public housing organisations.

The identification of useful actions and approaches—aimed at the comparative study of the entities participating in the project as well as the revision of the methods used—was a common thread found in all the research groups. The sources taken into consideration were the residents' experiences and the contributions of the volunteer associations operating in the territory.

With regard to quantitative methodologies, the use of census databases and health and municipal IT systems was quite common. The Bologna research group has also used a retrospective observational epidemiological study.

The Rome and Ascoli Piceno working groups used the questionnaires as research tools. The questionnaires concerned the evaluation and assessment of perceived health status, housing and context criticalities, health literacy, and aspects of daily life for families. In Rome, a questionnaire was also addressed to district social and health professionals in order to evaluate the perception of operators regarding work with individuals with social vulnerability. In the Ascoli Piceno project, particular attention was placed on the identification of climate-health indicators, with the aim of assessing mitigation and adaptation plans to climate change and identifying the most advantageous in terms of health effects. In general, personal, socio-economic and health data have been collected, processed and used to compare the areas of study with those nearby.

To date, the quantitative survey has involved different players. The participation of municipalities and local health authorities has been transversal to all group, in addition to the departments of Public Health and Epidemiology. The Rome research group included also the National Institute for Health, Migration and Poverty (INMP) and the University, while the Bologna group involved a social worker. Consequently, this group was able to collect data regarding the performance of social services in the area under study.

Lastly, the Milan project, which does not concern a particular neighbourhood of a city, is not comparable to the others from the point of view of the context characterisation due to its specificity, or lack thereof.

10.2 Urban-Architectural Area

There are different keys to reading the five studies. The information and data of each case were reported in the matrices with the use of synthetic descriptions useful for understanding the strategies implemented.

As a first element of the investigation, short descriptions offered a summary of the documents viewed and analysed from an urbanistic point of view (scientific research). Specifically, all the research-action groups carried out an urban and/or architectural analysis and the involvement of the communities aimed at the following: elaboration of strategies for urban regeneration in 40% of the cases (Rome and Trieste); development of service design in 40% (Ascoli Piceno and Milan); mapping of health determinants in 20% (Bologna).

The methodological analyses are followed by a description of the players involved, where it emerged that all groups made use of the participation of the inhabitants in the development of the design process. Four cases directly involved sports, religious and cultural associations rooted in the territory, the only exception being Bologna, which in any case included the participation of a local socio-educational centre. All groups saw the involvement of local authorities, including the ASL (Local Healthcare Company), the municipality (only in the cases of Ascoli Piceno, Rome and Trieste).

All studies (100%) implemented participated actions, such as meetings, interviews, questionnaires, focus groups, mappings aimed at the development of data collection and processing. More specifically, Rome and Trieste also made use of master's degree theses dedicated to the areas of study. Furthermore, these two cases developed actions aimed at the urban regeneration of spaces, such as the creation of urban gardens, soccer fields and playgrounds.With regard to the survey and analysis of each study case, 60% (Milan, Rome, Trieste) carried out photographic and/or architectural surveys, 60% (Ascoli Piceno, Bologna and Rome), in addition, implemented mapping of the territory, Ascoli Piceno and Rome through GIS (Geographic Information System) and BIM (Building Information Modeling) technologies. The Rome group also used software for environmental analysis such as Ecotect and Envimet. Finally, the Rome and Trieste groups carried out SWOT analysis (Strengths Weaknesses Opportunities Threats) and protocols for the regeneration process, while Milan developed an analysis of challenges and opportunities.

Moreover, 40% of the cases (Rome and Trieste) mentioned the use of the ISTAT (National Statistical Institute) source, also consulting urban planning tools on a regional and municipal level.

Lastly, only Ascoli Piceno and Rome made reference to European and international research work with regard to studies and analyses carried out on similar cases that led to the outline of the guiding principles for the elaboration of strategies, actions and experimental projects.

10.3 Community Involvement

When describing their projects, all four groups highlight the importance of involving the local population, for assessment needs as well as for the building of social capital and empowerment in order to create a proactive community.

First and foremost, particular consideration is given to meeting with and listening to the citizens in order to gain a greater understating of the context, with different timing and methods for each area. With this aim in mind, Rome and Ascoli Piceno describe sporadic meetings with the community (e.g. through community consultations, focus groups, etc.), while Bologna plans a weekly meeting aimed at collecting information on social needs. Trieste has continuous interaction with the inhabitants thanks to the constant interface with the micro-area headquarter referent, ensuring in this way a constant presence on the territory. Special attention is generally given to health needs and self-perception. However, Rome working group also planned participated activities aimed at analysing the physical and social environment of Bastogi in order to identify the critical issues of the inhabitants' living conditions. The Bologna working group, which also planned narrative meetings with the inhabitants regarding their experiences of health and disease, stresses the importance of listening to the community. Consequently, the Bologna group highlights that the participants report high satisfaction from finding a place in which they can talk and therefore decrease their sense of loneliness and isolation. In many of these areas, there is a clear sense of solitude and abandonment by the public institutions.

Furthermore, promoting community participation is fostered in order to create a dialogue and encourage the cooperation of the population in the development and growth of these projects. This collaboration among citizens, public administration and researchers is specifically pushed by Ascoli Piceno working group, which gives a great deal of attention to the citizens' participation and active involvement in the decision-making process for city policies and in the design of their own living environment. In Rome there was also the direct involvement of the community in the planning and renovation of the outdoor areas. The Milan group mainly involved the community (users, relatives and workers) through the dynamic mapping of the territories under study in a co-design process, which is a central point in the development of the project.

One of the main goals of community involvement is, for all of the working groups, the promotion of the social cohesion: internal meetings within the community have the power to increase the social relationships and mutual understating and sharing of community resources and to promote community integration and reduce conflict situations. Moreover, the Bologna group facilitated internal meetings within the area, while Trieste specifically planned self-help groups for this purpose. Along general lines, all projects planned different social, leisure and educational activities in order to increase the sense of community. This included: theatre and self-production workshops in Bologna; walking-groups and specific micro-projects for each micro-area in Trieste; physical education activities and community therapy interventions in Rome. Another widely used tool is the planning of different events: from the Christmas and chestnut parties in Bologna and the culinary events in Trieste—mainly addressed at the socialization—to the events dedicated to health promotion and proximity health assistance in Rome and the low-threshold health programs and socio-educational activities in Trieste. Given the importance of social capital, Trieste is using a tool developed with the University of Turin to measure the social capital generated within the micro-areas. This instrument could eventually be spread to the other contexts in order to offer a comparative study.

Lastly, the community was involved by every group for the communication of the aims of the research and the results of the projects. This is important not only for the inhabitants' understanding of the progress made, but also to gain their trust and increase their confidence in the working groups actions. Quite often, the users are described as being wary in the beginning.

The continuous communication of progress is particularly highlighted by the Ascoli Piceno group, through public meetings aimed at increasing the integrated and interdisciplinary cooperation among citizens, researchers and public administration.

In order to increase the community involvement and participation, some groups benefited from the presence and activity of groups rooted in the area. In the case of Bologna, neighbourhood volunteers and residents' committee were involved; in Trieste, there is the participation of cooperatives and community service operators. Instead, Ascoli Piceno group developed a smartphone App to facilitate the interaction, and promotes active communication through websites and posters.

Nevertheless, low community participation is the primary limitation listed by the groups, although some groups specifically chose to address target groups (e.g. in Ascoli Piceno there was the implementation of a protocol aimed at selecting the citizens) or, as in Rome, privileged individuals who could represent and lead larger groups. The main difficulty found by all four groups is the inclusion of those who are more isolated and therefore harder to reach.

10.4 Networking

All projects have worked to establish a network between the different institutional bodies involved and the private citizens in order to strengthen the partnership among the institutional and government bodies, while also raising awareness among local communities.

With regard to the players engaged, all four projects involved the regional health authorities (ASL) and municipalities. The participation of local public housing organisations was also included in some projects, such as Trieste and Bologna.

In most projects, including Rome, Bologna and Trieste, universities also participated. Moreover, Rome included also the National Institute for Health, Migration and Poverty (INMP), while the Bologna group involved community services and the neighbourhood committee president.

The institutional bodies involved in Rome, Trieste and Ascoli Piceno have signed a common agreement protocol—this ensures that every agency can act in an autonomous way and with a common purpose to be respected.

All projects sought to build a relationship of trust with the local population. This type of trust is often created starting from activities already rooted on the territory and organising events and periodical meetings.

The Bologna group focused mainly a communal participation approach. They organised meetings with the neighbourhood president, created events aimed at sponsoring the projects among private citizens and creating awareness of important aspects. The group also took part in joint events with other neighbourhoods. The Trieste group, on the other hand, has been organizing regular meetings through volunteer associations that know and understand the area. The Rome group, due to the housing and employment problems and the resulting mistrust of institutions, has tried to maintain a balance among the associations operating with the territory, institutional bodies and already existing social networks. Furthermore, they often involved local leaders in order to facilitate the population's involvement.

All the working groups expressed the perception that events aimed at sponsoring projects may be perceived as propaganda, and not of real interest to private citizens. For this reason, periodic meetings and the building of a trust-based relationship between institutions and resident population are essential.

Finally, all teams tried to extend the projects outside the specific area, with the purpose of promoting the projects to different institutional bodies that can implement and export them to different areas in Italy and abroad. For example, in June 2018, the Trieste group presented the results of ten years of research during a conference in which several institutional bodies, government agencies, and other associations were invited. During this conference, the signing of a memorandum of understating was carried out by all the members of the projects. Moreover, the Milan group organised seminars for partners and network members aimed at involving the institutional and third-party stakeholders.

With regard to publicising and spreading information on the projects' progress, Ascoli Piceno was the only group to use social media to transmit future results to the scientific community and decision-makers. In addition to national and international conferences and education activities on the territory, they also planned the use of website pages, facebook, personal social media, as well as digital newsletter to be published every four months (available online on the website of the university of Camerino, the regional health authority (ASUR) and the district of Ascoli Piceno).

In conclusion, all groups actively developed a solid network aimed at promoting the projects and building a strong bridge between the institutional players and the resident population.

Conclusions. Creating Social Capital: the Key Role of Public Policies and Services

Roberto Di Monaco

Abstract The social practices analyzed in this book suggest policies for the development of social networks, useful for promoting health and equity. They reinforce and specify many indications suggested by international literature [1]. Mainly, they help to better define the role that territorial actors could play in promoting health and equity. Moreover, these experiences explain more precisely the effect of local actions on social impact and therefore they propose guidelines for designing and evaluating intervention strategies. We will focus on the brief conclusions of the book on these issues.

Keyword Health inequalities · Social determinants · Social capital · Public health services · Community health care

The social practices analyzed in this book suggest policies for the development of social networks, useful for promoting health and equity. They reinforce and specify many indications suggested by international literature [1]. Mainly, they help to better define the role that territorial actors could play in promoting health and equity. Moreover, these experiences explain more precisely the effect of local actions on social impact and therefore they propose guidelines for designing and evaluating intervention strategies. We will focus on the brief conclusions of the book on these issues.

We know that social inequalities have strong effects on health inequalities [2]. These negative effects are not distributed homogeneously in the cities but are concentrated in specific neighbourhoods and areas, where poverty, environmental degradation and poor health rates reach high levels. This concentration generates further perverse effects: people with health problems tend to increase and the characteristics of the area worsen. For example, property values, private investments for redevelopment, business and commercial settlements, the infrastructure of proximity services tend to be reduced.

R. Di Monaco (✉)
Organization Sociology and of Leadership, University of Turin, Torino, Italy
e-mail: roberto.dimonaco@unito.it

A. Battisti et al. (eds.), *Urban Health*, Green Energy and Technology,
https://doi.org/10.1007/978-3-030-49446-9_17

Automatic processes to rebalance the social and welfare conditions of the population do not occur in these areas. On the other hand, the processes of environmental and social degradation produce further negative effects, as emerges from the cases examined. People cannot even use the resources normally available, such as essential services in homes (eg heating, condominium cleaning), the use of public spaces (eg gardens, squares), the use of services of proximity, health and personal safety services. Furthermore, conflicts between people and groups (young and old, natives and immigrants, etc.), social fragmentation, anger and isolation increase in these contexts.

In summary, people who live in marginal contexts not only have on average fewer resources and individual abilities but also have fewer social relationships useful for dealing with problems. When they are forced to face critical life situations, due to social or health problems (economic difficulties, job loss, family bereavement, difficulties in physical autonomy, etc.), they cannot manage the situation and fail to put in act low risk behaviors for one's health [3, 4].

Literature has recently focused on the key role that social capital plays in these critical situations, defined by Bourdieu [5] as "the aggregate of actual or potential resources linked to possession of a durable net-work". This would allow people to access many different types of resources through social relationships [6, 7].

The association between the level of social capital and the health of people was therefore verified by various researches. In integrated and cohesive communities, people have a greater capacity to cope with health problems, even when they have personal frailties. Exchanges, cooperation and shared meanings are practised by favouring processes that increase people's capabilities.

On the other hand, research continues to show deficiencies on two key aspects of social capital, which are very important from the point of view of public policies and services. First, the ways in which it would be possible to increase the social capital of a given community are not sufficiently theoretically investigated and empirically verified. Secondly, the role that public and private services can play in this direction, especially in the area of welfare and health, is not sufficiently explored and practised.

Precisely on these aspects the contributions presented in this book may provide some significant indications and may suggest the strategic options on which health policies and the fight against inequalities in urban environments should focus. We focus on a premise and three priorities for action.

The premise concerns the widely known limits of traditional bureaucratic services. To build quality relationships with people and to develop forms of individual and social empowerment, public and private welfare services should over-come the bureaucratic forms of the relationship within them, between themselves and with people. The bureaucracy is incapable of looking at people's needs, as well as activating, engaging and generating trust. Instead, traditional bureaucratic services push people to passivity: they often generate distance, poor listening, delayed response, welfarism, poor quality of service, inefficiency [8]. These services are often better used by people with more education and relationships, so they do not rebalance inequalities. This happens not only due to malfunctioning or overload, but because the traditional bureaucratic organizational model by definition is not oriented to the person and the quality of the relationship.

Instead, when policies and services are oriented towards the person and the community, they should invest in three directions, which clearly emerge in the experiences studied in this book.

The first orientation should be the initiative. Public and private operators should be the protagonists of the action and should start moving. This means moving to physical places and going to places where people live and work, in homes, communities and in areas affected by degradation. It also means meeting people, recognizing the symbolic universes of people and communities, putting themselves from their point of view, taking charge of what is valuable to them, recognizing their problems and their priorities. This requires operators, as well as public and private institutions to which they belong, a fundamental change of perspective [9]. When the person becomes the centre of attention, the service delivery processes should be rethought, integrated with each other and made as functional as possible to the new priorities. This is a radical cultural change in the organization and personnel of the services: it was implemented in an authoritative way by the 'pull system' strategy, proposed by the lean organization.

The second orientation concerns the activation of citizens. Generative welfare creates new social resources because people become protagonists. They guide the service by expressing their demand, but also by contributing their time, availability, exchanges and relationships. The processes of involvement of people create new social realities, where social capital grows and changes the capabilities [10], the concrete possibilities of the life of the people involved [11].

The third orientation concerns the process of empowerment, which develops both among the operators who lead the action, and between the people who participate in it. There is empowerment when people increase the degree of autonomy of their actions and when their capacity to manage them increases. In summary, individual and social learning processes are generated that change people's behaviour, in a framework of coherent relationships. The processes of learning from experience change the practices of life and work in a community: they re-quire people involved in processes of analysis, evaluation and experimentation, such as to favour the overcoming of critical events. These practices give new importance to data and information, which are not simply dropped from above but are produced and reworked with an active role of operators and citizens [12, 13]. They also give a different meaning to the evaluation actions, which support the action and the continuous improvement, and that help the subjects to elaborate new meanings and representations of the change [14].

The traits of the experiences, which we have underlined, are well represented by the methodological approach of action research [15]. It can be defined as a deliberate action, aimed at promoting a change in the real world, committed on a restricted scale but incorporated in a more general project, subjected to certain rules and disciplines to obtain knowledge or meaning outcomes [16,17]. It is a necessarily interdisciplinary action, which goes beyond the distance with the user, transversal to the boundaries of services and to the traditional articulations of policies, in strictly separate areas of competence.

Therefore, the challenge that emerges from the experiences reported in this book, in our opinion, concerns the need to extend the transformative logic of action research to the operating practices of all public and private subjects that deal with welfare and health in the territory.

The experiences show that the action of the operators can affect the social reality, through those that are defined in analytical sociology "social mechanisms". These are new interdependencies, created among the people who live in a particular place, who push their social relationships towards growth. Activation towards others, cooperation, trust, coordination and learning are among the most important social mechanisms. Thus, the operators who conduct the actions and manage services in the area can generate new social capital. This is because the operators perform the trigger function. They become activators of exchanges, dialogues and common actions, they become guarantors of trust with respect to the aims of cooperation and the commitment of the institutions they represent, they become builders of new meanings of common goods.

Two directions of development, towards which to direct the evolution of health intervention in critical urban areas, can be deduced from the experiences examined:

1. The improvement of the quality of the service process towards the needs of the person, in order to increase the value generated for the person himself. By quality we mean the technical-professional quality, but also the relational quality with the person and the quality achieved with the integration between different areas and professions in health services and with other services and policies;
2. The improvement of the quality of relationships in the community, where services and policies should generate activation of people and groups according to targets and problems, trigger social capital and open to people coordination, participation and decision on the problems they live.

The intersection of the two dimensions generates the following typology of strategic orientations, which could guide the evolution of services.

		Increased quality of service to people	
		Low	High
Generation of social capital in the community	High	Community practices are separated from the functioning of services They work to activate the community to deal with people's problems, not sufficiently treated by public services Situation: social projects that have the center of gravity on associations, groups, places of participation Services are absent, or participate only in formal agreements, or marginal commitment	Services are integrated and rooted in the community Quality processes are centered on the person (pull system strategy) and on the community (activation and cooperation) There are active community mechanisms generated by the action of public services, appropriately in relation to the target and the community Situation: services generate a growing flow of value for people and social capital
	Low	Welfare services are traditional and bureaucratic (fragmented, they do not take care of relationships with people) Many people's problems are not sufficiently treated, especially problems of the most fragile people. The community is kept out of the services provided to people. Sometimes the community protests, some people help others with volunteering Situation: services are traditional and do not develop innovations or systematic cooperation with the community	The services are of high quality and are able to integrate social-health and welfare benefits, focused on the person Community involvement is absent Situation: innovation concerns service processes and social-health integration

References

1. Kawachi I, Subramanian SV, Kim D (2008) Social capital and health. Springer, New York
2. Costa G et al (eds) (2014) L'equità in salute in Italia. Secondo rapporto sulle disuguaglianze sociali in sanità. Franco Angeli, Milano

3. Di Monaco R, Pilutti S (2014) Le azioni di correzione nel senso dell'equità delle politiche non sanitarie. In: Costa G et al (eds) L'equità nella salute in Italia. Secondo rapporto sulle disuguaglianze sociali in sanità. Franco Angeli, Milano, pp 137–165
4. Sen A (1986) Scelta, benessere, equità. Il Mulino, Bologna
5. Bourdieu P (1986) The forms of capital. In: Richardson JG (ed) The handbook of theory: research for the sociology of education, Greenwood Press, New York, pp 241–258
6. Coleman JS (1990) Foundations of social theory. Harvard University Press, Cambridge
7. Putnam R (1993) La tradizione civica nelle Regioni italiane. Leonardi Editore, Milano, p 196
8. Laverack G (2016) Public health. Power, empowerment and professional practice. Palgrave Macmillam Edition, New York
9. Di Monaco R, Pilutti S (2016) Scommettere sulle persone. La forza della leadership distribuita. Egea Bocconi, Milano
10. Van Der Gaaga M, Snijdersb TAB (2005) The resource generator: social capital quantification with concrete items. Soc Netw 27:1–29
11. Ostrom E (1990) Governing the commons. The evolution of institutions for collective action. Cambridge University Press, Cambridge (trad. it. Governare i beni collettivi, Marsilio Editore, Venezia)
12. Farnese ML, Centonze A (2016) Nonaka al lavoro: condizioni e azioni per lo sviluppo delle conoscenze nelle organizzazioni. Sviluppo e organizzazione 268:49–61
13. Nonaka I, Takeuchi H (1995) The knowledge creating company. Oxford University Press, Oxford
14. Weick K (1995) Senso e significato nell'organizzazione. Cortina, Milano
15. Manoukian F (2002) Presupposti ed esiti della ricerca-azione. L'intrapresa di percorsi di conoscenza insieme ad altri. Animazione Sociale 11:50–60
16. Dubost J (1984) Une analyse comparative des pratiques dites de Recherche-Action. Connexions 43:8–28
17. Dubost J, Levy A (2007) Origine e sviluppo della ricerca-azione. Spunti VIII(9):66–106

The manufacturer's authorised representative in the EU is Springer
Nature Customer Service Centre GmbH, Europaplatz 3, 69115 Heidelberg,
Germany. If you have any concerns regarding our products, please
contact ProductSafety@springernature.com

Printed and bound by CPI Group (UK) Ltd, Croydon, CR0 4YY
06/10/2026
02228459-0002